ACKNOWLEDGEMENTS
Rob Del Mundo would like to thank everyone at Indigo, especially Dominic Stones for enthusiastic support from the outset.
Thanks to Kathryn Zante and her excellent design work, when she wasn't at the kids' hockey practices. This project involved a tremendous amount of research. Thanks to everyone who responded to my questions with a quick e-mail, including D'Arcy Jenish, Joe Pelletier, Paul Patskou, and Mark Zwolinski. Two thumbs up to Rick Couchman and Stan Fischler for launching my sportswriting career.
My loudest cheering section, from first period to overtime, is my family: Dad, Mom, Mel, Jim, Justin, Megan, and Butch. Love you always.

PHOTO CREDITS

Hockey Hall of Fame Archives—6, 8, 11, 13-20, 22, 24, 28, 30, 32, 37, 41 (top, bottom right), 56, 57, 61 (top), 75, 77, 97, 110, 114, 132, 149 (right), 187 (top), 195, 197

Paul Bereswill/HHOF—35, 49, 59, 61 (bottom), 87 (HHOF-IIHF Images), 111, 115, 117, 121 (bottom), 122, 125, 134-37, 139, 146 (HHOF-IIHF Images), 148, 150, 155, 158, 159, 163, 169 (left), 173 (HHOF-IIHF Images), 176, 177

Dave Sandford/HHOF—10, 33, 41 (bottom left), 47 (both), 55, 69, 93, 123, 142, 151, 161 (topright), 165, 166, 172, 189, 193

Imperial Oil-Turovsky Collection/HHOF—26, 34, 36, 38, 40, 42, 43, 44, 46, 48, 50, 52, 54, 58, 64, 66, 68, 95, 203

Chris Relke/HHOF-IIHF Images—27, 29, 45 (left), 65, 79, 81 (left), 89, 101 (right), 161(top left, bottom)

Doug MacLellan/HHOF—7, 39, 45 (right), 85 (both), 91, 101 (left), 105, 107, 129, 162, 175, 185, 188, 196, 199

Graphic Artists/HHOF—74, 78, 80, 81 (right), 82, 88, 92, 121 (top), 127, 157, 171, 181 (left)

Frank Prazak/HHOF—9, 51, 62, 70, 72, 73, 83, 84, 108, 109, 119, 141 (left)

Lew Portnoy/HHOF—21, 63, 67, 76, 96, 103, 106, 114, 116, 118, 120

Miles Nadal/HHOF—23, 128, 149 (left)

O-Pee-Chee/HHOF—25, 131, 138, 145, 169 (right), 181 (right), 201

Fred Keenan/HHOF—86
Howie Borrow/HHOF—140
James Welch/HHOF—156
Josh Holmberg/HHOF—184
Matthew Manor/HHOF—12, 53, 194, 204 (Hockey Canada Images)
Mecca Collection/HHOF—90, 112, 124, 141 (right)
Richard Wolowicz/HHOF-IIHF Images—202
Roger St. Jean/HHOF—71
Steve Deschenes/HHOF—190
Steve Poirier/HHOF—160, 186, 205

Le Studio du Hockey/HHOF—60

Dennis Miles—98, 99, 104, 113, 129 (right), 130, 147, 167, 179, 187 (bottom)

Frank Lennon—94

Getty Images—31, 100, 102, 126, 133, 143, 144, 152, 153, 154, 164, 168, 170, 174, 178, 180, 182, 183, 191, 192, 198, 200

Library and Archives Canada Cataloguing in Publication
Del Mundo, Rob; Podnieks, Andrew
NHL: 100 Years of Hockey Glory
ISBN 9781552674109

Moydart Press
www.andrewpodnieks.com

First Printing 2015
Printed and bound in China

NHL

100
YEARS OF HOCKEY GLORY

Rob Del Mundo and Andrew Podnieks

MOYDART

Contents

The NHL Is Formed

The early years of the 20th century saw the birth of professional hockey, and in short order the best players had abandoned amateur play in favour of a career in which they could be paid to play the game.

Out of several smaller pro leagues emerged, in 1909, the National Hockey Association. Consisting of seven teams—three in Montreal and others in Ottawa, Cobalt, Haileybury, and Renfrew—the league had difficulties on many fronts, not the least of which were poor attendance and being raided of its star players by the rival Pacific Coast Hockey Association in Western Canada.

Frank Calder was the NHL's first president.

All problems paled in comparison, however, to its biggest headache, namely Eddie Livingstone, owner of the Toronto Shamrocks and later Toronto Blueshirts. Livingstone riled the other NHA owners on many fronts, raiding players, lying to league executives, threatening to move the Blueshirts to Boston, and filing a lawsuit against the NHA to aggressively intimidate the other owners.

The owners, in turn, were further furious when they realized the NHA constitution prevented them from simply throwing Livingstone out of the league, so instead they hatched a more subtle plan.

On October 19, 1917, the board of directors met and informed Livingstone's lawyer that Toronto had been suspended from the league for a year because it was too difficult to operate a league with five teams.

Livingstone then countered by saying he'd start another league and raid the NHA of all its players. One month later, at the next NHA meeting, Livingstone threatened to follow through on his promise to operate in Toronto.

It was the other owners, though, who got the last laugh. Representatives from the Montreal Canadiens, Montreal Wanderers, Ottawa Senators, and Quebec Bulldogs met at the Windsor Hotel in Montreal on November 22, 1917.

At that meeting they decided to withdraw from the NHA altogether and form another league, the National Hockey League. Four days later, the four teams signed on. Livingstone was furious and again took legal action, but Wanderers owner Sam Lichtenhein explained the situation clearly: "We didn't throw Livingstone out; he's still got his franchise in the old National Hockey Association. He has his team, and we wish him well. The only problem is, he's playing in a one-team league."

The Bulldogs were unable to ice a team for the 1917-18 season, so the NHL brought in a new Toronto entry. On December 19, 1917, the first NHL game was played at the Arena Gardens in Toronto, the home side losing a 10-9 decision to the Montreal Wanderers.

The Birth of the Montreal Canadiens

Towards the end of the 19th century, hockey was prevalent in Montreal, and the city was represented by three of the five teams in the Amateur Hockey Association: the Crystals, the Victorias, and the AAA Winged Wheelers. The latter club had won the first ever Stanley Cup awarded in 1893.

Three seasons later, the Crystals merged with the Montreal Shamrocks, and the new amalgamation adopted the Irish-oriented nickname to reflect the demographic of its players. The Victorias were comprised of players of Scottish descent, while the AAA club was a predominantly British-born team.

But there was no team to represent the French population, despite the fact that two-thirds of the city's inhabitants were Francophone. Teams such as the Nationals and the Montagnards were created to satisfy this market, but both were out of senior hockey by 1907. The few French players were left to play for either the Shamrocks, or another Montreal team – the Wanderers – that had joined the Federal Amateur Hockey League at the start of the 1904-05 campaign.

The Wanderers had forged a bitter rivalry with the Ottawa Senators, losing the Stanley Cup to their foes on the second-last day of the 1908-09 season in the Eastern Canada Amateur Hockey Association. At that league's annual pre-season meeting in November, held at Montreal's Windsor Hotel, expansion was on the agenda.

Ambrose O'Brien was in attendance to apply for a franchise for his hometown club, the Renfrew Creamery Kings. Meanwhile, the rivalry between the Senators and the Wanderers had extended from beyond the ice to the boardroom. Ottawa objected to Wanderers' owner Patrick J. Dolan's intent to use the Jubilee Arena as his team's home rink when the Westmount

Arena could accommodate more than twice as many fans. The reciprocal agreement among all four teams in the association provided for the sharing of gate receipts.

When the Senators, Shamrocks, and Quebec Bulldogs threatened to disband the ECAHA, those representing the Wanderers at the meeting stormed out in protest. But one of them, Jimmy Gardner, stayed behind and befriended O'Brien. Gardner pitched the idea of forming a league that would

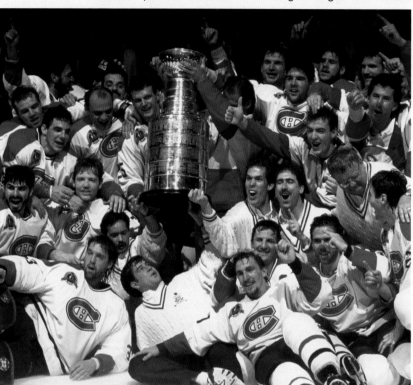

The Canadiens last won the Stanley Cup in 1993.

include Renfrew, Cobalt, and Haileybury. He also suggested adding a French team in Montreal to complement the existing English-speaking franchises.

The proposal was too good to pass up. O'Brien and representatives from the respective cities formed the National Hockey Association on December 2, 1909.

Two nights later, they announced the creation of a new team, "Le Club de Hockey le Canadien," a name represented by the "C" and the "H" in the logo of hockey's most storied franchise.

Wanderers Arena Burns Down

The Montreal Wanderers had been four-time Stanley Cup champions in the National Hockey Association. One of the five charter members of the NHL, the team was buoyed by hometown brothers Sprague and Odie Cleghorn.

But before the Wanderers even took to the ice for the new league's inaugural 1917-18 season, Sprague suffered a season-ending leg injury sustained after falling on an icy sidewalk. Then, Odie was lost from the roster to fulfill a condition that exempted him from serving in the military only if he didn't play hockey.

The Wanderers, managed and coached by Art Ross, had the support of English-speaking Montreal fans, while Francophones placed their support behind the Canadiens. Ross's team won its first game of the season, then lost its next three. On January 2, the Wanderers were scheduled to play their local rivals, with whom they shared the Westmount Arena on Rue St. Catherine.

The game itself became inconsequential when a fire broke out in the dressing room and quickly spread throughout the building. The fire department was dispatched, but to no avail. The roof collapsed and the arena was incinerated.

Two days later, league president Frank Calder called an emergency meeting at which Wanderers owner Sam Lichtenhein quickly disbanded the team. Citing losses of $30,000 since 1914, not including $1,000

Harry Hyland of the Cup-winning Montreal Wanderers.

lost in the fire that had claimed the team's sweaters and equipment, Lichtenhein felt he had no choice but to cease operations. The Wanderers' lifespan in the NHL lasted just six games, with the January 2nd and 5th games against the Montreal Canadiens and Toronto Arenas, respectively, listed as forfeits.

The 10,000-seat Westmount Arena was one of the first ever rinks designed solely for hockey and had been in operation since 1898. It featured four-foot high boards, allowing for the puck to be chipped out of the zone and along the rink's perimeter, an innovation at the time.

Ross played three games on defence in the Wanderers' brief NHL existence, scoring a goal while racking up twelve penalty minutes. Despite playing for several years in the amateur circuits, it was a brief NHL playing career for the man whose name is on the trophy presented annually to the league's scoring champion.

While the Wanderers folded, the Canadiens persevered. Owner George Kennedy moved his team into the Jubilee Arena, even borrowing equipment from local men's league teams for his own players.

Eventually the Canadiens moved into Mount Royal Arena, and in 1924 the team moved into the palatial Montreal Forum. The historic shrine was built one block east of where the ill-fated Westmount Arena once stood.

The Birth of the Toronto Maple Leafs

The NHL added three American teams in the summer of 1926, one of which was the New York Rangers. Running the team was Manhattan native Colonel John Hammond, who hand-picked the man to assemble his roster – Constantine Falkland Cary Smythe, known simply as "Conn."

Smythe's tenure with the Rangers didn't last long. Although Smythe successfully landed Bill and Bun Cook, Frank Boucher, and Lorne Chabot for the Blueshirts, he was fired before the Rangers' first game and replaced by Lester Patrick.

Returning to his sand and gravel business "C. Smythe for Sand," the entrepreneur had his interest piqued by the pending sale of the Toronto St. Patricks. Originally christened the Arenas when the NHL was formed, the St. Patricks were failing, having won just 12 of its 36 games the previous season, and playing before sparse crowds at Arena Gardens (later known as Mutual Street Arena).

Smythe met with Jack Bickell, a majority shareholder in the Toronto franchise. The two men made a deal in which Bickell would retain his share in the club – worth $40,000 – provided that Smythe could find $160,000 from other investors.

The transaction was successful, and Smythe was given full control of the team. On February 14, 1927, Smythe was named the team's coach and general manager. But beyond the happenings on the ice surface, a major alteration took place.

Smythe immediately changed the team's colours from the St. Patricks' green and white to the blue and white of his alma mater, the University of Toronto. Most importantly, he renamed the team the Maple Leafs. Smythe, who served in the Great War, had been inspired by the maple leaf worn by military servicemen overseas.

The new incarnation of the Toronto hockey club was, however, mired in mediocrity, finishing out of the playoffs in 1926-27, then winning just one playoff round over the next four years. But Smythe made several significant transactions to bring the team into Stanley Cup contention. He traded for Chabot, whom he had originally recruited for the Rangers. Then in 1930, Smythe used the winnings from a wager on a race horse named "Rare Jewel" to help pry defenceman King Clancy from Ottawa.

A year later, Maple Leaf Gardens was constructed at the corner of Church and Carlton Streets. The 1931-32 campaign ended with the Maple Leafs winning the Stanley Cup as they defeated Smythe's old team, the Rangers, in the finals.

Only two players on that victorious Leafs team, Hap Day and Ace Bailey, were holdovers from the St. Patricks.

The Leafs were Stanley Cup champions with captain George Armstrong in 1967.

1919 Cup Not Awarded

The 1918-19 Stanley Cup finals pitted the Montreal Canadiens against the Seattle Metropolitans of the Pacific Coast Hockey Association. The Habs were led by Newsy Lalonde – the league leader in goals, assists, and points. Montreal made quick work of the Ottawa Senators in the NHL finals series in five games, setting up the showdown with Seattle.

The Cup finals opened on March 19 at the Seattle Arena to the delight of the hometown fans who saw their team cruise to a 7-0 win. Goaltender Hap Holmes earned the shutout for the Metropolitans. The teams split the next two games, then played to a scoreless draw in Game Four that included a twenty-minute overtime.

On March 30, Montreal squared the series at 2-2-1 after Jack McDonald scored in overtime to give the Habs a 4-3 win in what turned out to be the final game of that historic playoff series.

Almost every Canadiens player had fallen victim to an epidemic of Spanish influenza that had swept across the globe. The Cup series was cancelled on the first day of April. Seattle refused to accept the title by default. As a result, the epidemic had an impact that neither of the two World Wars had; no winner of the Stanley Cup was named.

Defenceman Joe Hall, aged 36, succumbed to pneumonia in a Seattle sanatorium five days later. The NHL's penalty-minute leader in the league's first two seasons, Hall had stated at the beginning of the year that he felt like he could play ten more years of hockey.

Four other Montreal players—McDonald, Newsy Lalonde, Louis Berlinquette, and Billy Couture—were also stricken, the latter three serving as pallbearers at Hall's funeral.

General manager George Kennedy also fell ill. Although he recovered, Kennedy never regained his full health, passing away in 1921. His widow, Myrtle Kendall, sold the team to Joe Cattarinich, Leo Dandurand, and Louis Letourneau for the grand sum of $11,500.

The 1919 finals series had been hotly contested, with two of the games going beyond regulation. Lalonde had registered six goals over the five games while George Vezina had played in goal for all 336 minutes of the series, posting a 3.39 goals-against average. On Seattle's end, Frank Foyston led the way with nine goals and ten points while goaltender Holmes allowed just ten goals and recorded two shutouts.

The only other year in which there was no Stanley Cup champion was 2004-05 when the NHL season was cancelled in its entirety due to a labour dispute.

The 1919 Stanley Cup finals series was halted and never decided.

The Birth of the Original Ottawa Senators

More than a century before the franchise would be re-introduced into the NHL as an expansion team, the original Ottawa Senators were formed at the Montreal Winter Carnival in 1883. Initially dubbed the Ottawa Hockey Club, it was later nicknamed the Generals before adopting the Senators moniker in 1902.

The 1902-03 season marked the first year of a dynasty in which the Stanley Cup was claimed by the team playing in the nation's capital. Fans had come to label the team the "Silver Seven" instead of its official name. At the time, some of the players were paid with silver (contravening their supposed amateur status), and the rules of the sport called for a rover – a seventh man – on the ice. Ottawa swept the Rat Portage Thistles in a two-game series to claim its first Stanley Cup.

Two years later, the Silver Seven accepted a challenge from Dawson City, Yukon, whose players trekked some 6,400 kilometres across the country by, among other means, dogsled to play for the coveted trophy. But Ottawa gave the visitors a rude welcome in the first game with a 9-2 trouncing. In Game Two, Silver Seven forward "One-Eyed" Frank McGee was unstoppable. McGee scored an unbelievable 14 goals as his team coasted to a 23-2 demolition.

Ottawa had its string of championships broken in 1906 before reclaiming the Stanley Cup in 1909. By this time, the club's official nickname of Senators had been accepted into the mainstream. The following season saw the birth of the professional National Hockey Association, a seven-team league that claimed three of the teams from the Eastern Canada Amateur Hockey Association: two Montreal teams, the Shamrocks and Wanderers, and Ottawa.

The Senators claimed their only NHA Stanley Cup in 1910-11. This was the first season that featured three, 20-minute periods instead of two, 30-minute halves.

By the fall of 1917, Toronto Blueshirts owner Eddie Livingstone had fallen out of favour with his Montreal counterparts, Sam Lichtenhein of the Wanderers and George Kennedy of the Canadiens. The two Montreal clubs, along with the Senators and the Quebec Bulldogs, dissolved the NHA, leading to the formation of the National Hockey League.

Ottawa went on to win four Stanley Cups between 1920 and 1927. The Senators' star players included goaltenders Clint Benedict and Alec Connell, defencemen King Clancy and George Boucher, and forwards Cy Denneny and Frank Nighbor.

The franchise was a casualty of the Great Depression in the 1930s. The team was sold to St. Louis in 1934, where it lasted for one year as the Eagles before dissolving.

Alec Connell was the cornerstone of Ottawa's Cup wins in the 1920s.

Hart Trophy Introduced

Awarded annually to the NHL's most valuable player in the regular season, the Hart Trophy is named after Cecil Hart, who managed and coached the Montreal Canadiens. Hart was behind the Habs bench from 1926-27 to 1931-32, winning consecutive Stanley Cups in 1930 and 1931. He was talked out of retirement to begin the 1936-37 season, coaching an additional three years thereafter.

The trophy was donated to the league by Cecil's father, Dr. David Hart, in 1923. The elder Hart was a Jewish physician and was the first president of the Zionist Society of Montreal, while also being prominent in the Mason society. Dr. Hart intended the award to be handed to the NHL's most "useful" player, even though the criterion became adopted as the most "valuable" player.

The award's namesake, Cecil, was named a director to the Canadiens after being influential in the franchise's sale in 1921. Cecil Hart posted a record of 196-125-73 in 394 regular-season games. He was forced to retire midway through his final season, 1938-39, due to illness, and he passed away just a year later.

Frank Nighbor of the Ottawa Senators won the inaugural Hart Trophy in 1923-24. Nighbor collected eleven goals and 17 points over 20 games. The numbers were respectable, but not among the league leaders, thus supporting the "most useful" player definition over the "most valuable" player definition that was originally intended for the award.

The closest Hart Trophy vote in league history came in 2001-02 when Montreal goalie Jose Theodore and Calgary forward Jarome Iginla each finished with 434 points, based on a weighted voting system. Theodore edged Iginla by a razor-thin margin of 26 first-place votes to 23. In 1989-90, Mark Messier of Edmonton narrowly triumphed over Ray Bourque of Boston 227-225 to claim hockey's highest individual honour.

Wayne Gretzky's name is inscribed on the trophy nine times, including a run of eight consecutive honours, from 1979 to 1987. The leaders of the great Oilers dynasty of the 1980s, Gretzky and Messier are the only players to win the Hart Trophy with more than one team. The Great One took home the award in his first season with Los Angeles, 1988-89, while Messier had his name inscribed again after being dealt to the New York Rangers in 1991-92.

Since the 1967 expansion, only two defencemen have won the award. Bobby Orr, in his reinvention of the defence position with the Boston Bruins, won three straight Harts beginning in 1969-70. No other blueliner claimed the trophy until Chris Pronger of St. Louis did so in 1999-2000.

Dominik Hasek won the award in both 1997 and 1998. As such, he is the only goalie to win the Hart Trophy in consecutive years.

The Hart Trophy is one of the most important honours in the NHL.

The Quebec Bulldogs

Originally formed in 1878, the Quebec Bulldogs won consecutive Stanley Cups in the National Hockey Association beginning in 1911-12. This was the first year in which the rover position was eliminated, leaving six instead of seven men on the ice per team.

The Stanley Cup provision at the time was for the trophy to be awarded to the team that finished in first place after an 18-game regular season. Quebec won its last game of the year, 6-5, in overtime. Joe Hall provided the heroics, scoring the tying goal in the final minute before netting the overtime winner, placing the pressure on the Bulldogs' challengers, the Ottawa Senators, who were playing the Wanderers. But Ottawa couldn't handle the Montreal Wanderers, dropping a 5-2 decision to give the Stanley Cup to Quebec.

The 1912-13 campaign belonged to the defending champs. In a six-team NHA, the Bulldogs were the only team to finish above .500, cruising to a 16-4-0 record over a 20-game schedule. Goaltender Paddy Moran played in every game and led the league in goals-against average.

The Stanley Cup challenge featured the Bulldogs playing host to the Sydney Millionaires. The Nova Scotia team was no match for the host squad as Quebec won both games by scores of 14-3 and 6-2. Joe Malone scored nine goals in Game One of the series.

In the fall of 1917, Quebec became one of the five founding franchises of the National Hockey League. But the Bulldogs were depleted of players enlisted in the Great War and were unable to commit to participation in the inaugural season. As a result, the team suspended operations, leaving its players available in a dispersal draft.

Two years later, with the league in disarray and down to three teams after the Montreal Wanderers folded, the Quebec franchise was resurrected by manager Mike Quinn. But the fans who showed up to Quebec Arena witnessed more than their fair share of failure. The season opener on Christmas Day was a 12-5 pounding at the hands of the Montreal Canadiens and was a foreshadowing of a dreadful year. The Bulldogs won just four of their 20 games.

The team's only bright spot was the play of Malone, who scored an incredible 39 goals. Malone also registered ten assists to give him the scoring title by three points over his closest competitor, Newsy Lalonde of the Canadiens.

The 1919-20 season proved to be the only year of existence in the NHL for the Bulldogs. The team relocated to Hamilton in the fall and became known as the Tigers, where the franchise survived for five more seasons.

The Quebec Bulldogs were Stanley Cup champions in 1912 and 1913.

NHL Expands to U.S.

By the end of the 1923-24 season, the NHL had survived seven tumultuous years and had finally established four healthy franchises in Hamilton, Montreal, Ottawa, and Toronto. The league was ready to expand south of the border.

Charles Adams, a wealthy New England grocery-store entrepreneur, and Tex Rickard, a boxing promoter from New York, were both eager to bring hockey to the United States. As summer rolled around, league president Frank Calder was also reviewing applications for a second Toronto team and a team in Philadelphia, in addition to hearing the pitches from Adams and Rickard.

Rickard had withdrawn his application by late August, having grander plans to build a larger version of Madison Square Garden. Adams, however, was still very much interested in a franchise for Boston. In the fall, he came to terms with the league to acquire an expansion team for $15,000.

The Bruins were the first American team to join the NHL, in 1924.

Adams's first move was to hire Art Ross as coach and general manager. A multi-talented athlete with a pedigree that included boxing, baseball, and football, Ross had played for over a decade in the amateur leagues and in the National Hockey Association. His last appearance as a player was a three-game stint with the Montreal Wanderers in 1917-18.

Meanwhile, although the New York bid was postponed, a second Montreal team was interested in joining the NHL, presenting complications to Boston's ambitions in the process. Cecil Hart was actively gathering players for a franchise that would oppose the Canadiens in his hometown, even though the league hadn't officially given its approval.

Eventually, on October 12, 1924, the NHL awarded new franchises to both Boston and Montreal, which named their clubs the Bruins and the Maroons, respectively. Adams, who had affection for the colour brown, gave his team brown sweaters with gold stripes. The league's newest members faced off against each other for their inaugural games, in Boston, on December 1. The Bruins prevailed, 2-1.

It was a rough first year for the team in Beantown as the Bruins finished last in the six-team league with a record of 6-24-0. Playing before sparse crowds at Boston Arena, the team had fewer fans for their games than the local amateur teams were able to draw.

Unfazed, Ross was able to guide the Bruins to a fourth-place finish the next year, Sprague Cleghorn becoming a key off-season acquisition in boosting the team's fortunes. Legendary defenceman Eddie Shore came on board beginning in 1926-27.

Two years later, the Bruins were hoisting the Stanley Cup for the first time. By then, Boston was the elite team in a five-team American Division that included teams in New York, Detroit, Chicago, and Pittsburgh.

The Montreal Wanderers

Founded in December 1903, the same month as the birth of the airplane, the Montreal Wanderers enjoyed great success during the first decade of the 20th century. Informally nicknamed the "Redbands" because of their red and white uniforms, the Wanderers won four Stanley Cups between 1906 and 1910.

WANDERERS HOCKEY CLUB.
WINNERS OF STANLEY CUP AND WORLD'S CHAMPIONS.
1907

The Montreal Wanderers ceased operations after their arena burned down.

The team's inaugural season in the Federal Amateur Hockey League ended in controversy as it challenged the Ottawa Silver Seven for the Stanley Cup. The game, held on March 2, 1904, at Montreal's Westmount Arena, ended in a 5-5 tie, but the Wanderers refused to play two road games in Ottawa, forfeiting hockey's championship trophy to the Silver Seven.

A heated rivalry ensued between the two clubs, and a rematch was held two years later in a two-game, total-goals series for the Stanley Cup. The Wanderers won Game One handily, 9-1, as rushing rover Lester Patrick scored two goals. When Montreal scored the opening tally in Game Two, it seemed as though the team was on its way to an effortless series win. But the Silver Seven sparked a furious rally with nine consecutive goals. Fortunately for the Wanderers, they answered with two goals to clinch the 1906 Cup win.

The following season saw the Kenora Thistles defeat the Wanderers in a two-game Stanley Cup challenge series in January 1907, only to have Montreal exact their revenge on their opponents just two months later to reclaim the prize. At the celebratory parade, the Stanley Cup was somehow left behind and subsequently stolen. Luckily the trophy was returned when the thief realized that it had no exorbitant market value.

The Wanderers finished 8-2-0 in the Eastern Canada Amateur Hockey Association the next year to defend their title. Montreal was challenged four times for the Stanley Cup in the calendar year 1908 and won on each occasion, defeating teams from Ottawa, Winnipeg, Toronto, and Edmonton. Art Ross, who had come over from Kenora, became just the second player to win consecutive Stanley Cups while playing on different teams.

The 1909-10 season saw the formation of the National Hockey Association. The Wanderers, which came over from the ECAHA, finished 11-1-0 to take their fourth Cup title. Montreal faced one challenge for the Cup in March, easily defeating the Berlin Union Jacks, 7-3.

Hockey Hall of Fame member Dickie Boon managed the Wanderers through all four of their championships. Throughout their NHA existence, the offence was led by Harry Hyland, who collected 144 goals in just 117 games in seven seasons.

The Wanderers played just four games in the NHL's first season, 1917-18, folding after the Westmount Arena burned down.

The Death of Georges Vezina

Georges Vezina – for whom the trophy awarded annually to the NHL's best goaltender is named – was the Monteal Canadiens' cornerstone at his position for 15 seasons. Epitomizing the style of stand-up goalie in an era where netminders were forbidden to fall to the ice, Vezina played 328 consecutive games, all with the Habs.

Georges Vezina was the greatest goaltender of the early years of pro hockey.

Vezina first backstopped the Canadiens to the Stanley Cup in 1915-16. Montreal, the NHA champions, duelled with the Portland Rosebuds, the best team in the Pacific Coast Hockey Association, in a tightly-contested, five-game series. Montreal was victorious, 2-1, in the deciding game when Goldie Prodgers scored on an end-to-end-rush late in the third period.

The Habs appeared in two of the next three Stanley Cup finals but came away empty-handed. In 1917, the Seattle Metropolitans outlasted the Canadiens three games to one, becoming the first U.S.-based team to win hockey's hallowed trophy. Then, in 1919, the series between the same two teams was cancelled because of an influenza epidemic.

Vezina earned his second taste of victory in 1923-24. Leading all goaltenders in the regular season with three shutouts and a goals-against average of 1.97, the "Chicoutimi Cucumber" posted a perfect record in the playoffs. Montreal won two, two-game series against Pacific Coast Hockey League champions Vancouver, and Western Canada Hockey League champions Calgary, respectively, to reclaim the Stanley Cup. Vezina allowed just four goals in as many games, posting a shutout along the way.

The Canadiens failed to defend their title the next year, losing to the Victoria Cougars. Vezina was the goals-against average leader in the regular season for a second straight time.

As the 1925-26 season got underway, Vezina was in failing health. Looking pale and fragile and sweating profusely through workouts, he lost thirty-five pounds in training camp and had a high fever as he started the opening game against Pittsburgh on November 28. Vezina didn't play beyond the first period.

The following day, Vezina was diagnosed with tuberculosis. He was forced to retire from the game and paid one final visit to his teammates in the Montreal dressing room on December 3 before going home to Chicoutimi.

Vezina passed away on March 27, 1926, at l'Hôtel-Dieu hospital. He was 39 years old. He left behind his widow, Marie, along with the adoration of thousands of fans. Over 1,500 people attended his funeral.

Prior to the start of the next season, Canadiens owners Leo Dandurand, Louis Letourneau, and Joseph Cattaranich established the Vezina Trophy in memory of their late goaltender.

The Hamilton Tigers

After the demise of the short-lived Quebec Bulldogs franchise at the end of the 1919-20 season, NHL president Frank Calder faced new challenges from the league's old rival. Eddie Livingstone, who was left on the outside looking in when the NHL was first formed, was hoping to create a new league called the Canadian Hockey Association, with two teams based in Toronto along with franchises in Cleveland and Hamilton.

Calder was more than ready to spar with Livingstone once again and offered Hamilton the Quebec franchise for the NHL.

Meanwhile, the heart of Livingstone's entire operation hinged on control of Toronto's Mutual Street Arena, home to the NHL's St. Patricks. Livingstone had partnered with the rink's owner, Percy Quinn, to obtain a court order to lay claim to the rink. "Getting ice in Toronto or not getting it means the death of one league or the other," he told a reporter.

But Livingstone lost his bid when the presiding judge ruled against him. Thus, the former Bulldogs were resurrected as the Hamilton Tigers, and the Abso-Pure Ice Company became the new owners. The Tigers were coached and managed by Percy Thompson, who also ran the team's home rink, the Barton Street Arena.

Hamilton won its debut game against Montreal on December 22, 1920, by a score of 5-0. But the bright moments in the team's inaugural campaign were few and far between. The Tigers won just six of 24 games that season. Joe Malone was their leading scorer, collecting 20 goals in 28 games.

Thompson's squad finished in last place in each of its first four seasons. Then, in 1924-25, the Tigers were coached by Jimmy Gardner and featured a high-scoring forward line of Billy Burch centring brothers Red and Shorty Green. Hamilton vaulted to a 19-10-1 finish, the best record in the league.

But the team's much-anticipated appearance in the NHL finals against Montreal was cancelled when the Tigers players went on strike. Feeling that they had not been properly compensated for the increase in regular-season games, from 24 to 30, the players demanded an extra two hundred dollars each. They were rebuffed. Calder awarded the NHL championship to the Canadiens, who had beaten the St. Patricks in the semi-finals.

NHL adversary Livingstone resurfaced yet again, looking to put a team into the new Madison Square Garden in New York. Calder responded by awarding an NHL franchise to the Big Apple, where it became known as the New York Americans.

The Tigers were subsequently sold to the new club for $75,000, ending a five-year stay in Hamilton.

Hamilton, Ontario, had NHL hockey nearly a century ago, but for only five years.

NHL Controls the Cup

The 'holy grail' of hockey, the Stanley Cup, was donated by Sir Frederick Arthur Stanley, Lord Stanley of Preston in 1892. The trophy – which was initially nothing more than a silver bowl – was purchased for the equivalent of about 50 dollars, and was intended for "the championship club of the Dominion of Canada."

The Montreal Amateur Athletic Association was the first winner in 1892-93, finishing in first place in the five-team Amateur Hockey Association. Starting the following season, teams were able to challenge for the prize. The Montreal AAA team accepted a challenge from Osgoode Hall in Toronto, the champions of the Ontario Hockey Association. However, due to lack of available ice, the teams never got to compete.

Over the next several years, teams from across the country would throw down the gauntlet and make their bid to wrestle the Stanley Cup from its champion. Most notably, a team Dawson City, Yukon made a 6,400-kilometre journey in part by dogsled across the country to Ottawa in 1905 for the chance to capture the trophy.

In 1906, the Kenora (formerly Rat Portage) Thistles had a two-month reign as Cup champions, successfully defeating the Montreal Wanderers in a two-game series in January before losing a rematch in March, thus marking the shortest reign ever.

As the sport's elite players became professionals, the Cup was awarded based on the first-place finish in the top pro league, whether the Eastern Canada Amateur Hockey Association or the National Hockey Association. Then, for thirteen straight years ending in 1925-26, the NHA/NHL champion faced the best team from the Pacific Coast Hockey Association for the Stanley Cup. In time, challenges were accepted from American-based teams, changing the initial conditions that were set by Lord Stanley.

The Victoria Cougars were the last non-NHL team to compete for the prize, losing a best-of-five finals series to the Montreal Maroons in the spring of 1926. Nels Stewart led the way for Montreal with six goals in four games. Clint Benedict posted a 3-1 record in net, and all three victories were shutouts.

Starting with the 1926-27 season, the Stanley Cup has been exclusively awarded to the champion of the NHL.

The Ottawa Senators were the first team to retain the coveted trophy without having to fend off a challenger from another league. In that year's playoffs, the Senators posted a 2-0-2 record against Boston in the Stanley Cup finals. Game Three in Ottawa had to be halted after the first 20-minute overtime because of bad ice. Goalie Alec Connell had a magnificent series, allowing just three goals in fourteen periods of hockey.

The Stanley Cup is the most attractive trophy in all of sports.

The Montreal Maroons

Prior to the start of the 1924-25 season, league president Frank Calder awarded two new franchises to the NHL, the Boston Bruins and the Montreal Maroons. In Montreal, the Canadiens had been the city's pre-eminent team, earning the adulation of both English and French-speaking fans.

The landscape quickly changed, however, and the Maroons were established to represent the Anglophone part of the community. The team's founders—William Northey, Donat Raymond, and Edward Beatty—formed the Canadian Arena Company to build a new rink, the Montreal Forum, at the corner of Rue St. Catherine and Atwater.

Even though they weren't the Forum's first tenants, the crosstown rival Habs played the first game in the new arena, on November 29, defeating the Toronto St. Patricks, 7-1. The Canadiens' own rink, Mount Royal Arena, had a faulty ice-making plant, necessitating the change of venue.

Nicknamed appropriately for the colour of their uniforms, the Maroons hosted the Habs for the first time on December 27 playing to a heated 1-1 tie. The game was attended by 11,000 fans, setting a record.

The Maroons' first season ended in a disappointing fifth-place finish in the six-team NHL. But they recovered in the following year to take the NHL title. Led by Hart Trophy-winning Nels Stewart, who also won the scoring title with 42 points in 36 games, the Maroons fended off a challenge from Victoria for the Stanley Cup, beating the Cougars three games to one in the finals series. The English-speaking Maroons captured hockey's greatest prize without having a Frenchman on the roster.

The team returned to the finals against the New York Rangers in 1928, led by their potent "S" line of Stewart, Hooley Smith, and Babe Siebert. Because Madison Square Garden was booked for the circus, the Forum hosted all five games. Montreal lost Game Five in a heartbeaker, 2-1, the Rangers' Frank Boucher beating goalie Clint Benedict for the game-winner.

The Maroons' last hurrah came in 1934-35 when they swept the heavily-favoured Maple Leafs for the Stanley Cup. It was the first all-Canadian finals series since 1926. Goaltender Alec Connell allowed just four goals in the three-game sweep.

With the Great Depression taking its toll on the global economy, Montreal couldn't support two hockey teams. Players' salaries were escalating, and the cost of travelling was prohibitive.

STANLEY CUP PRESENTATION

Montreal's other team, the Maroons, were also Stanley Cup champions.

Following the Maroons' last-place finish in 1937-38, the team folded. Players were asked to leave their equipment behind but were permitted to keep their sweaters. Formally, the league suspended the franchise for a year, but it was never reinstated.

Forward Passing Allowed

The early years of the NHL were defence-oriented. While it's rare for a goaltender to post eleven shutouts or more in today's game, the feat was becoming the norm once the 44-game schedule was introduced in 1926-27.

Starting with that season, over the next three years, a goalie reached the eleven-shutout mark 15 times. Netminders including Alec Connell, Roy Worters, Clint Benedict, and Lorne Chabot were impenetrable walls between the pipes. George Hainsworth of the Montreal Canadiens established the all-time single-season mark with 22 shutouts in 1928-29, blanking the opponents, on average, every other game.

Goalscoring doubled when the NHL permitted forward passing in all zones.

Meanwhile the league had begun to institute forward passing as a means of generating more scoring. Beginning in 1927-28, forward passing was permitted in the neutral and defensive zones. The following season, the rule was amended to allow a forward pass into the attacking zone, but only if the receiver was still in the neutral zone at the time that the pass was made.

The results were still less than desired. In 1928-29, teams scored just 64 goals on average, and only 2.92 goals per game. Finally, for the next year, the league allowed forward passing in the attacking zone as well. However, such a play was still prohibited across the blue line. Officially the revised rule read, "No attacking player allowed to precede the play when entering the opposing defensive zone," essentially establishing the offside rule.

By finally permitting the forward pass in all three zones, the NHL achieved its objective of opening the game to more offence. Scoring doubled in 1929-30 as each team scored an average of 130 goals, and the goals per game average vaulted to 5.81.

Prior to that season, only three times had a team reached the 100-goal mark. But in 1929-30 each of the league's ten teams reached the century plateau. Even the lowly Pittsburgh Pirates, which won just five of 44 games, managed to find the back of the net 102 times. The Boston Bruins led the way with 179 goals.

The boost in individual production was also evident. The Bruins' Cooney Weiland won the scoring title with 43 goals and 73 points. By comparison, the previous season's champion Ace Bailey of Toronto had led all players with 22 goals and 32 points. Bailey's output would have been good for just 22nd place in 1929-30.

The introduction of the forward pass remains the single most important rule change in hockey. Look no further than Gordie Howe, Wayne Gretzky, or Sidney Crosby as evidence.

The Birth of the Vancouver Canucks

Before the Vancouver Canucks entered the NHL, they were a minor pro team, playing in the Pacific Coast Hockey Association for seven years beginning in 1945, and then the Western Hockey League starting in 1952.

The NHL had doubled in size from six teams to 12 as a result of the 1967 expansion, and Canucks president Cyrus McLean applied for a franchise one year later. After thoroughly reviewing the proposal, the league's governors agreed to make Vancouver, along with Buffalo, the next two teams to enter the league.

However, the league had to come up with a plan to align the divisions. The so-called "Original Six" teams had been placed in the East Division while the six new-comers from south of the border were all in the West Division. The governors decided to move Chicago to the West and put Vancouver and Buffalo in the East, an imperfect resolution considering the Canucks' relative geographic location.

But the Canucks encountered another major obstacle. The franchise fee was boosted to $6-million, an exorbitant sum for a minor league club. Fortunately, Vancouver had a white knight in Thomas Scallen, a lawyer and entrepreneur from Minnesota. Scallen, whose assets included an Ice Follies show, was enamoured by the city and invested without hesitation. The NHL officially awarded the two new franchises on December 2, 1969, and both teams were slated to make their debuts the next fall.

As a result, the 1970 Amateur Draft became all the more intriguing. Gilbert Perreault of the Montreal Junior Canadiens was the favourite to be the first-overall pick. The opportunity to draft the sure-fire prospect was determined by the spin of a roulette wheel. Vancouver was allotted the digits 1-10 while Buffalo was given the numbers 11-20.

The Canucks rejoiced when the wheel appeared to stop at number 1. But new Sabres general manager Punch Imlach protested, and correctly observed that the needle was pointing to 11, obscuring an extra '1.'

Buffalo celebrated and drafted Perreault, who became the franchise player for the Sabres on the way to a Hall of Fame career. For good measure, Perreault wore number 11 as a tribute to that fateful spin, and that number hangs today in the rafters in Buffalo as a retired sweater.

Vancouver chose defenceman Dale Tallon from the Toronto Marlboros with the second overall pick. Tallon went on to a very respectable NHL career with the Canucks, Blackhawks, and Penguins, playing 642 games over ten seasons.

But there's no question that the roulette wheel decided the fates of the league's 1970 expansion cousins for several years.

The Vancouver Canucks were the first new team in Canada since the Ottawa Senators folded in the 1930s.

Maple Leaf Gardens Opens

Conn Smythe needed a new home for the Maple Leafs, which were playing out of the 8,000-seat Mutual Street Arena. But in the midst of the Great Depression, funds were scarce. Food, not sports, was the priority in such troubled times.

Unwavering in spite of the harsh economy, Smythe, along with his assistant Frank Selke, devised a plan to hire construction workers who would be paid partially in stock in the new building. Then Smythe persuaded the T. Eaton Company to sell him the land located at the corner of Church and Carlton Streets in Toronto. Miraculously, he was also able to get financing from other investors, including Sun Life and the Bank of Commerce.

Just five months after the first shovel hit the ground, Maple Leaf Gardens stood erect at 60 Carlton Street. The arena had a capacity of over 13,000 and every hockey fan had an unobstructed view of the ice surface.

On November 12, 1931, the NHL season got underway with the Leafs hosting the Chicago Black Hawks in the Gardens' first game. The 48th Highlanders entertained the sellout crowd with their rendition of "Happy Days Are Here Again."

Above the rink, Foster Hewitt began his Hockey Night In Canada radio broadcasts, bringing his trademark play-by-play punctuated with, "He shoots; he scores!" to the country.

The puck dropped for the opening faceoff at 8:55 pm. Chicago's Harold "Mush" March scored 2:30 into the game, making history. Toronto tied the game when Charlie Conacher converted a pass from Joe Primeau at 18:42 of the second period.

Ultimately, the Black Hawks spoiled the party when Vic Ripley fired home the game-winner at 2:35 of the third period, rounding out the scoring in a 2-1 Chicago win. The inaugural Maple Leaf Gardens game was attended by 13,542 fans.

Despite the loss, Toronto – led by the Kid Line of Charlie Conacher, Joe Primeau, and Busher Jackson – finished second in the four-team Canadian division and posted a 17-4-3 record on its new home ice. The Leafs advanced to the Stanley Cup finals to face the New York Rangers, Smythe's previous employers.

Smythe exacted revenge on the team that fired him in favour of Lester Patrick, as the Leafs swept the series in three games. The scores of 6-4, 6-2 and 6-4 in the respective games gave the 1932 finals the nickname the "Tennis Series." Game Three was played in Toronto, and Ace Bailey scored the winner, clinching the city's first Stanley Cup championship in ten years.

Opening night of Maple Leaf Gardens, November 12, 1931.

The Birth of the Original Winnipeg Jets

Two of the most active voices in the formation of the WHA were those of "Wild Bill" Hunter and Ben Hatskin. Both men operated junior teams, located in Edmonton and Winnipeg, respectively.

Hatskin, a former football player with the Blue Bombers of the Canadian Football League, had owned the junior Jets since the mid-1960s. He gave the same nickname to his WHA team when the league began play in 1972-73.

The league's first season had twelve teams split into two divisions. Winnipeg was in the Western Division along with the Alberta (later Edmonton) Oilers, Chicago Cougars, Houston Aeros, Los Angeles Sharks, and Minnesota Fighting Saints.

The watershed moment for the upstart league came in June 1972 when Hatskin signed Chicago Blackhawks superstar Bobby Hull to a multi-million-dollar deal to play in Winnipeg. The departure of the "Golden Jet" from the NHL paved the way for other players to follow suit.

But the Jets' recruiting wasn't limited to one side of the Atlantic Ocean. Winnipeg pioneered the initiative to scout European nations for hockey talent. To start the 1974-75 season, the team acquired Swedish forwards Anders Hedberg and Ulf Nilsson and their countryman Lars-Erik Sjoberg on defence.

All three players had represented Sweden at the previous year's World Championships. Hedberg and Nilsson were assigned to play alongside Hull, the threesome becoming known as the "Hot Line," the league's most dangerous trio. Sjoberg, an outstanding blueliner, had served as captain of the Swedish national team. Eventually he became the first European to wear the "C" for both a WHA and NHL team.

The Jets ended the Houston Aeros' run of two straight AVCO Cup titles by winning the championship in 1976. It marked a run of three AVCO Cups in four years for Winnipeg, as the Jets also skated off the ice victorious in 1978 and again in 1979 for what would be the final WHA season. Winnipeg was one of four WHA teams that merged with the NHL.

The NHL incarnation of the Jets didn't enjoy the success of its predecessor. Winning just nine of 80 games in 1980-81, the team struggled to get above the .500 mark even as it drafted a franchise player in future Hall of Famer Dale Hawerchuk. Playing in the same division as powerhouses Edmonton and Calgary made it all but impossible for the Jets to advance far in the playoffs.

In 1996, a struggling Canadian economy forced the sale of the team and its relocation to Phoenix, Arizona but, two decades later, the city benefitted from the demise of the Atlanta Thrashers, which moved to Manitoba and was named, again, the Jets.

Teemu Selanne was one of the first superstars with the original Jets.

Howie Morenz Dies

Dubbed the "Mitchell Meteor" in honour of his Ontario hometown, Howie Morenz was the franchise player for the Montreal Canadiens from the late 1920s to the early '30s, in the same way that Rocket Richard, Jean Beliveau, and Guy Lafleur dominated their respective eras wearing the bleu, blanc et rouge.

In 1923-24 the rookie Morenz, along with Aurele Joliat and Billy Boucher, formed the youngest line in the league. The trio led the team in scoring in both the regular season and the play-offs as the Habs won their first Stanley Cup in eight seasons.

Morenz led the league in scoring twice and was the Hart Trophy winner three times. He went on to win two more Stanley Cups, in 1930 and 1931.

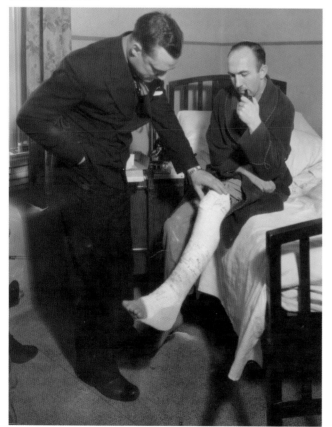

Howie Morenz in hospital, shortly before he died of a 'broken heart.'

By the end of the 1933-34 season, however, Morenz's scoring prowess was fading. The Montreal fans turned their wrath on their once-beloved superstar as the Canadiens suffered two first-round playoff exits in a row. Morenz was traded to Chicago, then played for the New York Rangers for half a season, before the Habs welcomed him back into the fold.

Morenz was elated to return to his original team. He was no longer the dynamic scoring threat who carried the offence, but he told sportswriters, "the spirit is back!"

Disaster struck on January 28, 1937, in a game between Montreal and Chicago. In a race with Black Hawks' defenceman Babe Siebert, Morenz slid into the end boards. Both players crashed at full speed, and Morenz's left leg snapped. The leg was fractured in four places, all but ending his hockey career.

Morenz was taken to Hôpital Saint-Luc to recover. Bedridden, he hung on to every last shred of hope of possibly returning to the team while visitors dropped in by the dozens to sign his cast. But in February he suffered a nervous breakdown, and on March 8, he suffered a fatal heart attack at age 34.

Two days later, Morenz's funeral was held at the Montreal Forum. Thousands of mourners lined up to pay their respects as the casket lay at centre ice. The rows of chairs on the rink surface were filled to capacity, while a massive crowd gathered outside. Morenz left behind his wife, Mary, and three children—Howie Jr., Donald, and Marlene.

Joliat, who had Morenz as a linemate during both of his fallen teammate's stints in Montreal, provided his personal insight. "When he realized that he would never play again, he couldn't live with it. I think Howie died of a broken heart."

The Birth of the Quebec Nordiques

When the first World Hockey Association general meeting was held in September 1971, Quebec was not on the list of the original ten cities that would be getting a franchise. However, Gary Davidson, one of the forerunners of the upstart league, did plan to operate a team in San Francisco upon the commencement of play the following season.

But the next twelve months weren't without obstacles, as the WHA tried to establish its footing. The Miami Screaming Eagles would never see the light of day, becoming the Philadelphia Blazers before even a single puck was dropped. Nor did the San Francisco team – the Sharks – ever participate in an opening faceoff.

Instead, a group of Quebec City businessmen that ran the junior Quebec Remparts—and was led by Marius Fortier—bought the Sharks. The Bay Area was losing its appetite for hockey after witnessing the failure of the NHL's California Golden Seals. Eccentric Seals owner Chuck Finley, who infamously ordered his team to dress in white skates, had failed to deliver a winning roster.

Fortier's group purchased the San Francisco team from Davidson for $210,000. They brought in wealthy businessman Paul Racine as an investor, and also had "Wild Bill" Hunter of the Oilers help guarantee Quebec's franchise fee.

The team, named the Nordiques because of its relative geographic location, was one of the WHA's twelve franchises when the first games were played in 1972-73. The team successfully persuaded Montreal Canadiens defenceman J.C. Tremblay to patrol its blue line. Tremblay had been a two-time All-Star Team selection and five-time Stanley Cup champion with the Habs.

However, the Nordiques were able to lure an even bigger Montreal name to their team. Maurice "Rocket" Richard was introduced as Quebec's first coach. But Richard's tenure behind the bench was short-lived. The Rocket, who tried to match lines as a coaching strategy, was a mere shadow of the man who could fire a slapshot past a goalie at will. He couldn't remember players' names, and he was losing sleep and eating poorly from the stress of his new post.

After losing their first game to the Cleveland Crusaders, the Nordiques shut out the Alberta Oilers for their first-ever win. Richard promptly stepped down and was replaced by Maurice Filion. The Rocket was too proud to accept the payment he was offered for his services.

The Nordiques' only AVCO Cup championship came in the 1976-77 season. They were admitted into the NHL along with three other WHA teams in 1979, playing in Quebec City for 16 seasons before moving to Colorado to become the Avalanche.

Hall of Famer Joe Sakic played his entire career with the Quebec/Colorado franchise.

All-American Hawks

Heading into the 1937-38 season, there was no reason to believe that the Chicago Black Hawks were Stanley Cup contenders. The team had finished 13 games under .500 and out of the playoffs the previous year. And the Black Hawks' offensive leader, Paul Thompson, about to turn thirty-one, was in the twilight of his career.

In fact, Chicago struggled through the '37-'38 campaign, finishing with just 14 wins and 37 points in a 48-game schedule. New York Rangers general manager Lester Patrick mocked the eight American-born players put on the roster by Chicago owner Major Frederic McLaughlin as a bunch of amateurs.

Still, Chicago qualified for the post-season, the only team with a losing record to so, ending up in third place in the American Division. The quarter-finals pitted the Hawks against the Montreal Canadiens.

The Habs had finished a dozen points better than Chicago in the regular season but lost the deciding game in the best-of-three series in overtime. Thompson, coming off an all-star year with Chicago, had the puck deflect off his skate past goalie Wilf Cude at 11:49 of overtime to send the Canadiens packing. Future Hall of Famer Aurele Joliat had missed the entire play-offs for Montreal with an injured shoulder and announced his retirement three days later.

Up next in the semi-finals was the New York Americans, and again the Black Hawks

stunned their opponents in three games, setting up a finals matchup against the Canadian Division's best team, the Toronto Maple Leafs.

To this point in the season, Black Hawks goaltender Mike Karakas – a native of Aurora, Minnesota – had carried the load in net. But just before Game One of the finals, doctors discovered that Karakas had a broken toe. Desperate to find a netminder, Chicago located former New York Americans' goalie Alfie Moore – in a Toronto bar according to urban legend – and signed him to a contract. Moore's appearance was a success as the Black Hawks won Game One, 3-1, at Maple Leaf Gardens.

Toronto evened the series when it shot five pucks past another hastily-acquired substitute goalie, Paul Goodman. By the time the series shifted to the Windy City, Karakas was fitted with a steel boot and ready to return to the lineup.

The Black Hawks won the next two games at home to win the unlikeliest of championships, becoming victorious with a roster entirely comprised of full or half-Americans.

So pessimistic was the NHL about the Black Hawks' chances that the Stanley Cup was never sent to Chicago, and the winners had no trophy with which to celebrate.

The Chicago Black Hawks won their second Cup in five years in 1938.

The Birth of the New Winnipeg Jets

After the original Jets were eliminated in Game Six of the 1996 Western Conference quarter-finals, a tearful crowd at the Winnipeg Arena bid farewell to their hockey club. Unable to keep up with mounting financial losses, then-owner Barry Shenkarow had sold the franchise, signifying what seemed like the end of NHL hockey in the Manitoba capital after 17 years.

The players saluted the fans while a banner that read "Our Jets Will Fly -4- Ever" streamed down from the upper seating level. The new owners, Richard Burke and Steven Gluckstern, had initial designs on moving the franchise to Minnesota before eventually relocating the team to Phoenix, where it became known as the Coyotes.

The small consolation for Winnipeg hockey fans was the immediate purchase of the International Hockey League's Minnesota Moose by Mark Chipman, the chairman of True North Sports and Entertainment. Chipman had been one of several businessmen who were behind the "Save Our Jets" rally to prevent the Jets' departure out of Winnipeg. While all efforts proved to be futile, Chipman nevertheless clung to aspirations of the NHL's return to the city someday.

Over the next four seasons, the NHL expanded by four teams, placing franchises in Nashville, Minnesota, Columbus, and Atlanta.

The Atlanta Thrashers entered the NHL in 1999-2000, playing eleven seasons in relative mediocrity. They made the playoffs just once, in 2007, and made a hasty exit in a four-game sweep at the hands of the New York Rangers.

And, just like the Flames who had attempted a foray into Georgia's hockey psyche in the late 1970s, the Thrashers were met with relative indifference. The hockey team was relegated to the back of the sports pages in a city preoccupied with the NFL Falcons, NBA Hawks, and the University of Georgia Bulldogs.

On May 31, 2011, the league approved the sale and relocation of the Thrashers to the Winnipeg-based True North group. The transaction came unexpectedly as it appeared at the time that the Coyotes – which also struggled financially – would be the next team to hire moving vans.

But Chipman had remained steadfast in his resolve that he had maintained ever since the original Jets had left town. In those intervening years, True North had since helped build the MTS Centre as a home for the Moose, replacing the Winnipeg Arena. The rink would now host NHL hockey, as envisioned by Chipman all along.

On October 9, 2011, the new Winnipeg Jets beat Montreal, 5-1, in their debut. Nik Antropov scored the first-ever goal for the reborn team.

Andrew Ladd captained the Jets during the 2014-15 season.

Kraut Line Goes to War

The Boston Bruins were Stanley Cup champions in 1940-41, marking their second title in three years. The dominant team had lost only eight of 48 games in the regular season and boasted one of the most dangerous forward units in hockey, the "Kraut Line."

The trio of Milt Schmidt, Bobby Bauer, and Woody Dumart was named because they were all of German descent and all hailed from Kitchener, Ontario, a city with a high German population once known as Berlin.

Buoyed with optimism in defending their title, the Bruins took to the ice in the fall to start the season. Sports created a brief diversion while the Axis and Allies were raging conflict in the Second World War.

But when the Japanese bombed Pearl Harbor on December 7, 1941 – the "day of infamy" as labelled by U.S. President Franklin D. Roosevelt – the landscape of the world was changed forever.

Schmidt, Bauer, and Dumart enlisted in the Royal Canadian Air Force while Boston goalie Frank Brimsek joined the U.S. Coast Guard.

On February 10, 1942, the Bruins hosted the Montreal Canadiens. It was to be the last game for the Kraut Line before the three left for their military service. Boston won the game easily, 8-1, Schmidt, Bauer, and Dumart combining for ten points in the dominating win.

At the end of the game, the crowd of 10,240 fans roared in appreciation. As thunderous applause echoed throughout the arena, the Kraut Line members were presented with their paycheques for the season, plus a generous bonus. Then the linemates were hoisted onto the shoulders of Bruins and Habs players alike as they were carried off the ice, possibly never to return.

The loss of Schmidt, Bauer, and Dumart was too much to overcome for the Bruins, which had compiled a 21-11-5 record before waving goodbye to their teammates. Over the remainder of the season, Boston went just 4-6-1.

In the playoffs, they defeated Chicago in the quarter-finals but lost to Detroit in the next round. Brimsek left to serve in the South Pacific following the season's end.

(l-r) Bobby Bauer, Milt Schmidt, and Woody Dumart of the great Kraut Line.

All four men – future Hall of Famers – stayed in military duty until the end of the war, thus missing the next three NHL seasons. When they did return to play in 1945-46, the skaters had trouble adjusting to the red line, which had been implemented two years earlier to speed up the game.

The Kraut Line disbanded with Bauer's retirement at the end of the 1946-47 season.

The Birth of the New Ottawa Senators

In the early days of the 20th century, hockey at its highest level was vibrant in the nation's capital. The original Ottawa Hockey Club, informally known as the Silver Seven, won four straight Stanley Cups, ending in 1906. Then, as the team formally adopted its Senators nickname, they added another six championships from 1909 to 1927, boasting players such as Cyclone Taylor, Frank Nighbor, and King Clancy in the mix.

But the Great Depression made it impossible for the team to survive, and the original Senators moved to St. Louis in 1934, playing for one season as the Eagles before the franchise dissolved.

For nearly six decades, Ottawa was left out of the NHL circuit. The city was granted one of the dozen inaugural WHA franchises, the Nationals, in 1972, but it became the Toronto Toros the following year.

Finally, in 1989, Bruce Firestone, chief executive officer of Terrace Investments, assembled a bid to bring professional hockey back to Ottawa. Submitting a letter of intent with the NHL for an expansion team, he also unveiled plans to build a 22,500-seat arena in the suburb of Kanata, west of the city. The Civic Centre, home to the junior 67's, was modest for its tenants but far below NHL standards.

On December 6, 1990, NHL president John Ziegler granted franchises to both Ottawa and Tampa Bay to begin play in 1992-93.

But the initiative spearheaded by Firestone met its challenges. The Ontario Agricultural Ministry had opposed construction on the Kanata farmland intended as the location for the Senators' new arena. There was also concern about vehicular congestion that the building would inevitably generate.

Eventually a compromise was reached by which Firestone agreed to reduce the capacity by 4,000, and the Ottawa Municipal Board gave their approval for construction to begin.

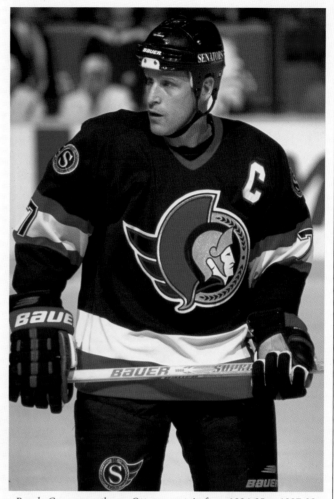

Randy Cunneyworth was Ottawa captain from 1994-95 to 1997-98.

In hockey-related manners, the team hired Mel Bridgman to be its first general manager and Rick Bowness as its first coach. While awaiting construction of the new arena – named the Palladium – the Senators played their first three-and-a-half seasons at the Civic Centre.

On October 8, 1992, the newly-incarnated Senators played their first game, hosting the Montreal Canadiens. Stanley Cup banners from the first edition of the team, plus a banner commemorating the retired number 8 of Frank Finnigan, were raised to the rafters.

Ottawa didn't disappoint the 10,500 fans in attendance, winning 5-3. Neil Brady got the Senators' first goal with a tap-in at the side of the net, a power-play marker that Montreal goalie Patrick Roy had no chance of stopping.

Leafs Rally From 3-0

The Toronto Maple Leafs got all that they could handle and more in the 1942 Stanley Cup finals. The Detroit Red Wings, which finished with a losing record and 15 points below the Leafs in the regular-season standings, had adopted a forecheck-heavy, offensive blueprint that Toronto coach Hap Day had difficulty countering.

As a result, the Leafs lost the first two games of the series at home, then lost the third game at Detroit's Olympia. On the brink of elimination, Day instituted some drastic changes, injecting some youth into the lineup. He shuffled a pair of defencemen, replacing Bucko McDonald with Ernie Dickens. But the shocker was the benching of one-time NHL scoring champion Gordie Drillon in favour of Don Metz.

Prior to Game Four, Day read to his players a letter written by a 14-year-old girl who expressed disappointment in the Leafs' play in the previous three games. Day's tactics seemed to spark his players as Toronto rallied from a 2-0 deficit to win Game Four by a 4-3 score. Metz's brother, Nick, had the game-winning goal.

Back at Maple Leaf Gardens, the Leafs won Game Five decisively by a 9-3 count. Nineteen-year-old Gaye Stewart made his only playoff appearance of the year, while Don Metz had an exceptional performance with a hat trick and five points.

In the next game, back in the Motor City, goalie Turk Broda

Syl Apps holds the Stanley Cup in 1942 after a most improbable comeback.

stifled the Red Wings at every turn on the way to a 3-0 shutout victory. Incredibly, the Leafs had evened the series, forcing a one-game showdown back at Maple Leaf Gardens for the Stanley Cup.

On April 18, the rink was filled to capacity, some 16,218 spectators watching history in the making. The attendance set a Canadian record for a hockey game. The Leafs fell behind 1-0 after one period but kept their composure. Sweeney Schriner, the franchise's first-ever Russian-born player, scored twice while unheralded centre Pete Langelle had the game-winner in a 3-1 victory.

The Leafs leapt over the boards in ecstasy, completing the most improbable of comebacks. As an added reward for their efforts, each player was given a gold coin that also served as a lifetime pass to Maple Leaf Gardens.

The feat of coming back from a 3-0 deficit to win a seven-game series had never been accomplished and has never been repeated since in the Stanley Cup finals.

Philadelphia rallied from 3-0 to defeat Boston in seven games in the 2010 Eastern Conference semi-finals. And the Los Angeles Kings, seemingly down-and-out against San Jose in the 2014 opening round, stormed back to win Games Four to Seven, carrying that momentum all the way to winning the Stanley Cup.

Best Players Born in
Montreal

MIKE BOSSY

Blessed with a lethal shot, Bossy recorded an NHL record nine consecutive 50-goal seasons beginning in his rookie year of 1977-78. His career goals-per-game average of .762 (573 goals in 752 games) is the highest of any player in league history with at least 200 goals.

MARTIN BRODEUR

The all-time goaltending leader with 691 wins and 125 shutouts, Brodeur backstopped the New Jersey Devils to three Stanley Cup championships. He led Team Canada to its first gold medal in 50 years at the 2002 Olympics in Salt Lake City and was victorious again at the 2010 Games in Vancouver.

RAY BOURQUE

Boston's anchor on defence for 21 seasons, Bourque excelled at both ends of the ice, earning an incredible 19 All-Star Team selections in his career, the most of any player at his position. A winner of five Norris Trophies, Bourque ended his career on a winning note, hoisting the Stanley Cup as a member of the Colorado Avalanche.

BERNIE GEOFFRION

Credited with perfecting the modern-day slapshot, Geoffrion terrorized goalies with his ability to fire pucks with tremendous velocity. "Boom Boom" won six Stanley Cups with the Habs.

DOUG HARVEY

Playing on the Canadiens' teams that dominated the mid-to-late 1950s, Harvey won seven Norris trophies, a mark bettered only by Bobby Orr and which has since been tied by Nicklas Lidstrom. His name is on the Stanley Cup six times.

MARIO LEMIEUX

"The Magnificent One," the all-time Penguins legend, Lemieux's combination of skill and strength was unequalled. He brought two Stanley Cups to Pittsburgh, winning three Hart Trophies and six scoring titles along the way. Lemieux's career points-per-game average of 1.883 is second only to Wayne Gretzky's (1.921).

MAURICE RICHARD

"The Rocket" was revered in Montreal like no other player before or since. With fiery determination, Richard was virtually unstoppable when driving to the net. The NHL's trophy awarded to the regular-season leader in goals is named in his honour.

LUC ROBITAILLE

The highest-scoring left winger of all-time, Robitaille racked up 668 goals and 1,394 points in 19 seasons. Although he never won a Stanley Cup with Los Angeles, where he played most of his career, he did achieve such glory in Detroit, in 2002.

GUMP WORSLEY

After a decade in New York, during which he quipped that the team gave him the most trouble was "the Rangers," Worsley was traded to Montreal where he won four Stanley Cups and two Vezina trophies. His career mark of 335 wins was 20th of all-time at the end of the 2014-15 season.

Mario Lemieux was one of the greats who grew up in hockey-mad Montreal.

Richard Scores 50 in 50

Hockey history may have unfolded very differently had Maurice "Rocket" Richard served in the military.

After an abbreviated 1942-43 rookie season with the Montreal Canadiens, Richard enlisted in the Canadian Army, following the lead of several NHL players at the time. But he was declared unfit for service after an examination of his medical history revealed that he'd suffered two broken legs.

Maurice Richard was the first player to score 50 goals in an NHL season.

That fall, Richard returned to the team. Coach Dick Irvin placed the right winger on a line with Elmer Lach at centre and Toe Blake on the left side. They collectively became known as the Punch Line, forming instant cohesion. The trio occupied the top three positions in scoring in both the regular season and play-offs as the Habs coasted to the Stanley Cup, losing just once in nine playoff games.

With explosive speed and unmatched determination, Richard was even more effective as the 1944-45 season got underway. On December 28, he victimized Detroit goalie Harry Lumley for five goals as the Habs thumped the Red Wings, 9-1.

By late January, Richard had bulged the twine 32 times in 30 games, scoring at a feverish pace. The individual record for most goals in a season was 44, set by another Canadiens player, Joe Malone, 27 years earlier.

It took just 40 games for Richard to tie Malone's record. Two games later, on February 25, the Canadiens hosted the Maple Leafs. Despite the best efforts of Toronto checking forwards Nick Metz and Bob Davidson to neutralize him, Richard finally set the all-time single season mark, unleashing a perfect shot past goalie Frank McCool for the record-breaking tally.

But there was one more benchmark to reach. The unprecedented 50-goal plateau would provide for perfect symmetry for a regular-season schedule that had as many games.

When Richard was just one goal shy of the mark, controversy ensued at the Montreal Forum. It was the penultimate game of the season, and the Rocket had an apparent goal disallowed by referee King Clancy. Despite the protests of the Habs' faithful fans, Richard's pursuit of history came down to game 50 in Boston, on March 18.

The Bruins held Richard in check for two periods. After Boston took a third-period lead, the record seemed more improbable with each passing second. But with just 2:15 left on the clock, Richard beat netminder Harvey Bennett for the elusive 50th goal.

No other player, including Richard himself, reached the milestone again until teammate Bernie Geoffrion did so, 16 years later in a 70-game season.

Hall of Fame brothers Frank and Lester Patrick were innovators in the sport, establishing the Pacific Coast Hockey Association in 1911. Introducing a fast-paced league that encouraged creativity, the Patricks also differentiated their brand of hockey from the game in Eastern Canada by introducing assists as an official statistic and placing numbers on the backs of players' sweaters.

Most significantly, the Westerners embraced the forward pass, a simple manoeuvre that was resisted by the National Hockey Association, and later the NHL, until the late 1920s.

By 1914-15, the Patricks had put together a free-wheeling team, the Vancouver Millionaires, that included speedy Fred "Cyclone" Taylor and versatile two-way forward Frank Nighbor. The Millionaires steamrolled their way to a PCHA championship with a 13-4 record.

Vancouver hosted the NHA champion Ottawa Senators for the Stanley Cup in 1915 in a best-of-five series. The series provided for two sets of rules, where odd-numbered games featured the western standards of an extra skater (a rover) but, more importantly, the forward pass. The even-numbered games would be played under eastern rules.

The Senators made the trek by rail to Vancouver, where the 10,500-seat Denman Street Arena hosted the first three games.

In Game One, it was ultimately the forward pass that worked to the Millionaires' advantage. Vancouver won handily, 6-2, as Ottawa had no strategy to defend their opponents' breakouts.

The Senators briefly gained momentum in the second game, vaulting to a 2-0 lead and taking liberties with Taylor, the Millionaires' star. But despite the eastern rules, Vancouver made the necessary adjustments, then countered with a barrage of offence en route to an 8-3 win.

Game Three was a lop-sided affair as the series reverted back to PCHA rules. Vancouver skated to an effortless 12-3 victory, Barney Stanley leading the way with four goals as the Millionaires' season ended triumphantly.

Each player was rewarded with $300 for his efforts, but there was no celebration with the Stanley Cup. The Senators, then the trophy's caretakers as NHA champions, had been so confident of victory that they had not brought the Cup from Ottawa.

While it was the eastern league that was eventually elevated to the highest level of professional hockey, the NHA – and subsequently the NHL – implemented many of the Patricks' innovations.

On March 26, 2015, exactly a century to the day that the Millionaires won the Stanley Cup, the Vancouver Canucks hosted the Colorado Avalanche in a commemorative game to mark the occasion. The Canucks' players wore heritage sweaters emblazoned on the front with their historical predecessors' "V" crest.

Vancouver's only Stanley Cup win came a century ago, in 1915.

Hall of Fame Established

The idea of building a hall of fame to honour hockey's greatest players started gaining momentum in the early 1940s. Baseball had opened its doors to a hallowed shrine in Cooperstown, New York, in 1939. Captain James T. Sutherland, a resident of Kingston, Ontario, and a former president of the Canadian Amateur Hockey Association, began spearheading the movement for a hockey version.

Sutherland had long advocated that Kingston was the birthplace of hockey. As a result, the city was established as the home to a new hockey hall of fame that was founded on September 10, 1943, in partnership with the CAHA and NHL. Kingston's mayor Stuart Crawford was appointed its first president.

Although construction of a building to house the game's artefacts was years away, the first Hockey Hall of Fame inductees were announced in 1945. The first members in the Players' Category were Dan Bain, Hobey Baker, Dubbie Bowie, Chuck Gardiner, Eddie Gerard, Frank McGee, Howie Morenz, Tommy Phillips, Harvey Pulford, Art Ross, Hod Stuart, and Georges Vezina.

Inducted into the Builders' Category were Sir Montagu Allan, and the donor of the Stanley Cup in 1893, Lord Frederick Stanley. Bobby Hewitson, who served as an NHL referee for ten years, was named the museum's first curator.

Additional inductions followed in 1947, 1950, and 1952. Players such as Eddie Shore, Cyclone Taylor, Newsy Lalonde, and Bill Cook, and Builders including Lester Patrick and Frank Calder, earned their due recognition.

But in 1958, with still no building in place because of construction delays arising from rising costs, NHL president Clarence Campbell moved the site of the hall from Kingston to Toronto. That same year saw another round of inductees that included Players King Clancy and Dick Irvin and Builders Frank Patrick and Conn Smythe.

It was Smythe who led the efforts to see the construction of a building come to fruition. By 1961, a museum had finally been built on the grounds of Toronto's Canadian National Exhibition. On August 26, Prime Minister John Diefenbaker was on hand for the ceremonial opening of the Hockey Hall of Fame. Over 750,000 visitors passed through the museum's doors in its first year of operation.

The Hockey Hall of Fame moved to its current location at Toronto's Brookfield Place in 1993. Located at the corner of Yonge and Front Streets, the building that now houses the game's most treasured collections was the former head office of the Bank of Montreal.

Kingston did get its own shrine in 1965, now known as the Original Hockey Hall of Fame and Museum.

The Hockey Hall of Fame opened on the grounds of the CNE in Toronto in 1961.

CANADA VS. SOVIET UNION

The 1987 Canada Cup delighted hockey fans with an epic showdown between the sport's two greatest powers, Canada and the Soviet Union. The decisive third game of the series was held at Copps Coliseum on September 15. Two nights earlier at the same venue, Mario Lemieux scored in overtime to draw Canada even at one game apiece.

But it was the Soviets who struck early, and often. Goals by Sergei Makarov, Alexei Gusarov, and Vyacheslav Fetisov propelled the visitors to a 3-0 lead by the eight-minute mark of the opening period, silencing the sellout crowd.

However, on a team stacked with future Hall of Famers such as Wayne Gretzky, Lemieux, and Mark Messier, it was the grinders – the secondary scorers – who sparked Canada's comeback.

Rick Tocchet was the first to solve goalie Sergei Mylnikov, connecting on a power play. His Flyers teammate Brian Propp pulled Canada to within one. Both goals were scored from just outside the crease, with little finesse.

But with 28 seconds left in the first period, Andrei Khumotov took advantage of a Ray Bourque turnover and beat Grant Fuhr on a breakaway to restore the Soviets' two-goal cushion.

The second period belonged to the Canadians. Larry Murphy and Brent Sutter each netted their first goals of the tournament, evening the score at 4-4. Then Dale Hawerchuk connected, recovering his own rebound behind the net after his initial shot was stopped by Mylnikov, then scoring on a wraparound to give Canada its first lead of the game.

With the game – and the series – on the line, both teams kept up the high-paced tempo for

the third period. Alexander Semak, the Soviets' overtime hero in Game One, tied the score with a one-timer from the slot with just over seven-and-a-half minutes left in regulation.

It appeared that the contest would go to overtime for a third straight game. But following a Team Canada icing came one of the most memorable plays in international hockey history.

Hawerchuk won the faceoff and got the puck to Lemieux, who banked it off the left boards to get by one defender as the Canadians broke out of their zone. Lemieux fed the puck to Gretzky, and number 99 carried the puck up the left wing. Suddenly Canada found itself on an odd-man rush, Murphy driving towards the net as another option for Gretzky.

But Gretzky found Lemieux trailing on the play and the "Great One" passed off to the "Magnificent One."

Lemieux made no mistake, finding the top corner of the net over Mylnikov's glove with 1:26 remaining, sending a nation into ecstatic celebration.

Mario Lemieux scored the game-winning goal at the 1987 Canada Cup in Hamilton.

Clapper's 20-Year Career

At 6'2", Dit Clapper towered over most players of his generation. Entering the NHL as a 20-year-old in 1927-28, Clapper went on to forge a career that lasted two decades on the strength of his durability and versatility.

Clapper was placed on the right wing along with centre Cooney Weiland and left winger Dutch Gainor to form the Dynamite Line. In his second season, Clapper contributed his first career playoff goal as the Bruins won the 1929 Stanley Cup, the first championship in the franchise's history.

The 1929-30 season was a breakout year for the Newmarket, Ontario native. Clapper and Weiland were a formidable duo, finishing as the NHL's top two goal scorers. Weiland, who was also the scoring champion with 73 points, netted 43 goals, beating Clapper's career-best total by two.

The next season, Clapper was named to the Second All-Star team. He repeated the selection again four years later, in 1934-35.

Then, in 1937-38, Clapper was shifted to defence. The Bruins had the Kraut Line of Milt Schmidt, Woody Dumart, and Bobby Bauer to carry the scoring and needed to fill a void on the blue line. Paired with Eddie Shore, Clapper was just as effective in preventing goals as he had been in scoring them.

Boston captured its second Stanley Cup in 1939. Clapper was named to his first of three consecutive First All-Star teams. He remains the only player in NHL history to be named to an All-Star Team on both forward and defence.

Another Stanley Cup followed in 1941. The next year, Clapper – for the first time in his career – had his season curtailed by a serious injury. He played just 32 of 48 games after a bad tendon kept him off ice. Nevertheless, Clapper persevered. In 1945-46, he took over duties from Art Ross behind the Bruins' bench, becoming a player-coach.

In 1946-47, Clapper played in his twentieth season, becoming  the first player in league history to reach the milestone. He played just six games that year, but he set a benchmark rare for any player to accomplish over any era.

One of Clapper's most infamous moments occurred when the Bruin punched a referee, incensed that a penalty wasn't called after Clapper had been butt-ended in the face by the Maroons' Dave Trottier. The official was future NHL president Clarence Campbell. Clapper escaped with a $100 fine.

Immediately after his retirement, Clapper was inducted into the Hockey Hall of Fame, becoming the first player to have the three-year waiting period waived.

Aubrey "Dit" Clapper was the first NHLer to play in 20 seasons.

Ottawa's HALL OF FAMERS

Players

Jack Adams, 1959

Clint Benedict, 1965

Frank Boucher, 1958

George Boucher, 1960

Punch Broadbent, 1962

Harry Cameron, 1962

King Clancy, 1958

Sprague Cleghorn, 1958

Alec Connell, 1958

Bill Cowley, 1968

Rusty Crawford, 1962

Jack Darragh, 1962

Cy Denneny, 1959

Eddie Gerard, 1945

Billy Gilmour, 1962

Dominik Hasek, 2014

Syd Howe, 1965

Bouse Hutton, 1962

Percy LeSueur, 1961

Frank McGee, 1945

Frank Nighbor, 1947

Tommy Phillips, 1945

Harvey Pulford, 1945

Gordon Roberts, 1971

Art Ross, 1949

Alf Smith, 1962

Hooley Smith, 1972

Tommy Smith, 1973

Bruce Stuart, 1961

Hod Stuart, 1945

"Cyclone" Taylor, 1947

Marty Walsh, 1962

Cooney Weiland, 1971,

Harry Westwick, 1962

Builders

Frank Ahearn, 1962

Roger Neilson, 2002

P.D. Ross, 1976

Carl Voss, 1974

King Clancy was a star with Ottawa before being traded to the Leafs.

Dominik Hasek was the most recent Senators alumnus inducted into the Hockey Hall of Fame.

Cy Denneny played 12 years with the Senators before and after the formation of the NHL.

Rookie Meeker Scores Five

After the Toronto Maple Leafs won the Stanley Cup in 1945, the team was enthusiastic about its chances of defending its title. Syl Apps, Don Metz, and Gaye Stewart, among others, were returning from military service that fall. Having been absent from the squad, they would only bolster the lineup with their presence. Or so it seemed.

But goalie Frank McCool sat out because of a contract squabble, and Turk Broda struggled in the Leafs' net. Ted Kennedy injured a tendon, and then Babe Pratt was suspended for gambling on hockey. Toronto's season that had started with such optimism ended with a whimper as the Cup champions missed the playoffs.

In 1946-47, Conn Smythe inserted six rookies into the roster. One of them was fresh-faced Howie Meeker from Kitchener, Ontario. A 22-year old who had excelled during his senior hockey playing days in Kitchener and Stratford, Meeker had been pulled into military service and almost never had the opportunity to play in the NHL.

While overseas, Meeker landed in hospital after a grenade exploded near his legs during a training exercise. He convalesced for four months, gradually regaining his strength. Returning to Canada, he played seven more games with Stratford, collecting eight goals and 13 points in those games and catching the eye of the Leafs. Toronto signed him to a contract in April 1946.

Meeker made his NHL debut centring a line with Ted Kennedy and Vic Lynn. The forward unit became known as the Tricky Trio Line. The Leafs were dominant over the first stretch of the year, vaulting to a 20-7-4 record over 31 games to stay just ahead of the rival Canadiens.

Then, on January 8, 1947, Meeker ran roughshod over the visiting Chicago Black Hawks, thrilling the crowd at Maple Leaf Gardens. Scoring five times against goaltender Paul Bibeault, Meeker tied the NHL mark for the most goals in a game by a player in his first season. Only Joe Malone, Harry Hyland, and Mickey Roach had previously accomplished the feat, and only Don Murdoch, in 1976, has done so since.

Diminutive rookie Howie Meeker had a huge game in his first NHL season, scoring five times.

Meeker finished the year with 27 goals and 45 points, taking Calder Trophy honours as the league's top rookie. He beat out Jim Conacher of Detroit and Cal Gardner of New York in the balloting, while a kid from Floral, Saskatchewan, named Gordie Howe wasn't even a finalist.

The Leafs reclaimed the Stanley Cup that season and went on to become the first team in NHL history to win three straight championships. Meeker earned four Cup rings between 1947 and 1951.

Toronto's Biggest Trades

▶ TOP TRADE

SEPTEMBER 10, 1943 Toronto Maple Leafs trade Frank Eddolls to Montreal for Ted Kennedy

One of the greatest Leafs of all-time, Ted "Teeder" Kennedy was originally a prospect in the organization of the archrival Canadiens. The deal was orchestrated by Toronto's acting general manager, Frank Selke, while Conn Smythe was serving in the military during the Second World War.

Kennedy's remarkable leadership qualities earned him the appointment as team captain in 1948. His brilliant play-making endeared him to the Toronto fans. The chant, "Come on, Teeder!" became a popular rallying cry at Maple Leaf Gardens.

Kennedy won five Stanley Cups between 1945 and 1951, establishing an all-time franchise mark with 23 career points in the finals. He is one of only two Leafs to win the Hart Trophy as the league's most valuable player, earning the honour in 1954-55, his last full season.

In 2014, Kennedy was posthumously named one of the first three Leafs alumni to be honoured on Legends Row outside of Air Canada Centre.

Eddolls lasted only three years in Montreal, playing a total of 57 games for the Habs before being dealt to the New York Rangers.

Although the Leafs were clear victors in the trade, Smythe felt that the trade made in his absence undermined his authority. Selke in turn resigned, and went on to become the architect of many great Montreal teams.

HONOURABLE MENTION

JANUARY 2, 1992 Toronto trades Gary Leeman, Alexander Godynyuk, Jeff Reese, Michel Petit, and Craig Berube to Calgary for Doug Gilmour, Jamie Macoun, Ric Nattress, Kent Manderville, and Rick Wamsley

The ten-player trade, the largest in NHL history, marked the arrival of a return to glory for the suffering Leafs franchise. Just seven months into his post as Toronto general manager, Cliff Fletcher traded for the beleaguered Gilmour, whose Flames days were all but over after the gritty centre lost a salary arbitration ruling a few months earlier.

Fletcher then brought in Pat Burns to take over the Leafs' coaching duties. In 1992-93, Toronto made a surprise playoff run to the semi-finals with Gilmour as the cornerstone of the offence. Gilmour set single-season team records for assists (95) and points (127), earning a Hart Trophy nomination and winning the Selke Trophy as the league's top defensive forward.

In five seasons with the Leafs, Gilmour appeared in 52 playoff games, setting franchise records with 60 assists and 77 points.

The trade was a complete bust for the Flames. Leeman never came to close to reaching the career-best 51 goals that he tallied during the 1989-90 season.

Ted Kennedy was acquired from Montreal for nothing more than Frank Eddolls.

Bill Cowley Top Scorer

While Wayne Gretzky dominated the game at a level unmatched by any player in hockey history, the pre-expansion equivalent of the "Great One" was Boston Bruins centre Bill Cowley. Gifted with uncanny playmaking ability, Cowley was easily the most productive player of his era.

A native of Bristol, Quebec, Cowley entered the league in 1934-35 with the St. Louis Eagles, the short-lived franchise that had transferred from Ottawa. When the Eagles folded at the end of the year, Boston claimed Cowley in a subsequent Dispersal Draft.

Three years later, in 1937-38, Cowley was named to the All-Star Team for the first time in his career. He followed that season with an outstanding campaign, leading all playoff scorers with eleven assists and 14 points as the Bruins won the Stanley Cup in 1939. Cowley had also been the regular-season assists leader, with 34 in as many games.

In 1940-41, Cowley had what can only be characterized as a dream season. Establishing a single-season record for assists with 45, Cowley won his first scoring title with 62 points and was also named the Hart Trophy winner as the NHL's most valuable player. His playoff action was limited to two games, but the Bruins ended up winning their second Stanley Cup in three years.

Cowley won another Hart Trophy in 1943 while leading the league in assists for the third time in five years. The following season, 1943-44, was one of the most productive years ever for an individual. Cowley was scoring at a torrid pace – well on the way to smashing former Boston teammate Cooney Weiland's points record – before he was sidelined a shoulder injury suffered in a game against Toronto on January 8.

He missed twelve games, returning with fervor and just missing out on the record by two points. Cowley finished the season with 71 points in 36 games. His mark of 1.97 points per game stood for 37 years before Gretzky became the NHL's first two points per game player over a season.

A gentlemanly player, Cowley accumulated just 143 penalty minutes in 13 years of NHL play. Although he never won the Lady Byng Trophy, he was often a candidate for the award.

On February 12, 1947, Cowley surpassed Syd Howe's career mark of 528 points to become the NHL's all-time scoring leader. He retired at the end of the season with 548 points in 549 regular-season games.

The mark wasn't overtaken for another five years before Elmer Lach of the Montreal Canadiens surpassed Cowley.

Few players could match the offensive skill of Boston's Bill Cowley.

Quebec/Colorado TOP DRAFT CHOICES

1979 – Michel Goulet, #20, Quebec

1981 – Randy Moller, #11, Lethbridge

1982 – David Shaw, #13, Kitchener

1984 – Trevor Steinburg, #15, Guelph

1985 – David Latta, #15, Kitchener

1986 – Ken McRae, #18, Sudbury

1987 – Bryan Fogarty, #9, Kingston

1988 – Curtis Leschyshyn, #3, Saskatoon

1988 – Daniel Dore, #5, Drummondville

1989 – Mats Sundin, #1, Nacka

1990 – Owen Nolan, #1, Cornwall

1991 – Eric Lindros, #1, Oshawa

1992 – Todd Warriner, #4, Windsor

1993 – Jocelyn Thibault, #10, Sherbrooke

1993 – Adam Deadmarsh, #14, Portland

1994 – Wade Belak, #12, Saskatoon

1994 – Jeffrey Kealty, #22, Catholic Memorial

1995 – Marc Denis, #25, Chicoutimi

1996 – Peter Ratchuk, #25, Shattuck-St. Mary's

1997 – Kevin Grimes, #26, Kingston

1998 – Alex Tanguay, #12, Halifax

1998 – Martin Skoula, #17, Barrie

1998 – Robyn Regehr, #19, Kamloops

1998 – Scott Parker, #20, Kelowna

1999 – Mikhail Kuleshov, #25, Cherepovets

2000 – Vaclav Nedorost, #14, Ceske Budejovice

2002 – Jonas Johansson, #28, HV 71 Jonkoping Jr.

2004 – Wojtek Wolski, #21, Brampton

2006 – Chris Stewart, #18, Kingston

2007 – Kevin Shattenkirk, #14, U.S. National U-18

2009 – Matt Duchene, #3, Brampton

2010 – Joey Hishon, #17, Owen Sound

2011 – Gabriel Landeskog, #2, Kitchener

2011 – Duncan Siemens, #11, Saskatoon

2013 – Nathan MacKinnon, #1, Halifax

2014 – Conner Bleackley, #23, Red Deer

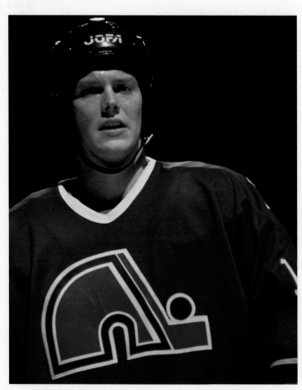

Mats Sundin was the first European to be selected first overall at the NHL Entry Draft, in 1989.

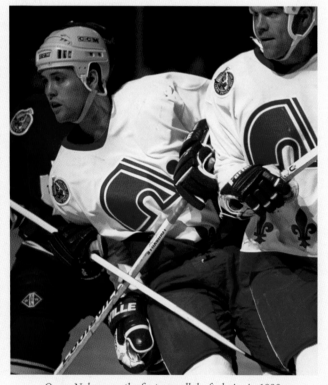

Owen Nolan was the first overall draft choice in 1990.

The Production Line

As the roster of the 1947-48 Detroit Red Wings began to take shape, the team was forming the nucleus of what was about to become a dynasty that would dominate the early 1950s.

First-year coach Tommy Ivan assembled a forward line that had Ted Lindsay, 22, on the left wing. At right wing was second-year pro Gordie Howe, while centring the bunch was veteran Sid Abel, 29. Collectively, they were dubbed "The Production Line."

By the end of their first season, Lindsay, Howe, and Abel occupied three of the top four positions in team scoring. Detroit was swept by Toronto in the Stanley Cup finals, but the young squad was quickly morphing into championship contenders.

The next year, 1948-49, saw the Red Wings achieve both team and individual success. Detroit, with 88 points, finished atop the NHL standings for the first time since 1943, which was

(l-r) Gordie Howe, Sid Abel, and Ted Lindsay formed the potent Production Line.

also the last year that the Red Wings had won the Stanley Cup. All three members of the Production Line were named All-Stars, Abel – also the Hart Trophy winner – on the First Team, and Howe and Lindsay on the Second Team.

But the Wings were still unable to dethrone their nemesis, the Leafs, and were swept in the finals for a second straight year.

Finally, Detroit reached the pinnacle of success the next season, and it was the Production Line that sparked the team offensively. Lindsay, Abel, and Howe finished as the league's top three scorers, each player also earning an All-Star Team berth.

The 1950 playoffs opened with the Red Wings once again taking on the Leafs. Controversy ensued early on when Howe missed a hard check on Toronto's Ted Kennedy and fell head-first into the boards. Howe was rushed to hospital and underwent surgery to relieve pressure in his bleeding brain. His life hung in the balance.

Howe recovered, but his playoffs were over. Nevertheless, Detroit took care of Toronto in the semi-finals, then defeated Montreal in Game Seven of the finals, thanks to the double-overtime heroics of Pete Babando.

Two years later, the powerhouse Red Wings became the first team in history to go undefeated in both best-of-seven playoff series to win the Stanley Cup. The Production Line was firing on all cylinders and was augmented by Red Kelly and Marcel Pronovost on defence and Terry Sawchuk virtually unbeatable in net. Detroit needed the minimum eight playoff games to win the 1952 title.

Abel's move to Chicago that summer signified the breakup of one of hockey's all-time greatest forward units.

Calgary's CAPTAINS

Brad Marsh, 1980-81

Phil Russell, 1981-82, 1982-83

Lanny McDonald, Doug Risebrough, 1983-84

Lanny McDonald, Doug Risebrough, Jim Peplinski, 1984-85 to 1985-87

Lanny McDonald, Jim Peplinski, 1987-88

Lanny McDonald, Jim Peplinski, Tim Hunter 1988-89

Brad McCrimmon, 1989-90

Alternating captains, 1990-91

Joe Nieuwendyk, 1991-92 to 1994-95

Theoren Fleury, 1995-96, 1996-97

Todd Simpson, 1997-98, 1998-99

Steve Smith, 1999-2000

Steve Smith and Dave Lowry, 2000-01

Dave Lowry, Bob Boughner and Craig Conroy, 2001-02

Bob Boughner and Craig Conroy, 2002-03

Jarome Iginla, 2003-04 to 2012-13

Mark Giordano 2013-14 to 2014-15

Todd Simpson captained the Flames from 1997 to 1999.

Jarome Iginla was the face of the Calgary Flames for more than a decade.

Suspended for Life

In March 1948 the NHL was rocked by a gambling scandal involving two Boston Bruins teammates, Billy Taylor and Don Gallinger.

The 28-year-old Taylor, a veteran of six seasons, had starred for the Leafs in the earlier part of the decade, winning a Stanley Cup in 1942. He was traded to Detroit four years later, and then spent a year with the Red Wings before being dealt to the Bruins.

Gallinger was just 22 but was already in his fifth NHL season. When Gallinger entered the league, he was an underage player who had been granted the opportunity because the Second World War had depleted many NHL rosters. Both Taylor and Gallinger eventually postponed their hockey careers to enlist in the military.

While in Boston, the two men became associated with James Tamer, a criminal and gambler living in Detroit. Taylor and Gallinger wagered on games against Boston, but only on games in which they expected the Bruins to lose. Gallinger also provided his team's injury information to men of ill repute.

Taylor was traded to the New York Rangers in February 1948, but on March 9, league president Clarence Campbell released the findings of an ongoing investigation, handing down the harshest punishment in league history in the process. Taylor was suspended for life. Gallinger – who steadfastly denied all clams – was suspended indefinitely, but subsequently also banned for life.

In a statement, Campbell acknowledged that no "fix" of a game was attempted by either player.

The following year, Gallinger finally confessed to the wrongdoings in the face of overwhelming evidence against him. Had Gallinger owned up immediately, he may have reinstated, just as Leafs forward Babe Pratt was, in 1946. Pratt had been found guilty of betting on NHL games, and while he initially faced expulsion, Campbell reduced the ban to nine games after Pratt immediately expressed his remorse.

Both Taylor and Gallinger are holders of NHL individual records. Taylor has the mark for most assists in a game, setting up seven goals while with Detroit on March 16, 1947, in a win over Chicago. The record has since been equalled three times, all by Wayne Gretzky.

On March 21, 1943, Gallinger, a month shy of his 18th birthday became the youngest player ever to score a playoff overtime goal, accomplishing the feat in the semi-finals versus Montreal.

Thus, by serving the league's longest suspensions, Taylor and Gallinger have the dubious distinction of having their names in the record book for both famous, and infamous, reasons.

The lifetime bans for both players were rescinded in August 1970.

Don Gallinger.

Quebec Milestones

MOST SEASONS JOE SAKIC (20)

Given his prolific career, Sakic was a virtual 'steal' at the 1987 NHL Draft even though he was selected 15th overall. The graduate of the Swift Current Broncos of the Western Hockey League wasn't even Quebec's first pick that year. The Nordiques had taken defenceman Bryan Fogarty in the ninth slot. Sakic is also the Quebec/Colorado franchise leader with 1,378 career games played. He was a first ballot Hockey Hall of Fame inductee in 2012.

MOST POINTS JOE SAKIC (1,641)

Sakic topped the 100-point mark six times in his career. His marks of 625 goals and 1,016 assists are also all-time franchise records. In 1996, Sakic captained the Colorado Avalanche to the first of two Stanley Cups. He led the playoffs that year with 34 points and set a record with six game-winning goals in one post-season (since broken by Brad Richards). Following the Avalanche's four-game sweep of Florida in the finals, Sakic was named the Conn Smythe Trophy winner.

In 2000-01, Sakic had a silverware-filled season, winning the Hart, Pearson, and Lady Byng Trophies. He capped off the magical year with another Stanley Cup win, making the victory all the more memorable by handing the trophy to first-time winner and seasoned veteran Ray Bourque.

MOST WINS PATRICK ROY (262)

The Nordiques/Avalanche all-time leader in every major statistical goaltending category, Roy had 478 appearances, 28,317 minutes played, and 37 shutouts in a Colorado uniform. The Avalanche obtained Roy in a blockbuster trade on December 6, 1995, just days after the netminder demanded a change of scenery after being humiliated in a game in Montreal. Roy backstopped the Avalanche to two Stanley Cup victories and was the playoff MVP in 2001.

MOST PENALTY MINUTES DALE HUNTER (1,562)

The Petrolia, Ontario, native was Quebec's second-round, 41st overall draft pick in 1980. Hunter not only had a propensity for dropping the gloves, but he could also find the back of the net

with consistency. In 1985-86, Hunter collected a career-high 28 goals while also accruing 265 penalty minutes. He also holds the franchise's iron-man record, playing 312 consecutive games between October 9, 1980, and March 13, 1984.

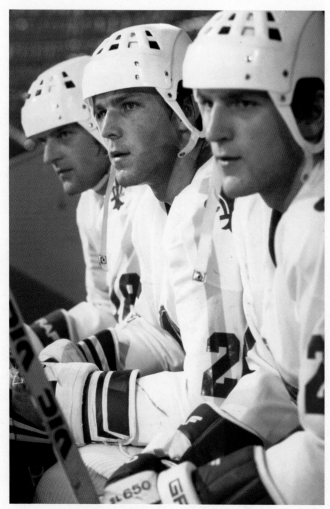

Peter Stastny (middle) flanked by brothers Anton (left) and Marian.

MILESTONES AND RECORDS

Peter Stastny recorded his 1,000th career NHL point on October 19, 1989, scoring a goal in Quebec's 5-3 win over Chicago. Stastny reached the milestone in just his 682nd career game.

Both Peter Stastny and his brother, Anton, hold the league record for most points in one road game. Each sibling scored eight points in Quebec's 11-7 win at Washington on February 22, 1981.

Stanley Cup Redesigned

The Stanley Cup, hockey's most famous trophy, has undergone several transformations since it was donated by Lord Stanley in 1893 as the ultimate reward for hockey supremacy.

The original trophy was a bowl in which the winning team had its name engraved. At Lord Stanley's suggestion, championship teams started adding rings to the base of the trophy. The most recent winner was inserted closest to the bowl, while the names of the other victors were moved down.

As the number of rings increased, the Stanley Cup became an elongated "stovepipe." When the Maple Leafs were hockey's best team, in 1944-45, their band was nearest to the bowl while the ring belonging to the 1927-28 Rangers was at the bottom.

At that point, the stovepipe has reached its capacity. Twelve months later, when the Canadiens were crowned champions, there was no room for another band, nor could their names be engraved anywhere else on the silverware.

On April 23, 1946, Stanley Cup trustee Cooper Smeaton wrote to his colleague P.D. Ross to address the issue: "As you know, the Cup now rests on a very ugly looking, elongated base and it occurred to me that it might be possible to get Henry Birks for instance, to design a nice big base which would permit space for sufficient shields."

Ross replied: "Why not have Birks make a new base, with a receptacle in the base for a 'golden book' to record all the past and prospective winnings of the Cup?

The book would only need to be of moderate size, a hundred pages or so, with the base detachable from the Cup of course, for purpose of transportation."

The idea was flatly rejected by the League's Board of Governors.

Finally in 1947, the NHL hired Carl Peterson of Montreal, a Danish-born silversmith, to redesign the trophy. Peterson was also the Cup's first, league-sanctioned engraver. The makeover called for a two-piece cigar-shaped trophy where the bowl and collar could easily be detached. The 1948 Leafs were the first team to be awarded with the newly-transformed Stanley Cup.

A decade later, the one-piece design was introduced, consisting of a five-band barrel. The newest bands are inserted at the base, and each band holds up to 13 winning teams.

Once the newest ring is filled to capacity, the oldest band is removed from the Cup and placed on display at the Hockey Hall of Fame. Then, the other four bands are moved up to make room for the new one.

This is the design to which the current generation of hockey fans has been accustomed.

The stovepipe Stanley Cup became unwieldy and was redesigned to perfection by Carl Peterson.

GREAT RIVALRIES Toronto vs. Montreal

The roots of hockey's oldest rivalry trace back to the NHL's foundation in 1917 when Toronto and Montreal were two of the league's inaugural four franchises.

For the past century the Maple Leafs (nee Arenas) and Canadiens have represented Canada's two most rabid hockey cities, generating an atmosphere of both excitement and hostility whenever they face off as opponents.

A turning point in the historic rivalry came in 1943 when Frank Selke, assistant to Leafs president Conn Smythe, acquired Ted Kennedy from Montreal in a trade. Although Kennedy went on to have an illustrious career in Toronto, Smythe – who had been overseas, serving in the military – lashed out at Selke for making the transaction without his approval.

Selke resigned from the Leafs and joined the Canadiens, serving as the team's general manager from 1946-47 to 1963-64. Under Selke's tenure, the Habs built a strong nucleus of players that included future Hall of Famers Jean Beliveau, Dickie Moore, Tom Johnson, and Jacques Plante.

Toronto and Montreal squared off in a famous 1945 semi-finals. The Canadiens, the defending Stanley Cup champions, were led by Maurice "Rocket" Richard and his historic season of 50 goals in 50 games. But they were ousted by the Leafs in the semi-finals, despite finishing 28 points ahead of Toronto in the regular season.

An ugly incident between combatants Ken Reardon of Montreal and Cal Gardner of Toronto occurred in 1949. Reardon shattered Gardner's jaw in retaliation for a high stick he had received from the Leafs player two years earlier. NHL President Clarence Campbell intervened, and insisted that Reardon post a $1,000 bond not to harm Gardner again.

In 1951, the Leafs and Habs played the only Stanley Cup finals in which every game went into overtime. Bill Barilko scored the overtime Cup-winner at Maple Leaf Gardens in Game Five.

By the end of the decade, Montreal had forged the greatest dynasty in hockey history, winning five straight Stanley Cups. The 1960 series was a four-game sweep over Toronto, after which Richard ended his Hall of Fame career.

The two teams were Stanley Cup finalists in 1967, the last season of the six-team era. George Armstrong's empty-net goal in Game Six completed the Leafs' upset of the Habs.

Since then, the franchises' fortunes have gone in different directions. Montreal won ten Stanley Cups in the next 26 years while the Leafs never even advanced to the finals during that time. In both 1978 and 1979, Guy Lafleur and the Canadiens ran roughshod over the Leafs in the playoffs on the way to winning the Stanley Cup.

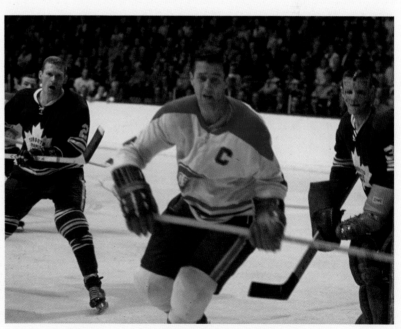

There is no rivalry in hockey that trumps Toronto-Montreal for history and national interest.

Barilko Ends OT Series in 1951

Nicknamed "Bashin' Bill" because of his devastating hip checks, Bill Barilko was a physical force on the Leafs' defence during their run of three straight Stanley Cups from 1947 to 1949.

In 299 regular season and playoff games over five seasons, Barilko scored 31 times. His final goal is forever immortalized in legend, photography, and song.

The 1951 Stanley Cup finals showcased bitter rivals Toronto and Montreal. Heading into Game Five at Maple Leaf Gardens, the Leafs held a three games to one lead in a tightly-contested matchup that could just as easily have been tilted in the Habs' favour.

Each of the first four games of the series had gone into overtime. Sid Smith, Ted Kennedy, and Harry Watson had game-winning goals for the Leafs, while Maurice Richard scored a fourth-period goal for the Canadiens.

Bill Barilko's Cup-winning goal defined his career and added poignancy to his early death.

Richard was unstoppable in the series. The Rocket opened the scoring in the second period of Game Five, collecting his fifth goal in as many games. The Leafs countered with a goal by Tod Sloan. The teams remained tied into the third period when Montreal's Paul Meger beat goalie Al Rollins, hoping with the rest of the Habs to send the series back to the Montreal Forum.

But with 31 seconds remaining in regulation, Sloan evened the affair with his second goal of the game, forcing a fifth consecutive overtime.

It took just two minutes and 53 seconds into the extra period for Barilko to seize the moment. After the Leafs' Howie Meeker out-duelled Canadiens defenceman Tom Johnson for the puck, he centred it from behind the Montreal goal to Harry Watson in front. Watson's shot then rebounded to the right of Habs goalie Gerry McNeil.

Barilko, who'd been warned by Leafs coach Joe Primeau not to pinch in from the point, ignored the bench boss's edict, drove towards the faceoff circle and blasted the puck, diving forward as he was shooting. As the puck sailed into the net past a helpless McNeil, Barilko, airborne, had both skates completely off the ice.

The goal clinched Toronto's fourth Stanley Cup in five years. Teammates rushed onto the ice in celebration to hoist Barilko onto their shoulders.

Barilko perished in a plane crash four months later while on a fishing expedition in Northern Ontario. His body, and that of his companion Dr. Henry Hudson, remained undiscovered for eleven years.

The photograph of Barilko's final goal is the most requested image from the collection at the Hockey Hall of Fame, while the story of his disappearance is the subject of the song "Fifty Mission Cap" by The Tragically Hip.

Sidney Crosby and the Golden Goal

February 28, 2010, was a transcendent moment for all Canadians.

For two and a half weeks, the finest athletes in the world had congregated in Vancouver for the XXI Olympic Winter Games. Going into the final day of competition, Canada needed one more gold medal to set a record for top-of-the-podium finishes by one country in a single Olympics.

To accomplish the feat, it would have to defeat the United States in the signature event of the Games – the men's hockey gold-medal game.

The Americans were seeking to avenge a loss on home soil to the Canadians eight years earlier in Salt Lake City. Led by coach Ron Wilson in 2010, the U.S. had trumped Canada, 5-3, in the preliminary round en route to a perfect 3-0-0 record in Group A. Canada finished second in the same pool as a result of that defeat.

The opening faceoff of the highly-anticipated game took place before a raucous sellout crowd at Canada Hockey Place, the vast majority of which was supporting Team Canada. Across the country, 21.5 million viewers were tuning in on television, more than two-thirds of the entire population.

Jonathan Toews pounced on a rebound to open the scoring for Canada in the first period. Corey Perry gave his team 2-0 lead in the second frame before Ryan Kesler finally responded for the United States.

Canada cautiously protected its 2-1 advantage throughout the third period. But with the gold medal so tantalizingly within their grasp, the Canadians allowed a goal by Zach Parise with 24 seconds left in regulation time and goalie Ryan Miller on the bench, sending the once-deafening crowd into shocked silence.

In the overtime, the United States almost spoiled the party when Joe Pavelski pounced on a Scott Niedermayer turnover for a breakaway. Pavelski was stopped by Roberto Luongo, and the play carried into the American zone, into the corner to the right of Miller.

Sidney Crosby, who had had, by his standards, a relatively quiet Olympics, passed the puck off to Jarome Iginla then darted for the net. Iginla completed the give-and-go as he was knocked to the ice by defenceman Ryan Suter.

Crosby converted the return feed, snapping the puck between the pads of Miller. The arena, and the entire nation, erupted in unified triumph. The 14th gold medal by Canada at the 2010 Olympics was a record-setter but was also the most coveted of them all.

Canadians who were too young to remember either Paul Henderson's 1972 Summit Series winner or Mario Lemieux's clinching goal at the 1987 Canada Cup were thankful to witness history made right in their own backyard.

Sidney Crosby scored the golden goal for Canada on home ice in 2010.

Mosienko's 21-Second Hat Trick

On the final day of the 1951-52 season, the Chicago Black Hawks paid a visit to New York to close out the year against the Rangers. The matchup was meaningless as both teams had failed to qualify for the playoffs. As a result, just 3,254 spectators were in attendance at Madison Square Garden.

In an inconsequential game, Rangers netminders Chuck Rayner and Emile Francis were rested in favour of seldom-used Lorne Anderson.

After forty minutes of play, New York appeared to be coasting to an easy win as the Blueshirts carried a 6-2 lead into the third period. But Chicago right winger Bill Mosienko not only sparked a remarkable comeback, he also scored his way into the NHL record book.

At the 6:09 mark of the final frame, Mosienko received a pass from linemate Gus Bodnar and wired a shot past Anderson

Fast-shooting Bill Mosienko scored three times in 21 seconds in an NHL game.

to get the Black Hawks to within three goals. On the ensuing faceoff, Bodnar won the draw, once again finding Mosienko, who had gotten behind the Rangers' defencemen. Mosienko got the better of Anderson at 6:20.

Bodnar again won the next centre-ice faceoff, feeding the puck to left winger George Gee. Gee set up Mosienko for the hat-trick goal at the 6:30 mark, just 21 seconds after the first goal. Carl Liscombe had held the previous hat-trick record, having potted three goals in 64 seconds in 1938 with Detroit.

Unfathomably, Bodnar nearly connected with Mosienko yet again, right after the next faceoff, but Mosienko's shot rang off the goal post. "It could have easily been four goals in 28 seconds," veteran author Stan Fischler told *The Hockey News*.

Energized, the Black Hawks scored another two goals to take the game away from their hosts by a score of 7-6. The game marked the third and final game of Anderson's NHL career. He spent the next three seasons with the Sudbury Wolves of the Northern Ontario Hockey Association.

Mosienko is most famously known for his record-setting achievement, but he was far from a one-game wonder. He had already been a two-time All-Star Team selection, also winning the 1944-45 Lady Byng Trophy. Over 711 career NHL games, Mosienko netted 258 goals.

In 1965, Mosienko was inducted into the Hockey Hall of Fame.

Canadiens legend Jean Believau has been the player to come the closest to equalling Mosienko's mark, scoring three goals in 44 seconds in 1955.

Entering the 2015 playoffs, Tim Kerr of Philadelphia held the record for the fastest post-season hat trick, scoring three times in 3:24 in 1985.

Best Players Born in
Toronto

PAUL COFFEY

The smoothest skating defenceman of his time, Coffey trails only Ray Bourque on the all-time scoring list among blueliners. He won four Stanley Cups and three Canada Cups in his storied career, making his way into the Hall of Fame in 2004.

CHARLIE CONACHER

Possessing an athletic pedigree just like his older brother, Lionel, Charlie Conacher skated his way to stardom with Toronto, winning a Stanley Cup in the first season of the operation of Maple Leaf Gardens, 1931-32. He was named an NHL All-Star at right wing for five consecutive seasons ending in 1935-36, the latter three selections being on the First Team.

BILL DURNAN

Durnan backstopped the Canadiens to Stanley Cup victories in 1946 and 1949. Over a Hall of Fame career that spanned seven seasons, he posted a record of 208 wins, 112 losses, and 62 ties with 34 shutouts.

DALE HAWERCHUK

After an outstanding junior career that included two Memorial Cup wins with Cornwall, Hawerchuk became the most prolific scorer in the history of the first Winnipeg Jets franchise in the NHL. His faceoff win in Game Three of the 1987 Canada Cup helped lead to Mario Lemieux's tournament-winning goal.

BUSHER JACKSON

Collectively, Jackson, Charlie Conacher, and Joe Primeau made up the Leafs' famous Kid Line that vaulted Toronto to a championship in 1932. Three times an All-Star Team selection at left wing, Jackson also played for the New York Americans and Boston Bruins during his fifteen seasons in the NHL.

LARRY MURPHY

An offensively-talented defenceman, Murphy amassed 1,216 points in 21 NHL seasons on his way into the Hockey Hall of Fame. He won two Stanley Cups in Pittsburgh before earning another two Cup rings in Detroit.

ADAM OATES

Unbelievably, Oates was never drafted, signing instead as a free agent with Detroit out of Rensselaer Polytechnic Institute. He was the perfect setup man for Brett Hull in St. Louis and enjoyed the same role with Cam Neely in Boston. Oates retired with the league's sixth-best career assists total.

BRENDAN SHANAHAN

Epitomizing the role of power forward, Shanahan is the only player in league history to accumulate 2,000 penalty minutes while scoring at least 600 goals. He is also a member of the exclusive Triple Gold club, having won a Stanley Cup, World Championship gold medal, and Olympic gold medal.

Brendan Shanahan won the Cup with Detroit and hopes to do the same in an executive capacity with the Maple Leafs.

STEVE SHUTT

The left winger on a Canadiens' top line that included Guy Lafleur and Jacques Lemaire, Shutt was an integral member of Montreal's dynasty that won four consecutive Stanley Cups to end the 1970s. He posted a season-high 60 goals in 1976-77.

Hockey Night in Canada Debuts

Foster Hewitt made himself famous over the radio airwaves by bringing his play-by-play to living rooms across the country. The advent of television made it possible to also capture images of the players who "shoot and score," as it were.

On October 11, 1952, the Montreal Canadiens hosted the defending Stanley Cup champions Detroit Red Wings. The marquee matchup, featuring rivals Rocket Richard versus Gordie Howe, marked the debut of *Hockey Night In Canada*.

The broadcast was produced by Gerald Renaud, a former Ottawa newspaper sports editor. He decided to use three cameras: one for wide-angle shots, one for medium shots, and one for close-ups, directly at centre ice.

At the microphone calling the game was Rene Lecavalier. He greeted the viewers with "Bonsoir, mesdames et messieurs." And as the on-ice war between the two famous number 9's Richard and Howe resumed, hockey broadcasting changed forever. Montreal won the game, 2-1.

Retailers thrived and televisions flew off store shelves everywhere. Consumers were all too eager to embrace the new medium from which to access news, sports, and entertainment. The 1952-53 inaugural season of *Hockey Night In Canada* was an unbridled success.

The Leafs' debut on *HNIC* occurred on November 1. Hewitt called the game from his gondola at Maple Leaf Gardens, greeting fans with his trademark welcome "Hello Canada!" The first English telecast was produced by George Retzlaff.

The broadcast began at 9:30 pm, midway through the second period. When the show went to air, it was just seconds after the Leafs' Bob Hassard had scored. Instant replay would not be available for another several years; therefore, households across the nation had been deprived – by the slimmest of margins – of seeing a live action Leafs goal. Toronto went on to defeat Boston, 3-2.

Over the years, *Hockey Night In Canada* tinkered with other innovations. An intermission panel called the Hot Stove League was introduced where experts discussed the game between periods. In Montreal, Renaud brought in a fourth camera at ice level to shoot game action around the nets.

Instant replay became a permanent fixture in 1965. The show brought in colour television for the first time in that same year during the playoffs between Toronto and Montreal.

HNIC is ingrained in the nation's psyche. The original instrumental theme song is iconic. Fans of a certain age recall when hosts wore unconventional, baby-blue blazers, yet those pale in comparison to Don Cherry's wardrobe currently on *Coach's Corner*.

No television program has lasted as long and has been as popular as CBC's Hockey Night in Canada.

Quebec/Colorado HALL OF FAMERS

Players

Rusty Crawford, 1962

Thomas Dunderdale, 1974

Peter Forsberg, 2014

Michel Goulet, 1998

Joe Hall, 1961

Guy Lafleur, 1988

Joe Malone, 1950

Paddy Moran, 1958

Joe Sakic, 2012

Tommy Smith, 1973

Peter Stastny, 1998

Bruce Stuart, 1961

Hod Stuart, 1945

Mats Sundin, 2012

Builders

Frank Ahearn, 1962

P.D. Ross, 1976

Carl Voss, 1974

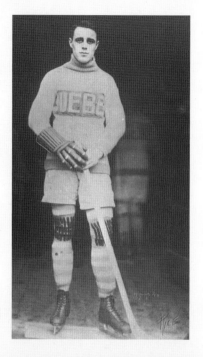

Joe Malone of the Quebec Bulldogs.

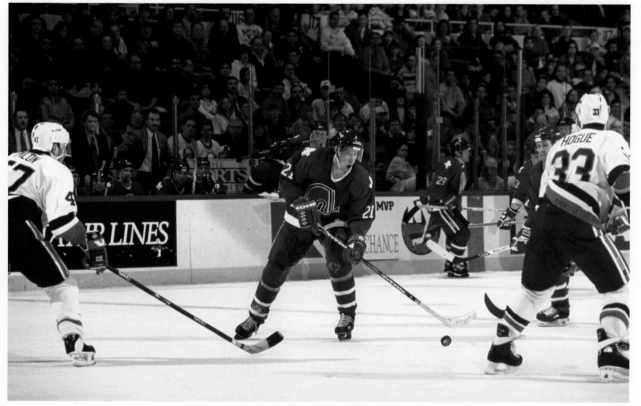

Peter Forsberg started his great career with Quebec.

Ted Lindsay Tries to Start a Union

Detroit's "Terrible" Ted Lindsay starred for the Red Wings on the team's top forward unit known as the Production Line. Away from the rink, however, he unified both the teammates with which he won Stanley Cups and the opponents whom he antagonized in an effort to ensure that all players be provided with fair working conditions.

Lindsay and Canadiens defenceman Doug Harvey were appointed to the NHL Pension Society Board in 1955. Rivals on the ice, the two men became allies after lobbying unsuccessfully for disclosure regarding how much money was in the players' pension fund. The request was more than reasonable considering that each player was paying $900 annually into the plan.

As fate would have it, Lindsay had a chance meeting in 1956 with Cleveland Indians pitcher Bob Feller, who was the president of the Major League Baseball Players' Association. Feller introduced Lindsay to New York lawyers Norman J. Lewis and Milton Mound, who had successfully negotiated a huge contract on the baseball players' behalf.

Lewis encouraged Lindsay to form a union, a suggestion that was taboo in the complicit culture of the NHL where players simply abided by the direction of their managers and coaches with nary a complaint.

Despite his initial misgivings, Lindsay proceeded with the initiative. At the 1956 All-Star Game in Montreal, he approached Harvey as well as players from each of the other four teams: Fern Flaman of Boston, Bill Gadsby of New York, Gus Mortson of Chicago, and Jim Thomson of Toronto.

Over the course of the next several months, the players solicited $100 in dues from each of their respective teammates. Then, on February 11, 1957, the group announced the formation of the first National Hockey League Players' Association.

The repercussions for the players – branded ungrateful militants – were harsh. One by one the men who were perceived as miscreants in the eyes of management were jettisoned from their clubs. A livid Jack Adams, the Red Wings' general manager, exiled Lindsay to the lowly Black Hawks in July.

The players fought back with an anti-trust suit filed in the fall, alleging that the NHL owners had monopolized the sport. The association appeared to be gaining momentum in November when the Maple Leafs voted to certify the association.

But nine days later, the Red Wings withdrew their support, effectively ending the bid started by their former teammate Lindsay.

Although Lindsay's plan didn't come to fruition for several years after it was first formulated, the Hall of Famer is acknowledged for his contributions by having the trophy presented annually to the most outstanding player, as voted by the NHLPA members, named in his honour.

Ted Lindsay was a sensational player on ice but a greater hero off ice for his efforts to start a players' union.

Montreal's TOP DRAFT CHOICES

1963 – Garry Monahan, #1, St. Michael's Juveniles

1965 – Pierre Bouchard, #5, St. Vincent de Paul Jr. B

1966 – Phil Myre, #5, Shawinigan

1969 – Rejean Houle, #1, Montreal

1969 – Marc Tardif, #1, Montreal

1971 – Guy Lafleur, #1, Quebec

1972 – Steve Shutt, #4, Toronto

1972 – Michel Larocque, #6, Ottawa

1972 – Dave Gardner, #8. Toronto

1973 – Bob Gainey, #8, Peterborough

1974 – Cam Connor, #5, Flin Flon

1974 – Doug Risebrough, #7, Kitchener

1974 – Rick Chartraw, #10, Kitchener

1974 – Mario Tremblay, #12, Montreal

1975 – Pierre Mondou, #15, Montreal

1976 – Peter Lee, #12, Ottawa

1977 – Mark Napier, #10, Toronto

1978 – Danny Geoffrion, #8, Cornwall

1980 – Doug Wickenheiser, #1, Regina

1981 – Mark Hunter, #7, Brantford

1984 – Petr Svoboda, #5, CHZ Litvinov

1984 – Shayne Corson, #8, Brantford

1985 – Jose Charbonneau, #12, Drummondville

1986 – Mark Pederson, #15, Medicine Hat

1993 – Saku Koivu, #21, TPS Turku

1995 – Terry Ryan, #8, Tri-City

1996 – Matt Higgins, #18, Moose Jaw

1998 – Eric Chouinard, #16, Quebec

2000 – Ron Hainsey, #13, U. Mass-Lowell

2000 – Marcel Hossa, #16, Portland

2001 – Mike Komisarek, #7, U. of Michigan

2001 – Alexander Perezhogin, #25, Avangard Omsk

2002 – Chris Higgins, #14, Yale

2003 – Andrei Kostitsyn, #10, CSKA 2

2004 – Kyle Chipchura, #18, Prince Albert

2005 – Carey Price, #5, Tri-City

2007 – Ryan McDonagh, #12, Cretin-Derham

2007 – Max Pacioretty, #22, Sioux City

2009 – Louis Leblanc, #18, Omaha Jr. A

2010 – Jarred Tinordi, #22, USA U-18

2011 – Nathan Beaulieu, #17, Saint John

2012 – Alex Galchenyuk, #3, Sarnia

2013 – Michael McCarron, #25, USA U-18

2014 – Nikita Scherbak, #26, Saskatoon

General manager Sam Pollock made brilliant moves to acquire the rights to draft Guy Lafleur.

Jacques Plante Wears a Mask

It's unfathomable today to think that hockey goaltenders played their position without facial protection, placing themselves in continuous peril while being bombarded with hard rubber pucks fired at high velocity.

Remarkably, such was the norm until Hockey Hall of Fame member Jacques Plante became the first netminder to use the mask as part of his standard equipment.

Entering the 1959-60 season, the Montreal Canadiens had won four straight Stanley Cups, and Plante was the Vezina Trophy winner in each of those years. Plante had been carrying a mask with him for several years, after suffering numerous injuries throughout his career.

But despite experimenting with the protective shield during practices, he never had the occasion to wear one during a game.

Jacques Plante was not only a great goaltender but a pioneer at his position.

He literally changed the face of goaltending during a game on November 1, 1959, when the Habs visited the New York Rangers.

Just over three minutes into the first period, hard-shooting Rangers right winger Andy Bathgate unleashed a slapper that struck Plante in the face, and the goaltender dropped to the crease in a pool of blood.

The crowd at Madison Square Garden watched in stunned silence as Plante, with a towel draped over his face, was helped off the ice by his teammates. An ugly gash extended from the left side of his mouth and through his nostril.

Twenty minutes later, Plante returned to the ice after receiving stitches. There was a buzz from the spectators as the netminder was wearing a mask.

Blake opposed the protective equipment, but Plante was unwavering. And the coach, whose only other option was to use a house goalie, wasn't in a position to argue. With their newly-masked goaltender securing the net, the Canadiens won the game, 3-1, Plante making 29 saves for the victory.

A short-lived showdown ensued between Blake and Plante. Blake was still vehemently against having his goalie wear a mask, opining that Plante was a weaker, more vulnerable netminder because of it. But Plante – the best backstop in the league – held all the cards, simply refusing to play if he weren't permitted to wear his prized possession.

Blake relented, and a happy Plante went on to win 40 games that season, plus a fifth straight Vezina Trophy. In the playoffs, the Canadiens swept both rounds to win their fifth Stanley Cup in a row.

While Clint Benedict was the first goalie to wear a mask in an NHL game in 1930, Plante was the pioneer who made the facial gear the rule, rather than the exception.

The All-Star Game in
Vancouver
★ ★ ★

JANUARY 25, 1977

The hometown Canucks were represented by defenceman Harold Snepsts of the Wales Conference. Three future Hall of Fame players didn't play. Leafs captain Darryl Sittler sustained a rib cartilage injury and was replaced by Ian Turnbull. Clark Gilles of the New York Islanders was also hurt, and had his spot filled by teammate Bob Nystrom. And with Steve Shutt of Montreal at the side of his wife who was about to give birth, his spot was filled by Bob Gainey.

Wales Conference coach Scotty Bowman raised a few eyebrows by using defenceman Larry Robinson on the left wing. But despite the unconventional strategy, the move paid off as "Big Bird" had two assists. Meanwhile, his makeshift French-Canadian line of Rick Martin centring Marcel Dionne and Guy Lafleur was effective, combining for five points.

The Campbell Conference lineup featured seven members of the Philadelphia Flyers and coach Fred Shero. Bernie Parent – the two-time playoff MVP during back-to-back Stanley Cups – was in goal, while tenacious centre Bobby Clarke was a First Team selection as voted by the NHL Writers' Association.

The teams were deadlocked 3-3 late in the third period when Martin, of the Buffalo Sabres, beat the Islanders' Chico Resch for the game-winner. For his efforts, Martin won a car as the game's most valuable player.

JANUARY 18, 1998

For the first time in history, the NHL All-Star Game instituted a North America vs. World format. The game was billed as a lead-up to the Olympic Games in Nagano, Japan, in which NHL players would be first-time participants.

In a foreshadowing of the Olympic men's hockey tournament to follow, goalies Patrick Roy of the Colorado Avalanche and Dominik Hasek of the Buffalo Sabres were opponents in the first period. Both netminders allowed three goals in a game that was exponentially inconsequential when measured against the Nagano semi-finals that unfolded a month later when Hasek got the better of Roy in a shootout win by the Czech Republic over Canada.

Anaheim superstar Teemu Selanne potted a hat trick and claimed a truck as the most valuable player of the game. Selanne went on to strike bronze at the Olympics.

The Canucks were represented by players on both teams. Pavel Bure, the "Russian Rocket," notched an assist for the World All-Stars, while on the North America side, Mark Messier – celebrating his 37th birthday – had the eventual game-winner in an 8-7 victory.

Teemu Selanne scored a hat trick and was named MVP of the All-Star Game in 1998.

Habs Win Five in a Row

How powerful were the Montreal Canadiens of the late 1950s?

Consider this: Their power play was so potent that the NHL had to institute a rule to allow a penalized player to return to the ice after a goal was scored with the man advantage because the Habs frequently scored more than once.

Until the end of the 1955-56 season, the player had to serve the full two-minute penalty. But with the likes of Jean Beliveau, "Rocket" Richard, and "Boom Boom" Geoffrion putting games out of reach on a single power play, the other teams successfully lobbied for the rule change, much to the Habs' chagrin.

Not that it mattered. The Canadiens dominated every aspect of the game. Their top scorers, Beliveau, Dickie Moore, and brothers Maurice and Henri Richard, were all destined for the Hockey Hall of Fame. Defensive forwards Floyd Curry and Don Marshall were outstanding penalty killers. The blue line boasted the legendary Doug Harvey and another future Hall of Famer, Tom Johnson. And the last line of defence in goal was Jacques Plante.

In 1959, Montreal became the first team in history to win four consecutive Stanley Cups. As the following season progressed, the Canadiens were comfortably in first place, but not without some controversy. Plante had a spat with coach Toe Blake after he was injured in a game versus the Rangers, refusing return to action until he was allowed to wear his famous innovation, the goalie mask.

The Habs encountered a mini-slump over the final ten regular-season games of the year, posting a 4-5-1 record. It appeared that the bleu, blanc et rouge wasn't so invincible.

But as the 1960 playoffs got underway, the Canadiens very quickly regained their form. They swept Chicago in the semi-finals, then made quick work of Toronto in the finals, taking the series in four straight games to win an unprecedented fifth consecutive Stanley Cup.

The Cup-clinching game was played at Maple Leaf Gardens. Captain Maurice Richard accepted the trophy from league president Clarence Campbell, then skated off the ice for the final time. Injuries, and age, forced the "Rocket" into retirement at the following season's training camp.

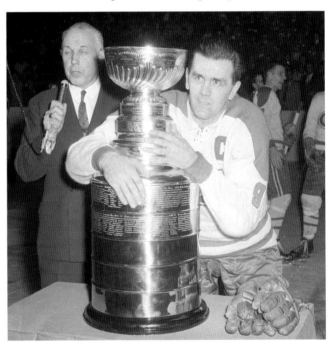

NHL president Clarence Campbell presented captain Maurice Richard with the Cup in 1960.

Between 1956 and 1960, the Canadiens won 40 of the 49 playoff games they played, posting a record of 20-5 in the Stanley Cup finals over that stretch.

Twelve men were part of all five championships: forwards Jean Beliveau, Bernie Geoffrion, Don Marshall, Dickie Moore, Claude Provost, Henri Richard, and Maurice Richard; defencemen Doug Harvey, Tom Johnson, Jean-Guy Talbot, and Bob Turner; and, goaltender Jacques Plante.

Toronto's CAPTAINS

Ken Randall, 1917-18, 1918-19

Frank Heffernan, 1919-20

Reg Noble, 1920-21, 1921-22

Reg Noble and Jack Adams, 1922-23

Jack Adams, 1923-24, 1924-25

Babe Dye, 1925-26

Bert Corbeau, 1926-27

Hap Day, 1927-28 to 1936-37

Charlie Conacher, 1937-38

Red Horner, 1938-39, 1939-40

Syl Apps, 1940-41 to 1942-43

Bob Davidson, 1943-44, 1944-45

Syl Apps, 1945-46 to 1947-48

Ted Kennedy, 1948-49 to 1954-55

Sid Smith, 1955-56

Jimmy Thomson, Ted Kennedy, 1956-57

George Armstrong, 1957-58 to 1968-69

Dave Keon, 1969-70 to 1974-75

Darryl Sittler, 1975-76 to 1980-81

Rick Vaive, 1981-82 to 1985-86

No captain, 1986-87 to 1988-89

Rob Ramage, 1989-90, 1990-91

Wendel Clark, 1991-92 to 1993-94

Doug Gilmour, 1994-95 to 1996-97

Mats Sundin, 1997-98 to 2007-08

No captain, 2008-09 to 2009-10

Dion Phaneuf, 2010-11 to 2014-15

Dave Keon wasn't big in stature but he was a fierce competitor who remains one of the greatest Leafs of all time.

$1 Million for Big M

The Toronto Maple Leafs had a rising superstar in left winger Frank Mahovlich of Schumacher, Ontario. The Calder Trophy winner in 1958, the "Big M" established a club record three years later with 48 goals in one season, in 1960-61. A year later, Mahovlich scored twelve points in as many playoff games as the Leafs ended an eleven-year Stanley Cup drought.

Following the celebratory 1962 summer, Mahovlich was unsigned at the start of training camp. No deal had been reached by the time the players gathered in Toronto for the All-Star Game to be played on Saturday, October 5. A pregame banquet held on the previous evening at the Royal York Hotel usurped all the headlines surrounding the game itself.

Frank Mahovlich was an enigma wrapped in hockey genius, cheered and booed for much the same reason.

Chicago Black Hawks' owner James Norris, whose team was beaten by the Leafs in the finals just six months earlier, coveted Mahovlich and offered Leafs vice-president Harold Ballard the princely sum of $1-million for the player's services. Ballard

gave his verbal confirmation, prompting Norris to reach into his wallet and pull out $1,000 in hundred-dollar bills as a downpayment.

Ballard then wrote on a piece of paper: "We except [sic] on behalf of Maple Leaf Gardens." The makeshift 'document' was also signed by Jack Amell of the Leafs' Silver Seven management group.

Given that the transaction was conducted over a dinner that went well into the night, its validity was dubious. But Norris asked the Black Hawks' publicity director Johnny Gottselig to relay the details to the media. Just before 1:00 am, *United Press International* and the *Associated Press* received word of the announcement.

Meanwhile, Leafs president Stafford Smythe arrived at the hotel. Upon hearing of the proceedings, he told Norris that there was no deal. Instead Smythe proposed that the principals meet at noon the next day, offering up the chance for Norris to make the same offer.

Sure enough, Norris and Black Hawks general manager Tommy Ivan walked into Maple Leafs Gardens precisely on time with a $1-million cheque in hand. Smythe rejected the offer and, just as expectedly, a furious Norris reverted to Ballard's slip of paper as written confirmation of the transaction.

Ultimately the issue was decided by NHL president Clarence Campbell at the urging of Norris. Campbell voided the sale saying that, "no responsible member of the Maple Leaf organization accepted the bid."

Mahovlich ended up signing a four-year contract for $110,000. Unlike the deal bartered between Norris and Ballard, the agreement between Mahovlich and Leafs general manager Punch Imlach was made in the clear light of day.

Ottawa Milestones

MOST SEASONS DANIEL ALFREDSSON (17)

At the recommendation of Senators director of player personnel John Ferguson, Alfredsson was selected in the sixth round of the 1994 NHL Draft. The Gothenburg, Sweden, native evolved into the face of the Ottawa franchise. Alfredsson served as team captain for 13 seasons while playing 1,178 career games in a Senators uniform, also a club record. His tenure in the nation's capital came to an end in July 2013 when he signed with Detroit as a free agent.

MOST POINTS DANIEL ALFREDSSON (1,108)

Alfredsson made an immediate impact in the NHL, collecting 61 points in his rookie season on the way to winning the Calder Trophy. In 2006, Alfredsson achieved his greatest success on an international stage by helping Sweden to an Olympic gold medal victory at the Winter Games in Turin, Italy. One year later, the captain led the Senators to an appearance in the Stanley Cup finals against Anaheim. Although the Senators lost to the Ducks in five games, Alfredsson, along with line-mates Dany Heatley and Jason Spezza, led the playoffs with 22 points each. 'Alfie' is also Ottawa's all-time leader in goals (426) and assists (682).

MOST WINS PATRICK LALIME (146)

Lalime was obtained by Ottawa from Anaheim – for whom he had never played a game – in June 1999. His best wins total came in 2002-03, when he posted 39 victories. In the playoffs, Ottawa lost a heartbreaking seven-game series to New Jersey in the conference finals. In five seasons in Ottawa, Lalime made 283 appearances and recorded 30 shutouts, both franchise records.

MOST PENALTY MINUTES

CHRIS NEIL (2,294, TO 2014-15)

The Senators long-time enforcer was a 6th-round draft choice in 1998. In ten of his first twelve NHL seasons, Neil was among the league's top seven leaders in penalty minutes. Neil has one career playoff overtime goal to his credit. He scored it in Game Two of the Eastern Conference quarter-finals against the New York Rangers, a game in which he fought Bryan Boyle in the

Daniel Afredsson was a much loved and respected captain during his many years with the Seantors.

first period. Neil, however, was held without an assist, thus missing out on a Gordie Howe hat trick.

MILESTONES AND RECORDS

Daniel Alfredsson registered his 1,000th NHL point on October 22, 2010, with a goal against the Buffalo Sabres. Exactly one month later, Alexei Kovalev reached the same milestone, scoring against Los Angeles.

In 2014-15, goaltender Andrew Hammond helped lead Ottawa to a miraculous playoff berth by allowing two or fewer goals in 12 consecutive games to start his career, tying a 76-year-old mark held by Frank Brimsek.

Glenn Hall's 502 Straight Games

Before teams had regular roster spots for backup goaltenders, Glenn Hall was a victim of the numbers game early in his career. The powerhouse Detroit Red Wings of the early 1950s had Terry Sawchuk as their unchallenged starting goalie. An All-Star Team selection in each of his first five full seasons, Sawchuk led the Wings to three Stanley Cups.

But towards the end of 1954-55, the last of those seasons that ended with a championship in the Motor City, general manager Jack Adams recalled Hall from the Edmonton Flyers of the Western Hockey League. The 23-year-old Hall won both games in which he played, surrendering just two goals.

Adams rolled the dice and traded Sawchuk in the prime of his career. Hall was anointed as Detroit's netminder for the new season, and the rookie was nothing short of superb, playing in all 70 games while posting 12 shutouts. As a reward for his efforts, Hall was named the winner of the 1955-56 Calder Trophy.

Using an unconventional butterfly stance that set the standard for future goalies, Hall dropped to his knees, spreading his legs like a butterfly to take away the bottom corners of the net from the shooter. He played every minute of the 1956-57 campaign, earning a First Team All-Star selection.

But when the Red Wings faltered in the first round of the playoffs versus Boston, Hall became a target of Adams's wrath. In a trade engineered to punish Detroit forward Ted Lindsay for trying to start a players' association, Adams dispatched "Terrible Ted" to Chicago on July 23, also sending Hall along in the deal.

Hall proved Adams wrong. Continuing to show his durability by playing in every minute of every game for the next five years, Hall was a stalwart in the Black Hawks net. In 1961, the Humboldt, Saskatchewan, native reached the pinnacle of success, backstopping Chicago to a Stanley Cup victory.

Finally, on November 7, 1962, Hall was forced to sit out because of a bad back, giving way to Denis DeJordy. Having played in 502 consecutive games, Hall established a record for goaltenders that will never be broken. Even more incredible is that Hall achieved it without wearing a mask.

Hall's final stop was in St. Louis after the Blues claimed him in the 1967 Expansion Draft. He led the team to the Stanley Cup finals, earning the Conn Smythe Trophy despite a sweep at the hands of the Canadiens.

In 16 seasons, Hall was a three-time Vezina Trophy winner and an All-Star Team selection on eleven occasions.

Gordie Howe was "Mr. Hockey," but Glenn Hall was "Mr. Goalie."

GREAT RIVALRIES Montreal vs. Boston

When the Canadiens eliminated the Bruins in a hard-fought, seven-game Eastern Conference semi-finals series in 2014, the 34th playoff series between the two teams was concluded. Indeed, Montreal and Boston are far and away the two most frequent playoff opponents in NHL history. The Habs have come away victorious 25 times in those series.

The 1946 Stanley Cup finals featured two of the most renowned forward units ever assembled: Montreal's Punch Line of Rocket Richard, Elmer Lach, and Toe Blake took on Boston's Kraut Line of Milt Schmidt, Bobby Bauer, and Woody Dumart. The Canadiens won the best-of-seven series in five games, winning two of those games in overtime.

The teams met again in the 1952 semi-finals. Game Seven is remembered for perhaps the most famous goal ever scored by Richard. The Rocket had been knocked unconscious in the first period after sustaining a punishing hit from Boston's Leo Labine. Richard didn't return until the third period with the score tied, 1-1.

With just under four minutes to play, Richard – still woozy from the hit – streaked towards the Boston goal, pushed away defender Bill Quackenbush, and fired the puck past goaltender Sugar Jim Henry for the eventual game-winner. In one of hockey's most iconic photographs, Richard and Henry shake hands while traces of blood on the Rocket's face are still evident.

Montreal earned an unlikely victory over Boston in the 1971 quarter-finals. The heavily-favoured Bruins scored a record 399 goals in the regular season and had the top four scorers in the league: Phil Esposito, Bobby Orr, John Bucyk, and Ken Hodge. But after dropping the first game, the Canadiens used a rally from a 5-1 deficit in Game Two to build their spirits. Led by rookie goaltender Ken Dryden, Montreal prevailed in seven games.

Arguably no playoff moment in Boston history is more infamous than the penalty that cost the Bruins the 1979 semi-finals. The Bruins led, 4-3, late in Game Seven at the Montreal Forum when they were called for too many men on the ice. Guy Lafleur tied the game on the resulting power play to force overtime. In the extra session, Yvon Lambert scored the winner, sending the Canadiens to the finals. Boston coach Don Cherry was fired after the season.

In 2011, the two teams battled to a seven-game showdown in the Eastern Conference quarter-finals. Nathan Horton of the Bruins scored the series winner in overtime. It was the first of an unprecedented three, Game Seven wins by the Bruins in one post-season on the way to a Stanley cup championship.

"Sugar" Jim Henry of Boston was a survivor between the pipes during the game's most competitive era.

Eagleson Gets Brewer Reinstated

The late Carl Brewer was a tough-as-nails defenceman with the Leafs, winning three Stanley Cups while finishing runner-up to Pierre Pilote for the Norris Trophy in 1963.

But while Brewer had his share of punch-ups on the rink, his biggest battles were fought off the ice. An intense man, Brewer often clashed with Toronto coach and general manager Punch Imlach.

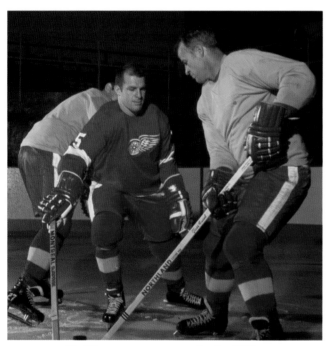

Carl Bewer was a rare example of an NHLer who was able to reclaim his amateur status.

The defenceman sat out the first part of the 1960-61 season following a disagreement over $100 in medical expenses that he felt that he was owed. Brewer announced that he would play football at Hamilton's McMaster University where he was earning a bachelor of arts degree. He returned to the Leafs after the team refunded him twice the disputed amount.

Even as the Leafs won three straight Stanley Cups, their on-ice success masked a bitter undercurrent within the walls of Maple Leaf Gardens. Imlach was perceived as a dictator by some

of the players, Brewer included. At one point, all-star Frank Mahovlich was on the verge of a nervous breakdown.

Brewer attended the team's training camp in Peterborough in 1965, but shortly afterwards he quit the team and retired following an argument with goaltender Johnny Bower. Citing irreconcilable differences between himself and Imlach, Brewer opted to enrol at the University of Toronto to finish his degree.

One year later, after Imlach failed to reach an agreement for Brewer to return, the player applied to be reinstated as an amateur so that he could join Canada's National Team. But the coach stubbornly refused to grant Brewer his release from the Leafs.

Frustrated but undeterred, Brewer enlisted the help of his agent, Alan Eagleson. The case went before the NHL Board of Governors in October 1966, five months before the start of the World Championships in Vienna, Austria. But no formal resolution came until December when Brewer was finally granted his wish.

At the 1967 World Championships, Brewer collected one goal and six assists in seven games as Canada won the bronze medal.

Eagleson publicly received much of the credit for Brewer's reinstatement. But, as written in *The Power of Two* by Susan Foster, Brewer`s life partner, the end to the standoff had more to do with legal concerns by the NHL more than Eagleson's persuasive abilities.

After Brewer permanently retired in 1980, he looked into Eagleson's business dealings and found them to be unscrupulous. Following an investigation by Russ Conway of the *Eagle-Tribune* (Lawrence, Massachusetts), Eagleson was convicted of fraud-related charges and sent to jail in 1998.

In 1911-12, the National Hockey Association implemented two major rule changes. The rover position was eliminated, leaving six players per team on the ice instead of seven. And, any challenge for the Stanley Cup had to wait until the end of the NHA regular season.

On the final day of the season, the Quebec Bulldogs vaulted into first place with an exciting 6-5 overtime win over the Ottawa Senators. Yet Ottawa was still left with a chance to overtake Quebec. If it could beat the Montreal Wanderers in the final game of the season, Ottawa would claim the Stanley Cup. It was, in fact, a replay of a protested game in which they used Cyclone Taylor in a game versus the Wanderers. Montreal still held Taylor's rights at the time, but Taylor refused to play for the team. Taylor and the Senators were fined, and the game was ordered by NHA executives to be replayed at the conclusion of the regular season.

Ottawa lost, 5-2, squandering its chance at the championship. Quebec was awarded the Stanley Cup based on its first-place finish.

In March, the Bulldogs faced a challenge from the Moncton Victorias of the Maritime Professional Hockey Association. The Victorias made the journey to Quebec for the best-of-three showdown.

The Bulldogs swept the series with a pair of blowouts. In the first game, Quebec's Jack MacDonald had four goals while teammate Joe Malone netted a hat trick in a 9-3 Bulldogs romp.

The second game was even worse for the Victorias. Quebec shelled Moncton, 8-0, MacDonald leading the way with a five-goal performance. Paddy Moran became the first goalie in history to record a shutout in Stanley Cup play.

Quebec defended its title the following season, coasting to the top of the NHA standings with a 16-4-0 record. In March, it faced a Stanley Cup challenge from the Sydney Millionaires.

The two-game, total-goals series was a mismatch in favour of the Bulldogs. Malone scored nine goals in the opening game, won by Quebec, 14-3. His younger brother and teammate, Jeff, also played in Game One. The second game ended in a 6-2 Quebec victory, led by a hat trick courtesy of Joe Hall.

Moran, the league's goals-against leader, played every minute in goal for his team for the second consecutive season. Quebec's reign as champions was ended by the Toronto Blueshirts, the 1913-14 NHA champions.

Five members from the Bulldogs' Cup-winning teams are in the Hockey Hall of Fame: Hall, Moran, Joe Malone, Rusty Crawford, and Tommy Smith.

JOE. HALL COVER-POINT

Joe hall passed away in 1919, forcing the cancellation of the Stanley Cup finals.

Masterton Dies of Injuries

The physical, often brutal, nature of hockey comes with inevitable consequences, most notably the potential for a career-ending or life-altering injury.

During the 1960s, when players routinely skated without helmets, an on-ice collision tragically cost one player, Bill Masterton, his life.

A Winnipeg native, Masterton played his junior hockey in neighbouring St. Boniface. He attended the University of Denver and helped the Pioneers to the 1961 NCAA championship. Masterton was the most valuable player in the playoffs and was also named an All-American.

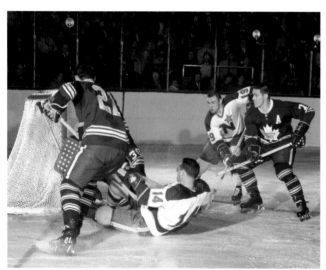

Bill Masteron (on the ice) was the first player to die as a result of injuries sustained during an NHL game.

He played one season for the Cleveland Barons in 1962-63 before retiring from professional hockey. Masterton joined technology company Honeywell while also playing for the United States National Team as an amateur.

However, when the 1967 expansion created 120 new jobs, his rights were purchased by the Minnesota North Stars from the Montreal Canadiens. Masterton suited up for each of Minnesota's first 38 games in their inaugural season. The last of those took place on January 13, 1968, against the Oakland Seals.

In the first period, as Masterton crossed the blue line, he was checked simultaneously by Seals players Larry Cahan and Ron Harris. A bare-headed Masterton fell backward, hit his head on the ice, and was rendered unconscious.

A horrified crowd at the Metropolitan Sports Center watched as Masterton was taken off the ice on a stretcher, blood pouring from his head. The player was rushed to Fairview Southdale Hospital. Masterton was attended by five physicians, but his condition was inoperable.

Two days later, Masterton, 29, succumbed to his injuries. He left behind his wife Carol, son Scott, aged three, and daughter Sally, aged one.

The tragedy had far-reaching effects. A trophy was instituted in Masterton's name to be awarded to the player who "best exemplifies the qualities of perseverance, sportsmanship, and dedication to hockey." Claude Provost of Montreal was the first winner of the award, in 1968.

In 1979-80, the NHL made it mandatory for all players entering the league to wear helmets. The rule did not apply to players who had signed their contracts before the regulation came into effect. Craig MacTavish, who retired in 1997, was the last skater to play in the NHL without a helmet.

A *Toronto Star* article published in 2011 revealed that a previously untreated concussion likely led to Masterton's death. Medical experts suggested that Masterton was suffering a brain injury when he stepped on the ice in what would be his final game. North Stars coach and general manager Wren Blair, and teammate goalie Cesare Maniago, also described Masterton as exhibiting symptoms related to concussions.

BEST GAME EVER IN WINNIPEG March 2, 1993

JETS VS. NORDIQUES

Teemu Selanne made his NHL debut in 1992-93 with a sensational rookie season that the league had never witnessed before and has not seen since. "The Finnish Flash" dazzled Winnipeg fans with his blazing speed and uncanny scoring abilities.

On February 28, Selanne had four goals in a 7-6 home win over the Minnesota North Stars. The hat trick marker was his 50th tally of the season in just his 63rd game of the year. The milestone broke the record, by three games, for the fewest number of games by a rookie to reach fifty goals, previously held by Joe Nieuwendyk.

Two nights later, Winnipeg Arena was abuzz in anticipation of Selanne reaching, or possibly even breaking, a long-standing mark for first-year players. Selanne needed just two goals to tie Mike Bossy's record of 53 goals by a rookie. The Islanders' Hall of Famer established the benchmark during the 1977-78 season.

If there were a hint that the evening was going to be special, it came no later than 15 seconds into the game. After the Jets won a faceoff in their zone, Selanne accepted a breakout pass from Phil Housley at centre ice. Selanne breezed past defenceman Curtis Leschyshyn for a breakaway chance and deked Nordiques goalie Stephane Fiset for the game's opening goal.

The Nordiques reeled off the next three goals. Andrei Kovalenko put his team up, 3-1, at the 16:21 mark of the second period. Just 18 seconds later, Selanne struck again. After Jets winger Darrin Shannon's shot went wide to Fiset's right, Selanne retrieved the puck from behind the net. With Fiset out of position on the far side, Selanne had a yawning cage into which he easily deposited the puck, tying Bossy's record.

Teemu Selanne was born to score, and with the Jets he scored a record 76 goals as a rookie.

The historic record-breaker came just before the midway point of the third period. Tie Domi dumped the puck out of the Winnipeg zone towards the Quebec side of the ice. Selanne streaked behind defenceman Adam Foote and was now in a foot race for the puck against Fiset who had stormed out of the goal towards the Jets forward.

Selanne easily got to the puck first. He lifted a backhander over Fiset and into the goal. In celebration, Selanne aimed his stick to the rafters of Winnipeg Arena. As 14,397 fans cheered, their voices hoarse, Selanne tossed his glove into the air before being mobbed by his teammates.

A banner proclaimed "52..53..54..Bossy's record is no more!"

Not even the Nordiques' 7-4 win could dampen the spirits of Winnipeg fans.

Berenson Scores Six Goals

Gordon "Red" Berenson was a standout at the University of Michigan where he played three seasons, posting an incredible 43 goals and 70 points in just 28 games in 1961-62. The Regina native became the first Canadian to go from a U.S. college team to the NHL when he turned professional with Montreal.

Berenson split his time with the Habs between the NHL and the minor leagues. With so much talent on the Montreal roster, particularly at centre where future Hall of Famers Jean Beliveau and Henri Richard were firmly secure atop the depth chart, Berenson saw limited action. Nevertheless, he earned a Stanley Cup ring in 1965.

Nicknamed the "Red Baron," the red-headed Berenson was traded to the New York Rangers, playing just 49 games in Manhattan over parts of two seasons before being dealt to St. Louis. While with the Blues, Berenson flourished, enjoying what would be the most productive time of his career.

He scored a career-high 35 goals in the 1968-69 season, but a half-dozen of those goals came on one historic night in Philadelphia.

On November 7, 1968, the slumping Berenson stepped onto the ice having found the net just three times in St. Louis's first eleven games. But he managed to get the better of Flyers goalie Doug Favell late in the first period to open the scoring.

In the second period, the "Red Baron" took over the game. Within a span of just over nine minutes, Berenson miraculously fired four shots past Favell to put the Blues up 5-0. The flurry of four goals in a period tied an NHL record held by "Busher" Jackson of Toronto (1934) and Max Bentley of Chicago (1943).

When Berenson's stick broke in the third period, the player feared that his spectacular output might be at an end for the evening. But sure enough, with 5:56 left in the game, Berenson beat a hapless Favell with a new stick for his sixth tally.

Berenson then came within an inch of tying Joe Malone's mark of seven goals in a game, set in 1920, but he hit the crossbar. The final score was 8-0 for the Blues. Berenson established a record by scoring six times in a road game. He finished the night with ten shots on goal.

Berenson scored 261 goals in 987 career NHL games. He also played in two of eight games for Team Canada in the 1972 Summit Series. On January 10, 2015, Berenson earned his 800th career win in his 31st season as coach of the University of Michigan hockey team.

Red Berenson's six goals in a road game remains an NHL record.

Toronto's HALL OF FAMERS

Players

Jack Adams, 1959
Glenn Anderson, 2008
Syl Apps, 1961
George Armstrong, 1975
Ace Bailey, 1975
Ed Belfour, 2011
Max Bentley, 1966
Johnny Bower, 1976
Turk Broda, 1967
Harry Cameron, 1962
King Clancy, 1958
Charlie Conacher, 1961
Hap Day, 1961
Gord Drillon, 1975
Dick Duff, 2006
Babe Dye, 1970
Fernie Flaman, 1990
Grant Fuhr, 2003
Mike Gartner, 2001
Doug Gilmour, 2011

George Hainsworth, 1961
Red Horner, 1965
Tim Horton, 1972
Busher Jackson, 1971
Red Kelly, 1969
Ted Kennedy, 1966
Dave Keon, 1986
Harry Lumley, 1980
Frank Mahovlich, 1981
Lanny McDonald, 1992
Larry Murphy, 2004
Reg Noble, 1962
Bert Olmstead, 1985
Jacques Plante, 1978
Babe Pratt, 1966
Joe Primeau, 1963
Marcel Pronovost, 1978
Bob Pulford, 1991
Borje Salming, 1996
Terry Sawchuk, 1971
Sweeney Schriner, 1962

Darryl Sittler, 1989
Allan Stanley, 1981
Mats Sundin, 2012
Norm Ullman, 1982
Harry Watson, 1994

Builders

Harold Ballard, 1977
J.P. Bickel, 1978
Pat Burns, 2014
Cliff Fletcher, 2004
Jim Gregory, 2007
William A. Hewitt, 1947
Foster Hewitt, 1965
Punch Imlach, 1984
Dick Irvin Sr., 1958
Roger Neilson, 2002
Rudy Pilous, 1985
Bud Poile, 1990
Frank J. Selke, 1960
Conn Smythe, 1958

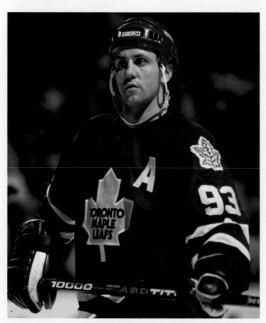

Doug Gilmour was the heart and soul of the Leafs during his time with the team.

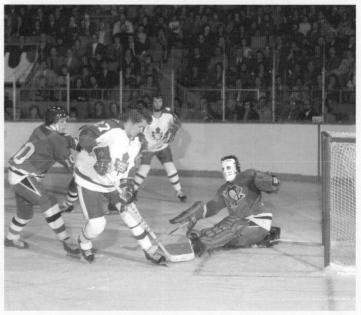

Darryl Sittler inherited Toronto's captaincy early in his career and led the team with class and dignity.

Green-Maki Incident

Regrettably, the NHL has had a small number of brushes with the law, where actions on ice have civic consequences. In 1988, for instance, Dino Ciccarelli was charged by Toronto police with assault after hitting Luke Richardson with his stick. Twelve years later, in a more vicious altercation, Marty McSorley had to answer for using his stick to strike Donald Brashear on the temple.

While both of those incidents were highly publicized, a stick-swinging duel that occurred decades earlier is not as thoroughly documented, mainly because the game in which it took place wasn't televised. But the actions and consequences were just as seious.

On September 21, 1969, the Boston Bruins and St. Louis Blues played an exhibition game in Ottawa. In the first period, Boston defenceman Ted Green collided with St. Louis forward Wayne Maki.

Ted Green's career suffered terrible damage after a stick-swinging incident with Wayne Maki.

Green wildly swung his stick at Maki. In retaliation, Maki used his lumber to swipe at Green. The stick caught the Bruins player squarely on his helmetless head. Green fell to the ice, barely conscious. He struggled to get to his feet, to no avail, as officials frantically called for a trainer and a doctor.

Immediately Green was rushed to the hospital where he was diagnosed with a compound skull fracture. The injury required two brain operations to save his life, and a metal plate had to be inserted.

The NHL suspended Green and Maki while fining them $300. Maki's ban was for 30 days while Green's suspension was for 13 days, "if and when he returns to hockey." Ottawa police laid assault charges against both men. Weeks later, however, the players were absolved of criminal wrongdoing.

Green's injury kept him from playing the entire 1969-70 season, the year that the Bruins claimed their first Stanley Cup in 29 seasons. After winning a championship with Boston in 1972, Green joined the World Hockey Association. He played for seven years with the New England Whalers and Winnipeg Jets.

Maki was claimed by Vancouver in the 1970 Expansion Draft. He was forced to retire two years later when doctors discovered that he had a cancerous brain tumour. Maki died in May 1974 at just 29 years old. His number 11 was retired by the Canucks until the sweater was reintroduced when Mark Messier signed with the team in 1997.

The infamous Green-Maki incident received a fraction of the scrutiny that it would have had had it occurred in today's age of social media. Not only is there no archival video footage of it available, but the only known photographs were taken by a 12-year-old spectator.

Montreal's Biggest Trades

▶ **TOP TRADE**

MAY 22, 1970 Montreal traded Ernie Hicke and the Canadiens' first-round pick in the 1970 draft (Chris Oddleifson) to California, for Francois Lacombe and the Golden Seals' first-round pick in the 1971 draft (Guy Lafleur)

Eccentric Golden Seals owner Chuck Finley had to be pleased with his team's second consecutive playoff berth in 1969-70. Optimistic about California's potential return to the postseason, Finley dealt away the first-round draft choice in 1971, not realizing its subsequent ramifications, for either his team, his trading partner, Montreal, or for hockey history.

California's 1970-71 campaign was disastrous. By late January, the Seals had won just 14 of 47 games, and a sure-fire prospect was setting junior hockey records for the ages with the Quebec Remparts—a kid from Thurso, Quebec, named Guy Lafleur.

Ken Dryden was property of the Boston Bruins before being traded to Montreal.

Montreal general manager Sam Pollock, who held the Seals' pick, orchestrated a subsequent trade to maximize California's chances of finishing in last place. He traded Ralph Backstrom to Los Angeles for Gord Labossiere and Ray Fortin in an attempt to help boost the Kings' offence.

Pollock's masterful plan came to fruition. In an era long before a lottery determined the first-overall pick, California's finish in the basement of the standings assured the Canadiens of their coveted spot in the draft.

Not surprisingly, Lafleur was selected first overall by Montreal in June 1971. A three-time Hart Trophy winner and all-time franchise scoring leader, Lafleur unquestionably stands as one of the Habs' all-time greats.

HONOURABLE MENTION

JUNE 1964 Boston Bruins trade Ken Dryden and Alex Campbell to Montreal for Guy Allen and Paul Reid

The NHL Amateur Draft was instituted to create parity among all franchises in what was then a six-team league. While the Leafs and Canadiens consistently built winning rosters by developing younger players through the junior and senior teams which they sponsored, opponents such as the Bruins and Black Hawks had no such luxury.

The year 1964 marked the second year that the NHL draft was held. Boston selected Ken Dryden with its 14th overall pick. A goaltender with the Etobicoke Indians of the Junior B circuit, Dryden had expressed interest in playing college hockey in the United States.

Boston traded Dryden to Montreal in a four-player swap. The future Hall of Fame netminder was oblivious to the transaction, admitting several years later that he'd always believed the Canadiens to be the team that had drafted him.

Dryden rose to prominence during the 1971 playoffs when he led the Canadiens to an unexpected Stanley Cup.

Orr Wins Art Ross

No player in the history of the game had a season as extraordinary as Bobby Orr in 1969-70.

Yes, "Rocket" Richard electrified the Montreal Forum patrons with his successful pursuit of 50 goals in 50 games, a quarter-century earlier. And, indeed, any of Wayne Gretzky's four, 200-point campaigns – four more than anyone else who has ever played – were borne of exceptional brilliance that may never be witnessed again.

But Orr's historic fourth professional year in hockey trumps them all. The Bruins' superstar single-handedly, superhumanly transformed the defenceman position. With exceptional skating, accurate passing, and a deadly shot, Orr reinvented the role of a blueliner from a player solely tasked to prevent goals to a skater who could consistently contribute to the offence.

By mid-January of 1970, Orr had recorded 51 assists to break the single-season record of assists by a defenceman, previously held by Chicago's Pat Stapleton. And there were still 36 games—almost half a season—remaining in the schedule.

Orr's remarkable compilation of points continued on March 15 against the Red Wings. The two-time defending Norris Trophy winner had two goals and two assists to become the first defenceman ever to register 100 points.

One week later, he matched the output of that night's scoresheet in a four-point effort versus Minnesota, giving him 79 assists. The mark established a record for most helpers in a season, by any player, either forward or defenceman.

By the end of the year, Orr had collected 33 goals and 87 assists for 120 points. He shattered his own mark of points in one season by a defenceman – 64 in 1968-69 – nearly doubling the tally. The next two highest-scoring rearguards that season were Oakland's Carol Vadnais and Toronto's Jim McKenny.

They each had 44 points, or just over one-third of Orr's historic total.

Orr became the first defenceman in the history of the game to win the Art Ross Trophy as the league's scoring champion, beating his teammate and runner-up Phil Esposito by 21 points. He was also named the Hart Trophy winner as most valuable player and easily claimed his third consecutive Norris award.

Then came the playoffs. The Bruins claimed their first Stanley Cup since in 1941, Orr flying through the air as he scored the winning goal in overtime. He capped off the season of a lifetime by earning the Conn Smythe Trophy as playoff MVP, becoming the first player in history to win four major awards in one year.

Only one defenceman has ever led the NHL in scoring, and Bobby Orr did it twice.

Calgary's TOP DRAFT CHOICES

1980 – Denis Cyr, #13, Montreal	**1999** – Oleg Saprykin, #11, Seattle
1981 – Al MacInnis, #15, Kitchener	**2000** – Brent Krahn, #9, Calgary
1983 – Dan Quinn, #13, Belleville	**2001** – Chuck Kobasew, #14, Boston College
1984 – Gary Roberts, #12, Ottawa	**2002** – Eric Nystrom, #10, U. of Michigan
1985 – Chris Biotti, #17, Waltham	**2003** – Dion Phaneuf, #9, Red Deer
1986 – George Pelawa, #16, Bemidji	**2004** – Kris Chucko, #24, Salmon Arm
1987 – Bryan Deasley, #19, U. of Michigan	**2005** – Matt Pelech, #26, Sarnia
1988 – Jason Muzatti, #21, Michigan State	**2006** – Leland Irving, #26, Everett
1990 – Trevor Kidd, #11, Brandon	**2007** – Mikael Backlund, #24, Vasteras
1991 – Niklas Sundblad, #19, AIK Solna	**2008** – Greg Nemisz, #25, Windsor
1992 – Cory Stillman, #6, Windsor	**2009** – Tim Erixon, #23, Skelleftea
1993 – Jesper Mattsson, #18, Malmo	**2011** – Sven Baertschi, #13, Portland
1994 – Chris Dingman, #19, Brandon	**2012** – Mark Jankowski, #21, Stanstead College
1995 – Denis Gauthier, #20, Drummondville	**2013** – Sean Monahan, #6, Ottawa
1996 – Derek Morris, #13, Regina	**2013** – Emile Poirier, #22, Gatineau
1997 – Daniel Tkaczuk, #6, Barrie	**2013** – Morgan Klimchuk, #28, Regina
1998 – Rico Fata, #6, London	**2014** – Sam Bennett, #4, Kingston

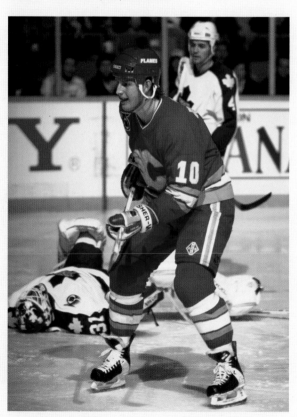

Few players had the perseverance to success as Gary Roberts.

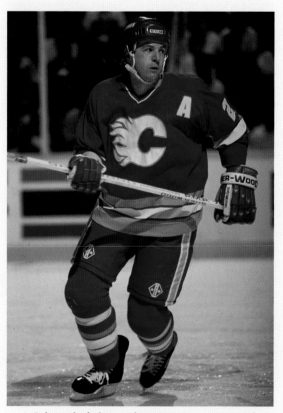

A Calgary draft choice, Al MacInnis was an essential member of the team's 1989 Cup run.

Orr Flies to Win Cup in 1970

Entering the 1970 playoffs, the Boston Bruins were riding a wave of regular-season triumphs. Bobby Orr, the scoring champion, was the game's most dominant player. Phil Esposito led the league in goals with 43. And, the team finished with 99 points in the standings, tied with Chicago, albeit officially in second place by virtue of the Black Hawks' five additional wins.

But the coveted Stanley Cup still eluded the Harry Sinden-coached squad. Boston was ousted in the semi-finals by Montreal the previous year, then watched enviously as the Habs swept St. Louis in the finals for their second straight championship.

In the 1970 quarter-finals, the Bruins drew the New York Rangers, the team that surprisingly edged the Canadiens for the final playoff spot in the East Division based on a goals-scored tiebreaker. After a six-game triumph, Boston quickly dispatched Chicago in a four-game sweep in the semi-finals.

The Cup finals matched Orr, Esposito, and the rest of the black-and-gold clad team against the St. Louis Blues, the West Division champions for a third consecutive year.

As in the previous two finals, which were both Canadiens sweeps of the Blues, this series exemplified the disparity between the pre-expansion East and expansion West divisions. Boston rolled over St. Louis in the first three games by margins of five, four, and three goals.

The fourth game was played on May 10 at Boston Garden, and the teams skated to a 3-3 deadlock through sixty minutes of regulation. Overtime lasted just forty seconds. Bruins forward Derek Sanderson aggressively led a forecheck into the Blues zone.

Orr, eager for redemption after being held without a goal in the first three games of the series, pinched along the right wing

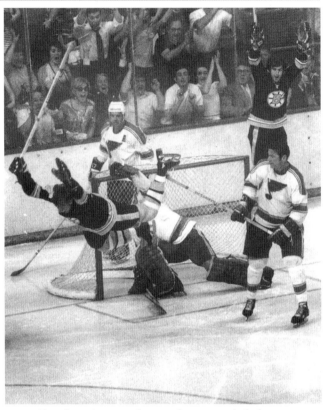

Few photos in sports photography can match the beauty of Bobby Orr flying through the air.

boards, getting the puck to Sanderson stationed behind the goal line.

As Orr passed off, he darted to the front of the goal, receiving a return feed from Sanderson a moment later. Orr fired the puck past Blues goalie Glenn Hall to clinch the game. In mid-celebration, his hands raised victoriously, Orr tripped over the stick of St. Louis defenceman Noel Picard, grinning ecstatically as he was sent airborne.

An appreciative Garden crowd erupted in pandemonium as Boston ended its 29-year Stanley Cup drought. Orr was named the Conn Smythe Trophy winner as the most valuable player in the playoffs, and the photograph of Orr's historic 'flying' celebration remains one of the most iconic images in all of sports.

The All-Star Game in
Quebec
Rendez-vous '87

★★★

FEBRUARY 11-13, 1987

In lieu of an intra-league event, the NHL hosted a two-game showdown against the best players from the Soviet Union. The international duel, staged at Le Colisee in Quebec City, did not disappoint as fans witnessed a spectacle that was a precursor to the Canada Cup later that year.

Jean Perron, coach of the defending Stanley Cup champion Montreal Canadiens, was behind the bench for the NHL All-Stars, while his USSR counterpart was the legendary Viktor Tihkonov.

In Game One, the first half was dominated by members of the powerhouse Edmonton Oilers. The line of Jari Kurri, Wayne Gretzky, and Esa Tikannen connected for the opening goal in the first period, Kurri getting the tally. The score held until Glenn Anderson made it 2-0 with three minutes to go in the middle frame. Meanwhile, Grant Fuhr was rock solid in net.

But the Soviets were hardly pushovers, and Alexei Kasatonov pulled the visitors to within a goal before the second period expired.

The teams went back-and-forth in the final period and were deadlocked at 3-3 with a five-minute sudden-death overtime looming, as per NHL rules. However, Dave Poulin found the back of the net of goalie Evgeni Belosheikin with 75 seconds remaining for the game-winner. Poulin, playing on a checking line with Dale Hawerchuk and Kevin Dineen, had helped neutralize the USSR's famous KLM line of Vladimir Krutov, Igor Larionov, and Sergei Makarov.

Game Two featured as much of the high tempo as the opener. Neither side gave an inch in the battle for hockey supremacy, regardless of the tournament's billing as an exhibition series. Once again, it was the Oilers connecting for the first goal, Mark Messier converting on a power play, assists going to Kurri and Gretzky.

Down 1-0 heading into the second period, the Soviets struck quickly. Both Valeri Kamensky and Krutov beat Fuhr two minutes apart to give the USSR the lead. Then for good measure, Kamensky scored with only 19 seconds left in the frame. It was a Canada Cup foreshadowing for the youngster who scored the tying goal in the first game of the September tournament, leading to a victory for his team.

The Soviets went on to prevail, 5-3. Messier and Makarov were named the most valuable players for their respective teams while Gretzky took tournament MVP honours.

"That was hockey the way it is supposed to be played," said Gretzky.

Very few people who watched the two games would disagree.

Marcel Aubut was a driving force behind Quebec City hosting Rendez-vous '87.

Esposito Scores 76 Goals

In one of the most one-sided transactions in NHL history, Bruins general manager Milt Schmidt fleeced his Chicago Black Hawks counterpart Tommy Ivan to obtain Phil Esposito in 1967.

At 6'1", 205 pounds, Esposito was immovable from the edge of the crease, or in the slot, where he earned his living. In 1968-69, his second season with the Bruins, the Sault Ste. Marie, Ontario, native not only won the Hart Trophy but set single-season records in both assists (77) and points (126).

Phil Esposito scored goals in a way no other player could, from the slot, with a quick shot.

Esposito led all scorers with 43 goals in the regular season the following year. He was sensational in the playoffs with 27 points – best among all players – as the Bruins won the Stanley Cup in 1970, ending a drought that lasted nearly three decades.

The Bruins were an offensive juggernaut in 1970-71, establishing a record by scoring 399 goals. The roster boasted the top four scorers in the NHL: Esposito, Bobby Orr, John Bucyk, and Ken Hodge.

Esposito was the cornerstone of the forward unit. A master at collecting the 'dirty' rebound goals around the net, Esposito generated an astounding 550 shots at opposing goaltenders, an average of more than seven per game.

As the Bruins embarked on a late season western road swing, Esposito was in hot pursuit of Bobby Hull's single-season mark of 58 goals. By the end of the Bruins' visit to Los Angeles on March 11, during which they demolished the Kings, 7-2, Esposito earned both his 59th goal and 127th point, establishing two new records.

Boston kept steamrolling, and so did Esposito. On March 20th, the Bruins won their 13th consecutive game. The team had put together a ten-game winning streak earlier in the season. Over the final eleven games of the regular season, Esposito found the back of the net an incredible 17 times. His totals for the season included 76 goals and 76 assists for 152 points.

In bettering Hull's previous goal mark by 18, Esposito's achievement was the highest margin in history by which the single-season goal record was surpassed.

Orr was named the Hart Trophy winner and Esposito the runner-up. However, a new award—the Lester B. Pearson Award—was introduced, to be presented to the league's best player as voted by members of the NHLPA. Esposito was named its inaugural winner.

For nearly four decades, no other player had taken more 500 shots on goal in a single season until Alex Ovechkin did so in 2008-09, firing the puck 528 times towards the net, still shy, however, of Espo's record.

Vancouver's CAPTAINS

Orland Kurtenbach, 1970-71 to 1973-74

No captain, 1974-75

Andre Boudrias, 1975-76

Chris Oddleifson, 1976-77

Don Lever, 1977-78

Don Lever and Kevin McCarthy, 1978-79

Kevin McCarthy, 1979-80 to 1981-82

Stan Smyl, 1982-83 to 1989-90

Dan Quinn, Doug Lidster and Trevor Linden, 1990-91

Trevor Linden, 1991-92 to 1996-97

Mark Messier, 1997-98 to 1999-2000

Markus Naslund, 2000-01 to 2007-08

Roberto Luongo, 2008-09, 2009-10

Henrik Sedin, 2010-11 to 2014-15

Longtime captain Trevor Linden is a superstar in Vancouver.

Dryden's Rookie Playoffs

The 1970-71 season was dominated by the record-setting Boston Bruins. The team won an unprecedented 57 games and boasted the league's top four scorers in the regular season. Boston was the clear favourite in its quarter-finals playoff series versus Montreal.

The Canadiens had a very respectable finish after missing the playoffs the previous year for the first time in over two decades, closing out the regular season with the NHL's fourth-best record. As they entered the post-season, the biggest question was whether their starting goaltender would be regular starter Rogie Vachon or backup Phil Myre?

And the answer was – neither! Instead, the Habs went with 23-year-old Ken Dryden, a Cornell University graduate who had spent most of the year with the Canadiens' minor league affiliate, the Montreal Voyaguers. Dryden had only six NHL regular-season games of experience to his credit, all played at the end of the season. He won them all, allowing only nine goals.

Dryden's playoff initiation was a baptism by fire as the net-minder was peppered with 42 shots in Game One, a 3-1 Boston win. The series turned in the second game as Montreal staged a miraculous comeback. Down 5-1 in the second period, the Canadiens stormed back with six unanswered goals to take the game and even the series.

Ultimately, Montreal prevailed in seven games, dethroning the defending champs. Dryden allowed 26 goals on 286 shots, a remarkable save percentage in an era of free-flowing hockey and smaller goalie equipment than is used today.

Dryden continued to play every minute in the Canadiens' net as the team took care of the Minnesota North Stars in six games in the semi-finals. In the finals, Montreal faced the Chicago Black Hawks, led by the "Golden Jet," Bobby Hull. Dryden's counterpart, Tony Esposito, was just as formidable between the pipes.

The series went the distance, and Game Seven was played at the Chicago Stadium on May 18. Although the Black Hawks jumped out to a 2-0 lead, the game turned when Jacques Lemaire's shot from centre ice somehow made its way past a bewildered Esposito, silencing the crowd.

Chicago couldn't recover from the blunder. Henri Richard scored a pair of goals, the latter holding up as the Cup-winner as Montreal claimed its unlikeliest of championships. Dryden was sensational in the final minutes of the third period, making several game-saving stops.

Dryden was awarded the Conn Smythe Trophy for his heroics. The next season, he took Calder Trophy honours as rookie of the year. No other player has ever won those two awards in that order.

Ken Dryden won the Conn Smythe Trophy before the Calder Trophy, a unique feat if ever there was one.

Calgary Milestones

MOST SEASONS JAROME IGINLA (16)

The Flames obtained Iginla in a trade with Dallas in December 19, 1995, sending Joe Nieuwendyk to the Stars. Although Calgary had to part with an integral part of its lineup, the transaction was more than worthwhile. Iginla evolved into the marquee player of the franchise, wearing the "C" for nine seasons.

MOST POINTS JAROME IGINLA (1,095)

Iginla also leads Calgary in all-time goals with 525. He collected a career-best 52 goals in 2001-02 while finishing with 96 points to capture the Art Ross Trophy. That same year, Iginla lost a narrow Hart Trophy vote to goaltender Jose Theodore of the Montreal Canadiens.

In the 2004 playoffs, Iginla lead the Flames to a surprising run to the Stanley Cup finals. Calgary came within one game of winning its first championship in 15 years, only to come up short in Game Seven against Tampa Bay.

MOST WINS MIIKKA KIPRUSOFF (305)

Kiprusoff was acquired from San Jose in November 2003, for a second-round 2005 draft pick (Marc-Edouard Vlasic). The native of Turku, Finland, was quickly anointed as the team's starter and took the Flames to the seventh game of the Stanley Cup finals.

In 2005-06, Kiprusoff won both the Vezina and Jennings Trophies while also being named to the First All-Star Team. Four years later, he helped lead his native Finnish team to a bronze medal at the 2010 Winter Olympics in Vancouver.

Kiprusoff's marks of 41 career shutouts and 33,779 minutes played for Calgary are also franchise highs.

MOST PENALTY MINUTES TIM HUNTER (2,405)

A native Calgarian, Hunter was a draft choice of the Atlanta Flames in 1979 before the franchise relocated to Alberta one year later. Hunter led the NHL in penalty minutes twice in his career, topping the 300-minute mark on three occasions.

In 1989 Hunter, along with co-captains Jim Peplinski and Lanny McDonald, joyfully hoisted the Stanley Cup at the Montreal Forum after Calgary's Game Six victory.

MILESTONES AND RECORDS

Lanny McDonald recorded his 1,000th NHL point by scoring against the Winnipeg Jets on March 7, 1989. Two weeks later, he registered the 500th and final goal of his illustrious career.

Jarome Iginla's 1,000th NHL point came on April 1, 2011, a goal versus St. Louis. On January 7, 2012, Iginla beat Minnesota's Niklas Backstrom for his 500th goal.

In the 1989 playoffs, Al MacInnis established a post-season record for defencemen with a 17-game point-scoring streak. He notched seven goals and 19 assists over that stretch on the way to taking Conn Smythe Trophy honours.

Theo Fleury wasn't tall but his tenacity on ice made him look like a giant.

WHA Legitimized as Hull Signs

Even before the opening faceoff in the first game of the World Hockey Association in the fall of 1972, the rival league hit a few obstacles coming out of the gate.

One of the inaugural franchises, the Miami Screaming Eagles, never got to see the light of day, instead moving to Philadelphia. And, although there were a few NHL players coming on board, the WHA still needed a marquee name to bring credibility to the new league.

In late June 1972, the WHA received the windfall that it so coveted when Chicago Black Hawks superstar Bobby Hull signed with the Winnipeg Jets.

Hull had just come off a 50-goal season with the Black Hawks, marking the fifth time in his illustrious career that he had reached the plateau. The 12-time All-star Team selection had not been offered a contract to continue playing in the Windy City beyond the final year of his deal, 1971-72.

There was also a history of animosity between Hull and Black Hawks' team president Bill Wirtz. The player had staged a bitter holdout two years earlier, embroiled in a contract dispute. Hull finally relented after a month off ice, but the strain on his relationship with Wirtz was irreversible.

Jets owner Ben Hatskin presented Hull with a very generous offer: a whopping $1-million up front – an unheard of sum in those days – plus $250,000 annually for five years. The deal also included a front-office position at $100,000 a year over the same term.

As the media assembled in Winnipeg for the signing, Hull grinned for the cameras, holding a huge cardboard novelty cheque for $1-million made out to Robert Marvin Hull.

The landmark signing had a domino effect on NHL players who had been indecisive about joining the WHA but who were now more than eager to follow Hull. Gerry Cheevers, Al Hamilton, and Gerry Pinder all left their respective NHL clubs to sign for bigger dollars. Derek Sanderson, Mike Walton, Dave Keon and a multitude of other players soon followed.

Although the WHA struggled to stay afloat, eventually folding while its four surviving clubs merged with the NHL in 1979, its rosters were comprised of high-calibre talent. Hull's initial signing enabled the WHA to lure some of the game's best players from the NHL on a consistent basis.

In the seven years of the WHA's existence, Hull played all of them with the Winnipeg Jets, winning three AVCO Cup championships along the way. He was named to the All-Star Team three times and had his most productive season in 1974-75 when he scored 77 goals in 78 games.

Bobby Hull gambled on the WHA and won. His signing effectively changed hockey forever.

92

GREAT RIVALRIES Edmonton vs. Dallas

While not historic adversaries or even geographic rivals, the Edmonton Oilers and Dallas Stars became familiar foes during a five-year stretch between 1996-97 and 2000-01 during which time they met every year in the playoffs.

Edmonton and Dallas have played several memorable playoff series in the last 15 years.

The 1997 Western Conference quarter-finals was a seeming mismatch. Edmonton, the seventh-seed, had finished the regular season with a sub-.500 record, 23 points behind Dallas. But the resilient Oilers managed to force a seventh game at Northlands Coliseum after overtime goals by Kelly Buchberger and Ryan Smyth helped keep them in the series.

Game Seven also went into sudden death after three periods. Dallas forward Joe Nieuwendyk appeared to have an open net to clinch the series, but he was denied by a miraculous save by Edmonton goalie Curtis Joseph, who dove from his left to his right to make a highlight-reel save on Nieuwendyk.

Moments later, Todd Marchant skated around defenceman Grant Ledyard down the right wing and scored a breakaway goal on Andy Moog to send the Oilers into the next round.

Dallas earned a measure of revenge the following season after eliminating Edmonton in five games. Benoit Hogue scored the only goal of Game Three in overtime. The defensive-oriented series was one in which neither team scored more than three goals in any game.

In 1999, the two teams played one of the most tightly-contested series to end in a four-game sweep. The Presidents' Trophy-winning Stars won each of the first three games of the opening round by just a single goal. By the time the puck dropped for Game Four, Dallas was missing several key regulars including Pat Verbeek, Guy Carbonneau, and Richard Matvichuk.

The Oilers weren't about to roll over, playing their opponents to triple overtime. At 17:34 of the sixth period, Sergei Zubov's point shot bounced off Nieuwendyk's leg and into the net past a heartbroken goalie Tommy Salo to complete the sweep.

"Next year somebody else can play this team," said Stars coach Ken Hitchcock after the game. "I mean, we've just about had it with these guys." Dallas went on to win its first Stanley Cup in franchise history.

However, Hitchcock's desire not to face Edmonton in 2000 went unfulfilled. Once again the Stars and Oilers duelled in the first round. Dallas took the series in five games on the way to its second straight appearance in the finals. The Stars were defeated by New Jersey in a six-game series.

The run of familiarity ended with a Stars six-game conference quarter-finals win over the Oilers in 2001.

1972 Summit Series

The eight-game showdown between Canada and the Soviet Union in 1972 was not only a heated competition for hockey supremacy; it was a clash of ideologies—West versus East, capitalism versus communism—staged in the middle of the Cold War.

Canada was more than eager to wager its international pride against its Soviet opponents in a best-on-best tournament. Out of protest against the International Ice Hockey Federation's refusal to allow Canada to use semi-professional players in competition, the country did not participate in hockey in the 1972 Olympics. The Summit Series was the perfect vehicle to settle the debate over which nation was the absolute hockey power.

Many pundits predicted an eight-game sweep for the maple leaf-crested roster. When Canada sprung to a quick 2-0 lead in Game One, the nation smugly—and prematurely—began to question their opponents' ability to stay competitive. Unfazed by the early deficit, the Soviets stormed back to take the game, 7-3, before a stunned crowd at the Montreal Forum.

The Canadians quickly realized that the Soviets, with their incredible passing and superior conditioning, weren't going to be pushovers. Peter Mahovlich scored a highlight-reel, short-handed goal in the second game in Toronto to help tie the series at one win each.

After the teams skated to a tie in Winnipeg, Canada was easy fodder in Game Four, prompting relentless, hostile boos for the home squad from the Vancouver fans. An irate Phil Esposito sounded off on national television in a post-game interview, incredulous at the lack of support for the team from Canadians from coast to coast.

The series shifted to Moscow for the final four games. In Game Five, the Soviets rallied with four consecutive goals in the third period for a 5-4 win. Over the final three outings, the physical war escalated on the ice.

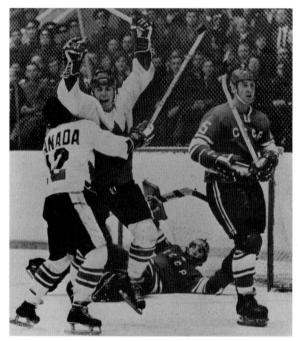

Paul Henderson scored the winning goal in the Summit Series, the most important eight games ever played.

Bobby Clarke slashed Valeri Kharlamov on the ankle in the next game, rendering the Soviet star forward ineffective. Canada won, 3-2. In Game Seven, a 4-3 Canada victory, Soviet captain Boris Mikhailov resorted to kicking Gary Bergman.

On September 28, the day of the eighth and deciding contest, businesses and schools across Canada shut down to witness the events unfolding from Luzhniki Ice Palace in Moscow. Trailing 5-3, the Canadians got third-period goals from Phil Esposito and Yvan Cournoyer to tie the game.

Then, with 34 seconds remaining in the game, there came the shot heard 'round the world. Paul Henderson, from the edge of the Soviet crease, lifted the puck past goalie Vladislav Tretiak to win the game, and the series, for Canada.

It was the most important sports victory in the country's history.

Best Players Born in
Winnipeg

ANDY BATHGATE

One of the all-time great New York Rangers, Bathgate had a slapshot that was his most dangerous weapon. The Hart Trophy winner in 1958-59, he famously struck Jacques Plante with a shot in the face that prompted the goalie to introduce the mask into the NHL.

ART COULTER

Coulter won a Stanley Cup with Chicago in 1934 and another championship with the Rangers in 1940. His Hall of Fame career included four Second Team All-Star selections on defence.

FRANK FREDRICKSON

The World War One veteran was one of the best amateur players ever to play for Canada. He was captain of the 1920 Winnipeg Falcons that won the Allan Cup, then won the gold medal at the Olympics that year, the first true international hockey tournament.

HERB GARDINER

The defenceman starred for the Calgary Tigers of the Western Canada Hockey League before he was sold to the Montreal Canadiens in 1926. The following year, Gardiner was named Hart Trophy winner.

CHING JOHNSON

A punishing, hard-hitting defenceman on the New York Rangers, Johnson finished among the league's top three leaders in penalty minutes four times in his career. He won Stanley Cups in 1928 and 1933 playing for the Blueshirts.

BILL MOSIENKO

Best known for scoring the fastest hat trick ever, Mosienko played 14 seasons for Chicago and rarely spent time in the penalty box. He won the Lady Byng Trophy in 1944-45 playing all 50 games without incurring a single penalty. The Hall of Famer was twice named a Second Team All-Star.

KEN REARDON

A five-time All-Star Team selection, Reardon was a physical defenceman on the Canadiens' blueline in the 1940s. His career was interrupted for three years while he served in the military. Reardon was inducted into the Hockey Hall of Fame in 1966.

TERRY SAWCHUK

Sawchuk's career mark of 103 shutouts was the NHL standard for nearly three decades before it was bettered by Martin Brodeur in 2009. A four-time Stanley Cup champion, Sawchuk had his finest performance in the 1952 playoffs with Detroit, winning eight consecutive games including four shutouts.

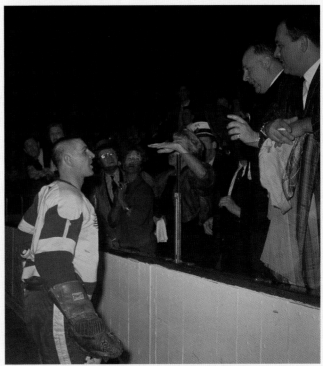

Terry Sawchuk was an incredible goalie whose threshold for pain was illogical.

JONATHAN TOEWS

A dynamic player who excels at both ends of the ice, Toews had won two Stanley Cups with Chicago and two Olympic gold medals with Canada by the time he reached his 26th birthday. In 2010, he was named the Best Forward at the Olympic Games in Vancouver. Toews followed that performance by winning the Conn Smythe Trophy as playoff MVP.

Salming Earns Respect

During the early 1970s, NHL rosters were still almost exclusively comprised of North American players. But, in 1973, the Maple Leafs' Gerry McNamara scouted a prospect, an immensely talented defenceman, from the Swedish Elite League.

McNamara was so impressed that he signed the player, Borje Salming, to a contract, paving the way for future Swedes to follow.

Salming had played internationally for Tre Kronor at the World Championships in 1972 and 1973. His goal in the latter tournament sealed the silver medal for Sweden. Both Salming and countryman Inge Hammarstrom joined the Leafs for the forthcoming season in the fall.

In Toronto's second game of the year, the Leafs visited the Spectrum in Philadelphia. The Flyers of the era were known as the Broad Street Bullies for their combative style of play.

Swedish defenceman Borje Salming was not just a smooth skater—he was tough as nails.

Leading that team, and the league, with 258 penalty minutes the previous year was Dave "The Hammer" Schultz.

A rookie and a foreigner, Salming was an easy target for the rugged, bruising Flyers, who took liberties against the 22-year-old blueliner. But at 6'1", Salming was not to be intimidated. In the first period, Salming answered a challenge from Schultz, the most feared enforcer in hockey. The two combatants exchanged slashes, and then were entangled in an altercation until separated by the linesmen.

"He looks like a real good one if he can stand up to the rugged going in this league," Flyers captain Bobby Clarke told the *Toronto Star*. "Everyone will try him until he proves he won't back off."

In 76 games in his rookie campaign, Salming registered 46 points while accruing 48 penalty minutes. He finished third in the voting for the Calder Trophy, but another upstart defenceman, Denis Potvin of the New York Islanders, won the award.

The Leafs and Flyers established a bitter rivalry, clashing in the playoffs in 1975 and 1976. Both series featured many fights. Salming, his teammate Tiger Williams, and opponents Schultz and Mel Bridgman all engaged in the combative play. Toronto came out on the losing edge of both series but, literally and figuratively, went down swinging.

Salming played 17 seasons in the NHL, pioneering the way for Swedish-born players to play in the NHL. He was named to the First All-Star Team once and to the Second All-Star Team five times. He was also a Norris Trophy finalist twice.

In 1996, he became the first Swedish player to earn induction into the Hockey Hall of Fame.

The first team in the nation's capital to win the Stanley Cup, the Ottawa Silver Seven, had a stranglehold on the trophy for four straight seasons.

With the offence led by 'One-Eyed' Frank McGee, Ottawa thumped the Montreal Victorias in a best-of-two, total goals series in March 1903 to claim the Cup. They then swept the Rat Portage Thistles 2-0 in a subsequent challenge series.

Frank Nighbor was an early star with the Ottawa Senators.

Between December 1903 and March 1904, the Silver Seven fended off challenges from the Winnipeg Rowing Club, the Toronto Marlboros, the Montreal Wanderers, and Brandon to defend the trophy.

The team faced its furthest geographic opponent the following year. In January 1905, a team from Dawson City, Yukon, travelled some 6,400 kilometres to throw down the gauntlet for hockey's most coveted prize. While the journey itself was a remarkable feat, Dawson City's on-ice performance was no match for Ottawa. The Silver Seven won the two games by a combined score of 32-4. Ottawa then retained the Cup with a 2-1 series win over Rat Portage in March.

The last of the Silver Seven's titles came in 1906 after the team defeated both Queen's University and Smith Falls in consecutive challenges. In all, McGee collected 15 goals in four challenge games played. Harry Westwick was part of a Cup-winner for a third straight year. Although Westwick had been on the 1903 roster, he had missed the playoffs that year with an ankle injury.

In 1909, the Ottawa Senators – the team now known by its formal nickname – finished on top of the Eastern Canada Amateur Hockey Association standings to win the Stanley Cup. Two years later, the Senators finished first in the NHA for the championship, then won two, one-game challenges versus Galt and Port Arthur.

The Senators won back-to-back titles in 1920 and 1921. In the former year, Frank Nighbor led the team with seven points in the finals series, won by Ottawa four games to one against the Seattle Metropolitans. Ottawa defeated the Vancouver Millionaires in five games in 1921.

Clint Benedict had been the goaltender in both series and backstopped the Senators to another Cup win in 1923. Over the course of that year's playoffs, King Clancy – normally a defenceman – played all six positions, including goaltender.

The Senators were the first team to win the Stanley Cup after the trophy came exclusively under NHL control, in 1926-27. Ottawa defeated Boston with two wins and two ties in the finals. Alec Connell was undefeated in the Senators' goal, and Cy Denneny led the team in scoring with four goals.

The Broad Street Bullies

The Philadelphia Flyers were the first expansion team to win the Stanley Cup, capturing consecutive titles in 1974 and 1975. Coached by future Hall of Famer, Fred Shero, the team's modus operandi was a style of play based on physical intimidation. Infamously, the squad was nicknamed the Broad Street Bullies.

Upon entry into the NHL, Philadelphia faced its 1967 expansion cousins, St. Louis, in the playoffs in the first two seasons of the 12-team era. The Blues came away victorious both times. Believing their inferior physical play was their downfall, the Flyers began building a team around skaters who played with more aggression.

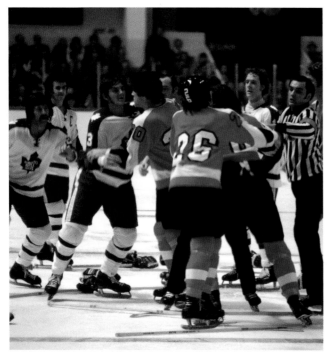

The Philadelphia Flyers in the mid-1970s inflicted almost irreparable damage to the NHL's reputation.

In the 1969 Amateur Draft, Philadelphia selected Dave Schultz in the fifth round and Don Saleski in the sixth round. One year later, the team made Bob Kelly a third-round selection. Then, in 1972, they made a trade with St. Louis for Andre Dupont.

These players were among the core of the Broad Street Bullies, living up to their moniker by employing their pugilistic tactics on a nightly basis. Opposing players visiting the Spectrum were known to contract a psychological ailment known as the "Philly Flu," informally defined as the fear of skating onto the ice in preparation for the cross-checks, high sticks, elbows, and punches that would be delivered by the hosts.

Schultz, known as "The Hammer," was the main enforcer. In 1974-75, he set an NHL single-season record, collecting 472 penalty minutes. Over his career, Schultz dropped the gloves most often versus fellow fighters Garry Howatt of the Islanders, Terry O'Reilly of the Bruins, and Harold Snepsts of the Canucks.

Andre "Moose" Dupont was no stranger to the penalty box, finishing second in the league to Schultz in penalty minutes in the latter player's record-setting year. His only career playoff overtime goal eliminated the Maple Leafs in the 1975 quarter-finals.

On defence, the Flyers' most feared combatant was Ed Van Impe. His punishing bodycheck on Soviet forward Valeri Kharlamov in an exhibition game in 1976 left the star motionless for several minutes. The incensed Red Army team briefly left the ice in protest over the unpenalized hit.

Philadelphia also had players whose talents went beyond what they could do with their fists. Captain Bobby Clarke was an outstanding two-way player and three-time MVP. Goaltender Bernie Parent backstopped the team in goal to both of their championships, winning the Conn Smythe Trophy both times.

But the Broad Street Bullies will forever be known as the team that used brawn, rather than skill, as their primary method of winning games.

BEST GAME EVER IN MONTREAL June 3, 1993

CANADIENS VS. KINGS

In the 1993 Stanley Cup finals, the Montreal Canadiens were aiming for a 24th banner to be raised to the rafters of the Forum. Standing in their way were the Los Angeles Kings, a team that had outlasted Toronto in the conference finals.

Both teams were riding the crest of a wave. Montreal entered the series having won an amazing seven straight overtime games. The Kings had the ever-dangerous Wayne Gretzky leading the offence. His four-point effort led Los Angeles to a 4-1 win in the series opener.

In Game Two, the Habs peppered Kings goalie Kelly Hrudey in the first period, but despite building a 15-3 edge in shots on goal at one point, Montreal continued to be held off the scoresheet.

Finally, with time winding down in the opening period, the Habs opened the scoring after winning a battle along the boards. As Stephane Lebeau knocked the puck off Darryl Sydor, Vincent Damphousse found it, passing it to Eric Desjardins at the left point. Desjardins slapped a hard shot past Hrudey at 18:31 for the game's first goal.

The Kings tied the game in the second period. On a Montreal power play, Patrice Brisebois fumbled the puck at the left point. Dave Taylor pounced on the turnover for a breakaway down the right wing and beat Patrick Roy between the pads while short-handed.

Los Angeles then took the lead at 8:32 of the third. After Taylor tried to jam the puck past Roy, the rebound went to Pat Conacher who converted a backhand.

As the seconds ticked away on the Forum scoreboard, the Kings appeared to be on their way to a commanding 2-0 series lead heading back to Los Angeles. But with 1:45 left in regulation, Habs coach Jacques Demers asked for a measurement on Kings enforcer Marty McSorley's stick.

It was a gutsy gamble, to be sure. A legal stick would have resulted in a power play for Los Angeles and effectively given the game to the Kings. But Kerry Fraser found the curve on McSorley's stick to exceed the allowable limit, sending the disgruntled forward to the penalty box.

As if summoned by the ghosts at the hallowed Forum, Desjardins tied the game on the ensuing power play, sending a shot through a maze of players parked in front of Hrudey. Desjardins completed his hat trick in overtime, becoming the first defenceman in Stanley Cup finals history to score three goals in one game.

The penalty to McSorley changed the momentum of the series, which the Habs proceeded to win in five games en route to the Stanley Cup championship.

Defenceman Eric Desjardins is the only blueliner to score a hat trick in a Cup finals game.

Fog and Bat Game

Buffalo's Memorial Auditorium played host to one of the most bizarre games in Stanley Cup playoffs history.

The finals series matched the Sabres—led by the French Connection Line of Gilbert Perreault, Rene Robert, and Richard Martin—versus the defending champion Philadelphia Flyers. Buffalo lost the first two games at the Spectrum, hoping to gain redemption as they returned home for Game Three on May 20, 1975.

The "Aud" did not have air conditioning, a luxury that would have certainly altered the events of the humid night. As the teams squared off in the first period, a small bat flew down from the rafters towards the ice, perhaps seeking cooler temperatures.

Prior to a faceoff, Sabres forward Jim Lorentz knocked the bat out of the air with his stick, killing it instantly. Philadelphia's Rick MacLeish picked up the dead rodent with his glove and brought it to the penalty box, much to the squeamish chagrin of the spectators in the vicinity.

As the game progressed, fog permeated the ice surface, drastically reducing—and in some cases eliminating—visibility. Not only was the action indiscernible on television, but watching from the seats, or even skating on the ice, was no different. The players were indistinguishable from the officials, and the puck was all but lost on the white ice. During stoppage, the players skated around the ice in circles to attempt to, literally, clear the air.

Miraculously, the game went on, and the teams skated to a 4-4 impasse after regulation time. With one minute left in the first overtime period, the French Connection Line prevailed. Martin fed the puck to Perreault, who then found Robert

in the corner, near the goal line. Robert, thinking that any shot directed towards the goal in the foggy conditions had a chance of beating the goalie, fired the puck on net. He was right. The bad-angle shot eluded Bernie Parent for the game-winner.

"I didn't see Perreault's pass," Parent said after the game. "I saw Robert's shot too late for me to come out and stop it. I'm surprised the overtime took so long. It was hard to see the puck from the red line. A good shot from the red line could have won it."

The teams split the next two outings. Game Six was back in Buffalo, where a crude, fan-made sign mocked the Flyers' anthem singer, proclaiming "Philly has Kate Smith, but we have an old bat, too."

Unimpressed, Philadelphia closed out the series, winning the Stanley Cup at the Aud under bat-free circumstances, in clear visibility.

Foggy conditions in Buffalo during the 1975 playoffs were enough to drive Flyers' goalie Bernie Parent to distraction.

Calgary's HALL OF FAMERS

Players

Doug Gilmour, 2011

Al MacInnis, 2007

Lanny McDonald, 1992

Joe Mullen, 2000

Joe Nieuwendyk, 2011

Builders

Cliff Fletcher, 2004

Harley Hotchkiss, 2006

Bob Johnson, 1992

Daryl "Doc" Seaman, 2010

Joe Mullen was a Hall of Famer as of the year 2000.

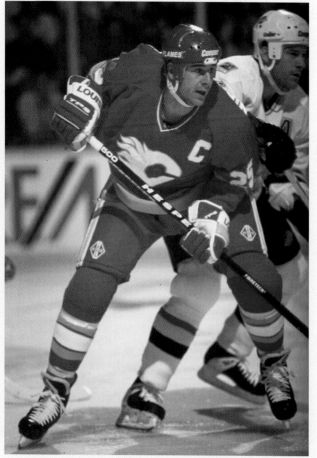

Joe Nieuwendyk was a 50-goal scorer and Stanley Cup winner with Calgary.

New Year's Eve, 1975

Three years after Team Canada squeaked out a victory over the Soviet Union in the 1972 Summit Series, the Cold War was still raging. For an encore of the historic showdown, the Super Series was held during which NHL clubs went head-to-head with their counterparts from the USSR.

The third game of the eight-game series pitted the Montreal Canadiens against the Central Red Army on December 31, 1975, at the Forum. The Habs were forming the nucleus of a dynasty that would see the Habs win the Stanley Cup for the next four years.

Guy Lafleur was on the way to his first scoring title. Montreal's defence was led by the Big Three—Larry Robinson, Serge Savard, and Guy Lapointe. In goal, Ken Dryden posted a miniscule 1.79 goals-against average through his first 31 starts of the season.

The Montreal-Red Army game from 40 years ago remains the finest of its kind.

The Soviets boasted a powerhouse roster of their own. The Red Army's top line had future Hall of Famer Valeri Kharlamov alongside Boris Mikhailov and Vladimir Petrov. Between the pipes was the man who ended up being the difference-maker in the game, Vladislav Tretiak.

The Montreal Forum was filled to capacity as 18,975 fans passed through the turnstiles. Goals by Steve Shutt and Yvon Lambert vaulted the Canadiens to a 2-0 lead before the game was seven-and-a-half minutes old. The score held after the first period, and the Habs outshot the visitors, 10-4.

In the middle period, the Soviets found a crack in the armour of the supposedly impenetrable Dryden. Mikhailov opportunistically managed to beat the Habs netminder with the Red Army's first shot of the second period, at the 3:54 mark. But, at the midway point, Yvan Cournoyer snapped a wrist shot past Tretiak on a Canadiens' power play to restore his team's two-goal lead.

Montreal continued to mount enormous pressure against the Soviets, but Tretiak held the fort. Kharlamov pulled the Red Army to within a goal at 16:21. Dryden faced just three shots in the second period, but two of the pucks eluded him.

Then, in the third, 20-year-old Boris Alexandrov converted a two-on-one pass from Viktor Zhluktov to tie the game. From then onward, the Canadiens attacked the Soviets' net looking for the game winner, but Tretiak was equal to the task, withstanding the onslaught.

At the sound of the final buzzer, the score-clock showed a 3-3 tie. The Canadiens wound up with a dominant 38-13 margin in shots on goal. Those fortunate enough to witness the game marvelled at its speed and skill, counting the matchup as the greatest exhibition game ever played.

The All-Star Game in Calgary

★ ★ ★

FEBRUARY 12, 1985

The hometown Flames were well-represented on the blue line by Paul Reinhart and future Hall of Famer Al MacInnis. For the first time in history, honourary captains were named for both rosters. The Campbell Conference named legendary goalie Glenn Hall to serve in that position, while the Wales Conference selected Guy Lafleur, who was less than three months removed from retirement.

Lafleur, the Montreal Canadiens great, did lace up the skates again, with the New York Rangers and Quebec Nordiques, accomplishing the unprecedented act of playing in the NHL after serving as an honourary All-Star Game captain.

Canadian astronaut Marc Garneau was on hand for the ceremonial faceoff, using a puck that he had taken with him into outer space. In addition, both players chimed in with their rendition of "Tears Are Not Enough" by Northern Lights, an initiative undertaken by producer David Foster to engage Canadian musicians to assist famine relief in Ethiopia.

Although Calgary played host, the Campbell Conference roster was filled with players from the hated provincial rivals, Edmonton. Eight Oilers, including goalies Grant Fuhr and Andy Moog, suited up on the Campbell bench that was guided by none other than their club's coach, Glen Sather.

On the Wales Conference side, Al Arbour was leading a team that featured 19-year-old Mario Lemieux, who was making his All-Star Game debut. Lemieux played on a line with Kirk Muller, who was the second-overall pick in the 1984 draft after Mario. Anders Hedberg of the Rangers, a former star in the World Hockey Association, complemented the trio, which had an outstanding game.

After 40 minutes of play, the Wales Conference had a 4-2 lead. Gretzky pulled the Campbells to within a goal at the midway mark of the third period, only to be answered by a goal from his heir apparent, Lemieux.

Wayne Gretzky was great when the All-Star Game was in Calgary, Edmonton's rival city.

The sides exchanged goals by Winnipeg's Randy Carlyle (Campbell) and Mike Gartner of the New York Rangers (Wales) to round out the scoring in a 6-4 Wales victory. Boston's Ray Bourque finished with four assists for the Campbells, and the Oilers' Mike Krushelnyski answered with three helpers of his own.

But the night belonged to Lemieux, whose two goals earned him the most valuable player award and a new car. He ended up promising the vehicle to his older brother, Alain, then a St. Louis Blues forward who wound up playing 119 career NHL games in the towering shadow of his sibling.

1976 Canada Cup

For the first time ever, an international tournament was staged featuring the top players from six nations: Canada, Czechoslovakia, Finland, Sweden, the Soviet Union, and the United States.

The Canadian team was a collection of players many of whom became honoured members of the Hockey Hall of Fame. Bobby Orr declared himself well enough to play despite knee injuries that had limited him to just ten NHL games in the 1975-76 season. Seven members of the Stanley Cup champion Montreal Canadiens were called to represent their country including Larry Robinson, Steve Shutt, and Guy Lafleur, the Art Ross Trophy winner.

Pundits predicted that the Soviet Union would provide Canada's toughest opposition. But the USSR was in transition after an upset loss to Czechoslovakia at the 1976 World Championship. Several mainstays from the once impregnable team were absent, including Valeri Kharlamov and Vladimir Petrov.

The Czechs surprised the Canadians with a 1-0 shutout win in the round-robin portion of the tournament, the only blemish on the host country's record through five games. Goaltender Vladimir Dzurilla had proven invincible and got the call between the pipes once again as Czechoslovakia and Canada faced each other in the best-of-three finals.

But Canada solved Dzurilla in Game One, shooting four pucks past the goalie in the first period, ending his night early. Coach Scotty Bowman's squad skated to an easy 6-0 win at Maple Leaf Gardens as Rogie Vachon posted his second shutout of the tournament.

The scene shifted to the Montreal Forum for the second game. Dzurilla was given a shot at redemption and did his part to keep the Czechs in the series as the teams were tied 4-4 after regulation.

Overtime was split into two ten-minute halves. Montreal defenceman Guy Lapointe nearly won the game in front of the home fans, but the officials ruled that the first half buzzer sounded before Lapointe's shot entered the goal.

The game, and the tournament, was decided shortly after the teams changed ends. Darryl Sittler took the puck down the left wing, then faked a slapshot, forcing Dzurilla to over-commit. Sittler calmly cradled the puck to the right side of the helpless goalie and made no mistake in depositing the puck into the open net to seal the win for Canada.

Orr finished with two goals and nine points in seven games and was named the tournament's most valuable player. Milan Novy was named the Czechoslovakia MVP while Borje Salming earned similar team honours for Sweden.

Sixteen members of the Team Canada roster were inducted into the Hockey Hall of Fame at the ends of their careers.

Darryl Sittler was the hero for Canada against Czechoslovakia in the Canada Cup finals in 1976.

Montreal's CAPTAINS

Jack Laviolette, 1909-10

Newsy Lalonde, 1910-11

Jack Laviolette, 1911-12

Newsy Lalonde, 1912-13

Jimmy Gardiner, 1913-14, 1914-15

Howard McNamara, 1915-16

Newsy Lalonde, 1916-17 to 1921-22

Sprague Cleghorn, 1922-23 to 1924-25

Bill Coutu, 1925-26

Sylvio Mantha, 1926-27 to 1931-32

George Hainsworth, 1932-33

Sylvio Mantha, 1933-34 to 1935-36

Babe Siebert, 1936-37 to 1938-39

Walt Buswell, 1939-40

Toe Blake, 1940-41 to 1946-47

Toe Blake and Bill Durnan, 1947-48

Butch Bouchard, 1948-49 to 1955-56

Maurice Richard, 1956-57 to 1959-60

Doug Harvey, 1960-61

Jean Beliveau, 1961-62 to 1970-71

Henri Richard, 1971-72 to 1974-75

Yvan Cournoyer, 1975-76 to 1977-78

Yvan Cournoyer and Serge Savard (interim), 1978-79

Serge Savard, 1979-80, 1980-81

Bob Gainey, 1981-82 to 1988-89

Guy Carbonneau and Chris Chelios, 1989-90

Guy Carbonneau, 1990-91 to 1993-94

Kirk Muller and Mike Keane, 1994-95

Mike Keane and Pierre Turgeon, 1995-96

Pierre Turgeon and Vincent Damphousse, 1996-97

Vincent Damphousse, 1997-98, 1998-99

Saku Koivu, 1999-2000 to 2008-09

No captain, 2009-10

Brian Gionta, 2010-11 to 2013-14

Alternating captains P.K. Subban, Andrei Markov, Tomas Plekanec, and Max Pacioretty, 2014-15

Jean Beliveau won the Stanley Cup ten times as a player.

1979 Challenge Cup

As a result of the significant interest in international hockey garnered by the 1972 Summit Series and 1976 Super Series and Canada Cup, the NHL attempted to whet the appetites of fans across the globe even further.

In 1979, the league's All-Star Game was replaced by a best-of-three showdown at New York's Madison Square Garden between the best from the NHL and the Soviet Union.

The makeshift NHL roster was coached by Scotty Bowman and included a starting lineup voted on through fan balloting: defencemen Denis Potvin and Larry Robinson; left winger Steve Shutt; centre Bobby Clarke; and, right winger Guy Lafleur.

Tony Esposito was voted into the goaltender's position, but Bowman—who had the final say—elected to use Ken Dryden and Gerry Cheevers instead.

The Soviets were missing Alexander Maltsev, who had a broken wrist. Also, Boris Alexandrov—who scored the tying goal in the 1975 New Year's Eve classic versus Montreal—had been suspended for violating the team's drinking policy. Nevertheless, the USSR boasted a host of stars who hadn't played in the 1976 Canada Cup, including Vladimir Petrov, Boris Mikhailov, and Valeri Kharlamov.

Game One took place on February 8 as Dryden once again went head-to-head against Tretiak in an international duel. Mike Bossy of the New York Islanders had a goal and an assist to lead the NHL All-Stars to a 4-2 win. Lafleur, Bob Gainey, and Clarke Gillies also scored.

Two nights later, both Bowman and USSR coach Viktor Tihkonov used the same goaltenders. In an intense, tightly-contested affair, the Soviets rallied from a two-goal deficit for a 5-4 victory. Alexander Golikov's tally early in the third period held up as the game-winner. The visitors had nearly twice as many shots on goal, outshooting their NHL opponents, 31-16.

In a surprise move, Tihkonov—buoyed by his confidence in his team's chances of winning the deciding game—rested Tretiak in favour of Vladimir Myshkin. Bowman also made a goalie switch, inserting Cheevers into the lineup.

The ending of the Challenge Cup didn't go so well for the NHL as it lost the decisive game, 6-0.

Goaltending was hardly a factor in the game as the Soviet Union demolished the NHL All-Stars, 6-0. Six different shooters found the net for the USSR, putting an anti-climactic end to the series. Myshkin had little trouble with any of the 24 shots that he faced in recording the shutout.

The embarrassing end to the tournament identified a glaring miscalculation by the league in believing that it could hastily assemble a team to gel after only three practices, while expecting to be competitive against a Soviet squad that trained and played together year-round.

Edmonton Milestones

MOST SEASONS KEVIN LOWE (15)

While teammate Paul Coffey led the rushes up the ice, Lowe was the defensive anchor of the Oilers' blue line during their championship dynasty. A first-round pick in 1979, Lowe played in six All-Star Games as an Oilers player and was part of Canada's winning entry at the 1984 Canada Cup.

In December 1992, Lowe was traded to the New York Rangers. He added to his Stanley Cup collection as a member of the Blueshirts in 1994.

MOST POINTS WAYNE GRETZKY (1,669)

Gretzky's accomplishments in the game are simply unparalleled. The "Great One" is the only player to ever score at least 200 points in a season, and he reached the plateau on four occasions. By the time he was traded to Los Angeles in 1988, he had rewritten the record book several times over.

His single season marks of 92 goals and 212 points (both in 1981-82) and 163 assists (1985-86) will almost certainly never be equalled, nor will his 51-game point streak of 1983-84 likely be challenged.

MOST WINS GRANT FUHR (226)

The Spruce Grove, Alberta, native backstopped the Oilers to four Stanley Cups in five years between 1984 and 1988. Even as Edmonton regularly played back-and-forth, high-scoring games, Fuhr's strength was in not allowing a goal in a game's critical moments, late in the third period.

Fuhr's 423 appearances are second all-time to Bill Ranford (449) on Edmonton's all-time list. With nine career shutouts, Fuhr ranks third among Oilers goalies behind Tommy Salo (23) and Curtis Joseph (14).

MOST PENALTY MINUTES
KELLY BUCHBERGER (1,747)

Buchberger was part of Edmonton's Stanley Cup victories in 1987 and 1990, and he captained the team for four seasons beginning in 1995-96. He was also part of Team Canada's gold medal-winning entry at the 1994 World Championship.

In Game Three of the Western Conference quarter-finals against Dallas in 1997, Buchberger scored the overtime winner. It was one of three overtime goals scored by the Oilers on the way to a massive seven-game upset over the Stars.

MILESTONES AND RECORDS

Wayne Gretzky is the fastest player to reach two of hockey's coveted milestones. The Great One's 1,000th point – an assist – came in just his 424th career game on December 19, 1984, against Los Angeles. His 500th career goal was an empty-netter versus Vancouver on November 22, 1986, in only his 575th game.

Jari Kurri earned his 1,000th point on an assist in a 6-4 Oilers win over St. Louis on January 2, 1990.

Mark Messier's 1,000th point came on an assist on January 13, 1991, as Edmonton defeated Philadelphia 5-3.

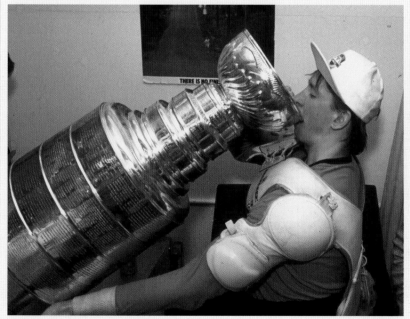

Given his extraordinary career, Wayne Gretzky earned every sip of the Cup he got.

Cherry's Too Many Men Penalty

The 1979 Stanley Cup semi-finals matched two of the league's elite teams, the Montreal Canadiens and Boston Bruins. Finishing second and third overall, respectively, in the regular season, both squads reached the 100-point plateau.

Montreal was gunning for a fourth straight Stanley Cup. Led by Ken Dryden in goal, the Habs needed a pair of overtime games to sweep the Leafs in the quarter-finals.

Meanwhile, Don Cherry's Bruins were looking to avenge the previous year's Stanley Cup finals defeat at the hands of the Canadiens. The balanced roster featured eight players who scored 20-or-more goals during the regular season.

The home team won each of the first six games of the series, setting the stage for a decisive Game Seven at the Montreal Forum on May 10. One of the Bruins' toughest challenges was to attempt to neutralize Guy Lafleur, the dynamic superstar who had just produced his fifth consecutive 50-goal season.

These efforts proved successful through the first 58 minutes of the game. The Bruins carried a 3-1 lead into the third period on two goals by Wayne Cashman and one from Rick Middleton. Resilient, the Canadiens responded with tallies from Mark Napier and Guy Lapointe before the midway mark. Middleton put Boston ahead once again, with 3:59 left in regulation time.

As the seconds ticked away on the Forum scoreboard, the Bruins inched that much closer to a berth in the Stanley Cup finals where the New York Rangers were awaiting. But disaster struck for Cherry's squad with 2:43 left on the clock. Bruins forward Stan Jonathan jumped on the ice too early during a chaotic line change. Linesman John D'Amico had no choice but to assess a bench-minor penalty for too many men on the ice.

Under the watchful eyes of the fabled Forum ghosts, the Canadiens seized the opportunity on the resultant power play. Lafleur, with his trademark, helmetless stride, accepted a drop pass from Jacques Lemaire just inside the Bruins blue line and unleashed a powerful slap shot past goalie Gilles Gilbert to force overtime.

The deflated Bruins never recovered. Yvon Lambert potted the series-winning goal just over nine-and-a-half minutes into the extra session. Jubilant, the Habs went on to defeat the Rangers to claim their fourth Stanley Cup in a row.

Game Seven was Cherry's last assignment behind the Boston bench. He was fired two weeks later.

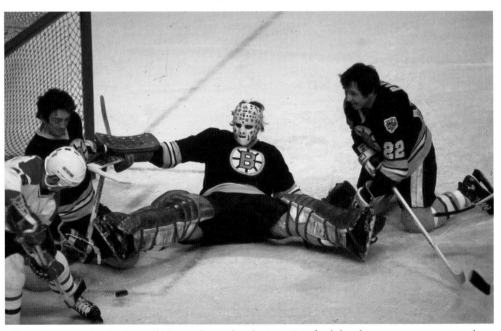

Don Cherry's Boston Bruins might have advanced to the 1979 Cup finals but for a too-many-men penalty.

GREAT RIVALRIES Ottawa vs. Toronto

They may be the only two NHL teams in the province of Ontario, but the Senators and Maple Leafs are idolized by polarized fans who are just as different as the Peace Tower is from the CN Tower.

Since the new incarnation of the Senators entered the league in 1992-93, the team has won one Presidents' Trophy and advanced to one Stanley Cup finals. The Leafs have not been able to boast either accomplishment in that time. However, when it comes to head-to-head playoff battles, Toronto has the decisive edge.

The two provincial rivals first tangled in the playoffs in 2000. Steve Thomas capped off a thrilling Game Five overtime at Air Canada Centre, converting a two-on-one feed from Sergei Berezin to give the Leafs a 3-2 lead in the series. Toronto eliminated Ottawa in the next game.

In 2001, the Senators were expected to exact revenge in a second consecutive, first-round matchup against their rivals. But the Leafs pulled off an unexpected four-game sweep.

Mats Sundin and Cory Cross had overtime goals in Games One and Three, respectively.

The teams played to a gruelling seven-game series in 2002. Daniel Alfredsson earned the wrath of the Air Canada Centre faithful in the fifth game after hitting Darcy Tucker from behind just before scoring the game-winning goal. Ottawa had a chance to clinch the series on home ice. But with the Senators holding a 2-0 lead, defenceman Ricard Persson drew a boarding major on Toronto's Tie Domi. The Leafs rallied on the strength of two power-play goals to force a seventh game, which they won to take the series.

The bitter feud reached a peak in 2004. On January 8, Alfredsson enticed further boos from the Toronto fans by pretending to toss his broken stick into the crowd, mocking countryman Mats Sundin. The Leafs captain had been suspended from one game for throwing a stick into the stands in his previous outing.

Three weeks later, during an on-ice brawl, Ottawa defenceman Zdeno Chara used his tremendous size to throw Bryan

McCabe around like a rag doll. Within a week, the teams staged a rematch at the Corel Centre. Toronto rallied for an overtime win after several Senators were felled by a flu bug. Leafs forward Owen Nolan simply shrugged off his opponents' ailment with an unsympathetic, "boo hoo."

In the playoffs that year, Joe Nieuwendyk scored not one but two very stoppable goals on Ottawa goalie Patrick Lalime to win Game Seven, clinching the Leafs' fourth straight playoff win versus the Senators.

Few rivalries of the 21st century rival Toronto's with Ottawa.

NHL-WHA Merges

From its inception in 1972, the World Hockey Association proved effective as a viable alternative to the NHL. The promise of more lucrative salaries was the fledgling league's key selling point. Bobby Hull became the WHA's first big-name superstar, lending credibility to the NHL rivals.

But the league was plagued with instability and insolvent franchises. Several teams struggled to meet its payroll. Toronto, Ottawa, Minnesota, Los Angeles, New York, and a host of other cities lost their clubs.

When John Ziegler replaced Clarence Campbell as NHL president in 1977, he began spearheading a movement for a merger with the WHA. The ongoing feud between the two leagues was not only costing millions of dollars but polarizing the pool of talent of hockey's best players.

Dave Keon returned to the NHL with Hartford after four WHA teams joined the league in 1979.

By August 1977, an agreement was in place for the NHL to admit six teams: Edmonton, New England, Quebec, Winnipeg, Cincinnati, and Houston. But a vote among the league's governors fell one short of the three-quarters' majority required for ratification.

The WHA played another full season before the issue was revisited in March 1979. Thirteen of seventeen votes in favour of the merger were needed, but again the proposal was defeated by a single vote. The dissenting clubs were Boston, Los Angeles, Toronto, Montreal, and Vancouver. Leafs owner Harold Ballard—a staunch opponent of the merger—didn't hide his merriment. "I feel so elated. It's just like the North beating the South in the Civil War," he said.

The public in Edmonton, Quebec, and Winnipeg reacted with outrage when word leaked that Montreal and Vancouver voted against the merger. The target of angst was Molson Breweries, the owners of the Canadiens. The company was swiftly boycotted in the prospective NHL cities. An anonymous bomb threat was made to the Molson brewery in Quebec City, and a bullet was fired through the window of a Molson plant in Winnipeg.

Two weeks later, in the wake of the backlash, Montreal and Vancouver relented. On March 22, the NHL voted to admit Edmonton, Hartford (formerly New England), Quebec, and Winnipeg. Each of the four teams paid $6 million in expansion fees. Each new franchise was permitted to protect two skaters and two goaltenders, and the Oilers, as expected, protected the cornerstone of the franchise, 18-year-old Wayne Gretzky.

The last WHA game was played on May 20, 1979, when Winnipeg defeated Edmonton in the sixth and deciding game of the AVCO Cup finals. Dave Semenko—who became one of Gretzky's bodyguards in the NHL—scored the last-ever goal in the league.

Best Players Born in
Edmonton

DAVE BABYCH

The second-overall pick of the Winnipeg Jets in 1980, Babych was an offensive threat from the blue line. He reached double-digits in goals in seven of his first ten seasons and had a career high of 74 points in 1982-83.

JAY BOUWMEESTER

Bouwmeester is one of only a handful of Canadians to play in the World Junior Championships as a 16-year-old. The durable defenceman compiled a 737-game iron-man streak in ten seasons with Florida, Calgary, and St. Louis. He won a gold medal with Team Canada at the 2014 Olympics.

JOHN BUCYK

The all-time Bruins leader in goals with 545, Bucyk was one of the most prolific left wingers of all time. He was twice named to the All-Star Team and won two Stanley Cups with Boston, in 1970 and 1972, also earning two Lady Byng Trophies along the way.

NEIL COLVILLE

The Colville brothers, Neil and Mac, formed the Bread Line along with Alex Shibicky on the New York Rangers. The trio was instrumental in guiding the Blueshirts to the 1940 Stanley Cup. Neil Colville was inducted into the Hockey Hall of Fame in 1967.

KELLY HRUDEY

Hrudey, a veteran of 14 NHL seasons, compiled a career record of 271 wins, 265 losses, and 88 ties playing with the Islanders, Kings, and Sharks. He backstopped Los Angeles to the 1993 Stanley Cup finals.

JAROME IGINLA

Although he was born in Edmonton, Jarome Iginla became the foundation of the provincial rivals in Calgary where he spent nine seasons as captain of the Flames. Iginla is the franchise's all-time leader in games played (1,219) and goals (525). Internationally he has won two Olympic gold medals, a World Cup of Hockey championship, and World Championship gold at both the junior and senior levels.

MARK MESSIER

The only player in NHL history to captain two different Stanley Cup-winning teams, Messier displayed a superb blend of scoring prowess and toughness with both the Oilers and the Rangers. "The Moose" retired as the league's second-overall all-time scorer with 1,887 points and is also second only to Gordie Howe with 1,756 games played.

Mark Messier was one of the greatest players to play in the NHL.

SCOTT NIEDERMAYER

With superior speed and natural hockey smarts, Niedermayer won championships at every level at which he played. From his Memorial Cup-winning days as a junior with the Kamloops Blazers, to four Stanley Cups with New Jersey and Anaheim, to Olympic and World Championship gold with Team Canada, his dominance on the blue line is of the rarest kind.

PETE PEETERS

A winner of 246 regular-season games in his career, goaltender Peeters had his best year in 1982-83 with Boston, winning the Vezina Trophy. He led the league with 40 wins and eight shutouts and was the Hart Trophy runner-up to Wayne Gretzky.

Gretzky Plays Against Howe

When Wayne Gretzky was ten years old, he sent a photo to his idol Gordie Howe. Howe signed and returned it. It was merely the beginning of a fruitful friendship that would last a generation.

Gretzky finally met Howe for the first time when Mr. Hockey paid a visit to Brantford, where the young boy's family lived. The two of them—both smartly dressed in a suit and tie—posed for a picture featuring Howe playfully wrapping a hockey stick around Gretzky's neck. Decades later, it has become one of the game's iconic photographs.

The friendship continued as Gretzky and Howe crossed paths whenever the Detroit Junior Red Wings, featuring Howe's sons Mark and Murray, played in Brantford. Gretzky was also a teammate of Howe's other son, Murray, on the Junior B Toronto Nationals in 1975-76.

When a 17-year-old Gretzky joined the WHA's Indianapolis Racers in 1978, he faced Howe as an opponent for the first time. The veteran of over three professional decades was a right winger on the New England Whalers. Gretzky stole the puck from Howe in the first period and received a trademark Howe elbow in return for daring to upstage the immortal one.

Under friendlier circumstances, the two men were teammates at the 1979 WHA All-Star Game, the last of its kind. Gretzky had been sold to Edmonton after the Racers folded. Later that year, Edmonton and Hartford (nee New England) joined the NHL as part of the WHA merger. On November 17, the two teams faced off at the Hartford Civic Centre. An 18-year-old Gretzky and a 51-year-old Howe were on their respective benches.

The veteran got the better of the rookie, earning an assist in the Whalers 4-0 win. Less than a month later at Northlands Coliseum, it was the Oilers who posted a shutout. Gretzky scored a goal to help Edmonton come out on top, 3-0. At the time, Gretzky had but eleven career goals, a fraction of Howe's career total of 797.

Edmonton and Hartford met twice more that season; a 3-3 tie on January 2, 1980, and a 6-2 Whalers win on February 19. Gretzky and Howe were also opponents at the 32nd NHL All-Star Game in Detroit, where Howe received a thundering ovation in his return to the Motor City.

Howe retired at the end of the 1979-80 season. Gretzky, of course, went on to shatter his idol's all-time scoring records. The "Great One" finished his career with more assists (1,963) than Mr. Hockey had points (1,850).

The WHA-NHL merger allowed a 19-year-old Wayne Gretzky to play against a 52-year-old Gordie Howe.

Hockey Hall of Fame Builder Cliff Fletcher was the architect of a Calgary Flames franchise that evolved into championship contention in the mid-1980s. The Flames made an unexpected run to the Stanley Cup finals in 1986, aided by Edmonton defenceman Steve Smith's infamous own goal that eliminated his team in the second round. But Calgary lost to rookie Patrick Roy and the Montreal Canadiens in five games of the Cup finals.

The powerhouse Oilers, however, continued to be a perennial nemesis for the Flames. Edmonton won the next two Stanley Cups as the Oilers' provincial rivals watched in envy. But the resilient Flames became even stronger. Joe Nieuwendyk was the rookie of the year in 1987-88. The following season, Fletcher acquired veteran defenceman Rob Ramage in a trade that saw Brett Hull go to St. Louis. Then, when Wayne Gretzky was traded by Edmonton in the summer of 1988, a huge window of opportunity opened for Calgary.

The Flames posted a 54-17-9, 117-point record in 1988-89 to win their second consecutive Presidents' Trophy. In the first three rounds of the playoffs, Calgary defeated Vancouver, Los Angeles, and Chicago in impressive fashion, earning a Stanley Cup finals rematch with Montreal.

Finishing just two points behind the Flames in the regular season, the Canadiens had the best defence in the league. With Patrick Roy in goal and Chris Chelios and Larry Robinson patrolling the blue line, Montreal gave up just 218 goals, the fewest in the NHL.

Calgary won Game One at the Olympic Saddledome. Rookie Theo Fleury's goal just past the midway mark of the second period held up as the game-winner in a 3-2 victory. Two days later, the Habs countered with a 4-2 win.

The series moved to Montreal where the home team moved ahead in the series following an overtime goal by Ryan Walter in the third game. Calgary evened things up with 4-2 win on the strength of a two-goal effort by Joe Mullen.

In the fifth game, back in Calgary, defenceman Al MacInnis extended his point streak to 16 games with a game-winning, first-period goal, giving his team a chance to clinch the Cup on Montreal ice.

The Flames fell behind 2-1 in Game Six, but the game turned in their favour when veteran Lanny McDonald, coming out of the penalty box, scored the equalizer. The third period belonged to Doug Gilmour, whose two goals helped seal the victory. Calgary was finally the Stanley Cup champion after years of living in the Oilers' shadow.

McDonald, having finally earned the trophy that eluded him over an 16-year career, announced his retirement on the highest note.

Calgary won its first and only Cup on Montreal ice in 1989.

35 Games Without a Loss

The 1979-80 Philadelphia Flyers weren't projected to be contenders. The team ended the previous year with a disappointing thud, bowing out to the New York Rangers four games to one in the quarter-finals. Pat Quinn was effectively a rookie behind the bench, embarking on his first full season as an NHL coach after replacing the fired Bob McCammon in January 1979.

Bobby Clarke (left) and Bill Barber helped the Flyers play a record 35 games without a loss.

After winning their season opener at home, the team travelled to Atlanta where the Flyers were hammered, 9-2, by the Flames. Philadelphia didn't lose another game for the next three months.

Led by their captain and future Hall of Famer, Bobby Clarke, the Flyers put together a remarkable 35-game unbeaten streak. The record-setting run began on October 14 with a 4-3 win over Toronto. Four days later, Philadelphia avenged the loss to Atlanta, winning 6-2 at the Spectrum.

As the streak progressed, Quinn alternated goalies, using the tandem of Pete Peeters and Phil Myre equally, an uncommon practise, to be sure. The Flyers didn't have a point-per-game player on their roster, but rather a balanced complement of four lines. Their top two forward units consisted of Bobby Clarke centring Bill Barber and Reggie Leach, and Ken Linseman between Brian Propp and Paul Holmgren.

On November 15, Philadelphia beat Edmonton, 5-3, for its season-high ninth straight win, extending the undefeated streak to thirteen games. The run of success garnered ever greater scrutiny and attention as the Flyers approached the record of 28 unbeaten games set by the Montreal Canadiens in 1977-78. The Spectrum hosted the state rival Pittsburgh Penguins on December 20 for the potential record-tying game.

Indeed, Philadelphia made history that night, but not without controversy. Trailing 1-0 late in the third period with the streak in jeopardy, the Flyers evened the score on a goal by Behn Wilson with 4:08 remaining. However the Penguins protested, to no avail, that the goal was kicked in. Philadelphia hung on for the tie, preserving the streak.

Two nights later, Quinn's squad rolled into Boston Garden and defeated the Bruins, 5-2, to surpass the Canadiens' mark. The magical run came to an end on January 7, 1980, when the Flyers were dumped, 7-1, in a visit to Minnesota. After 25 wins and ten ties, Philadelphia had gone 35 games – or almost half the season – without a loss.

With a record of 48-12-20, the Flyers finished atop the NHL's overall standings. The momentum from the spectacular year carried the team all the way to the Stanley Cup finals. Unfortunately for Philadelphia, they lost to the New York Islanders in six games.

BEST GAME EVER IN TORONTO April 25, 1967

MAPLE LEAFS VS. CANADIENS

The last Stanley Cup finals in the six-team era pitted long-time rivals the Toronto Maple Leafs and Montreal Canadiens, in 1967. Toronto coach and general manager Punch Imlach fired a shot across the bow when he referred to Habs rookie netminder Rogie Vachon as a "Junior B goaltender."

After Vachon led Montreal to a 6-2 pasting of the Leafs in Game One at the Forum, Imlach feigned an apology, saying that Vachon was instead at "Junior A" level. Toronto goalie Johnny Bower evened the series with a 31-save shutout in the second game as the Leafs won, 3-0.

The series shifted to Maple Leaf Gardens where 16,000 fans passionately cheered their home team, dubbed the "Over-the-Hill Gang." Ten players on the Toronto roster were 30 years of age or older. But to a man the Leafs showed no signs of aging in Game Three, an epic clash.

Jean Beliveau opened the scoring for Montreal on the power play. Le Gros Bill had an easy tap-in after taking a cross-ice pass from Bobby Rosseau. Six minutes later, the Leafs answered on a power play of their own. Defenceman Larry Hillman fired a rolling puck from the left point that was deflected by Pete Stemkowski to tie the score.

The Leafs grabbed the lead after Jim Pappin found a loose puck in the slot and whipped a backhand that eluded Vachon between the pads. But in the final minute of the period, John Ferguson equalled the score after the Canadiens won a faceoff in the Leafs zone.

Both goalies were flawless in the third period. Bower thwarted Yvan Cournoyer on a partial breakaway late in regulation time with a patented pokecheck. At the other end of the ice, Dave Keon missed a glorious chance for the game-winner with only one second remaining.

The superb netminding continued in overtime. It wasn't until just before midnight, at 8:26 of the second overtime period, that the game was decided. Stemkowski's centring pass deflected off the skate of Montreal's Terry Harper to Pappin. Pappin passed to Bob Pulford stationed off to Vachon's right. Pulford promptly deposited the puck into the goal for a winning score that Vachon had no chance of stopping.

It was the second-longest game in the history of Maple Leaf Gardens. Bower made 60 saves while his counterpart Vachon turned aside 51 Toronto shots. The line of Pappin, Pulford, and Stemkowski led the playoffs in scoring on the way to a Leafs Stanley Cup victory.

Bob Pulford celebrates his game-winning goal during the 1967 Stanley Cup finals.

Billy Smith Scores a Goal

Hockey Hall of Fame goaltender Billy Smith backstopped the New York Islanders to four straight Stanley Cups to begin the 1980s. Earning a Vezina Trophy, Jennings Trophy, and Conn Smythe Trophy during his storied career, Smith holds a unique record among his many achievements. He is the first NHL goalie to have been credited with scoring a goal.

The unusual event occurred on November 28, 1979, as the Islanders visited the Colorado Rockies. Smith came into the game to replace Glenn "Chico" Resch in the second period after coach Al Arbour decided that his starter was having an off night.

Trailing 4-3 in the third period, the Islanders were called for a delayed penalty. The Rockies pressured New York in their zone while netminder Bill McKenzie left the Colorado net in favour of a sixth attacker.

Rockies defenceman Rob Ramage pinched behind the goal line and passed the puck to the point. But the feed missed its intended recipient, sending the puck the length of the ice and into the vacated Colorado net to tie the game, much to the dismay of the crowd at McNichols Sports Arena.

The goal was originally credited to Islanders defenceman Dave Lewis. However, after television replays showed that Smith was the last New York player to touch the puck, the official scorer awarded the goal accordingly.

Despite the unlikely tally, the celebration was short-lived. Colorado regained the lead for good on the ensuing power play en route to a 7-4 victory. Amidst all the hoopla surrounding his goal, Smith ended up being the losing goaltender in relief.

Smith posted a 15-14-7 record in 1979-80 with two shutouts. He was named the Islanders' starting goalie for the playoffs and did not disappoint, winning 15 games while losing only four. Bob Nystrom's overtime goal in Game Six of the finals clinched the first Stanley Cup in team history and began a dynasty on Long Island.

Billy Smith of the Islanders was the first NHL goalie to be credited with a goal.

While Smith's marker came as a result of an opponent's miscue, the first goaltender to shoot the puck into the goal was Ron Hextall of the Philadelphia Flyers. Hextall achieved the feat late in the third period on December 8, 1987, against Boston, after the Bruins brought Reggie Lemelin to the bench in an effort to tie the game. Hextall scored again during the 1989 playoffs, against Washington.

Martin Brodeur is the first NHL goalie to be credited with three career goals. His first goal was scored in a New Jersey win against Montreal in the 1997 Eastern Conference quarter-finals.

Edmonton's TOP DRAFT CHOICES

1979 – Kevin Lowe, #21, Quebec	**2000** – Alexei Mikhnov, #17, Torpedo Yaroslavl 2
1980 – Paul Coffey, #6, Kitchener	**2001** – Ales Hemsky, #13, Hull
1981 – Grant Fuhr #8, Victoria	**2003** – Marc Pouliot, #22, Rimouski
1982 – Jim Playfair, #20, Portland	**2004** – Devan Dubnyk, #14, Kamloops
1983 – Jeff Beuekboom, #19, Sault Ste. Marie	**2004** – Rob Schremp, #25, London
1984 – Selmar Odelein, #21, Regina	**2005** – Andrew Cogliano, #25, St Michael's Jr. B
1988 – Francois Leroux, #19, St. Jean	**2007** – Sam Gagner, #6, London
1990 – Scott Allison #17, Prince Albert	**2007** – Alex Plante, #15, Calgary
1991 – Tyler Wright, #12, Swift Current	**2007** – Riley Nash, #21, Salmon Arm
1991 – Martin Rucinsky, #20, Litvinov	**2008** – Jordan Eberle, #22, Regina
1993 – Jason Arnott, #7, Oshawa	**2009** – Magnus Paajarvi, #10, Timra
1993 – Nick Stajduhar, #16, London	**2010** – Taylor Hall, #1, Windsor
1994 – Jason Bonsignore, #4, Niagara Falls	**2011** – Ryan Nugent-Hopkins, #1, Red Deer
1994 – Ryan Smyth, #6, Moose Jaw	**2012** – Nail Yakupov, #1, Sarnia
1995 – Steve Kelly, #6, Prince Albert	**2013** – Darnell Nurse, #7, Sault Ste. Marie
1996 – Boyd Devereaux, #6, Kitchener	**2014** – Leon Draisaitl, #3, Prince Albert
1997 – Michel Riesen, #14, Biel-Bienne	**2015** – Connor McDavid, #1, Erie
1999 – Jani Rita, #13, Jokerit Helsinki	

Grant Fuhr was drafted by Edmonton and led the Oilers to four Stanley Cups.

NHL Entry Draft Goes Public

The NHL Entry Draft is one of the most anticipated events on the calendar. The two-day affair is attended by prospects, families, scouts, executives, and thousands of fans, and the results are sent instantaneously over the Internet to the rest of the world.

The ubiquity of information today is in stark contrast to when the event—first christened the NHL Amateur Draft in 1963—was in its infancy. When there were but six teams in the league, the first four drafts were low-key, private affairs lasting no longer than 24 total selections.

By 1969, the NHL had not only doubled in size but had also ended sponsorship of amateur hockey. As a result, the draft was expanded to ten rounds, then to thirteen rounds the following year.

Perhaps the most significant change to the draft occurred in 1979. For the first time ever, teams were permitted to select

The NHL Entry Draft used to be a closed-doors event; now it attracts a worldwide audience.

players who had previous experience with another professional league; specifically, the recently-defunct World Hockey Association. This revision necessitated a name change for the event, now known as the NHL Entry Draft.

Just as significantly, in a move initially spearheaded by underage junior Ken Linseman, the NHL lowered the draft age from 20 to 18. Linseman successfully challenged in court the NHL rule that prohibited him from being drafted as an 18-year-old.

As the draft evolved, the process was still very much secluded. It was held in Montreal, at one of three venues: the NHL's head office, the Queen Elizabeth Hotel, or the Mount Royal Hotel. Finally, in 1980, in a move engineered to generate fan interest, the draft was opened to the public and hosted in an arena – the Montreal Forum.

Coincidentally, the Canadiens held the first-overall selection. The Colorado Rockies finished in the basement of the standings the previous season, and their pick was held by Montreal. The Habs had acquired the Rockies' pick four years earlier, for Ron Andruff, Sean Shanahan, and Colorado's first-rounder.

Montreal selected Doug Wickenheiser, a centre with the Regina Pats of the Western Hockey League. In hindsight, while Wickenheiser had a respectable career, the Habs missed a glorious chance to draft a junior player from within Montreal's city limits – future Hall of Famer Denis Savard.

The draft has since rotated around the pool of NHL cities. The first such event outside of Montreal was held at the Toronto Convention Centre in 1985.

The BB&T Center, home to the Florida Panthers, was the locale of the 2015 draft, where highly-touted sensation Connor McDavid was selected first overall by Edmonton.

The All-Star Game in
Toronto
★★★

OCTOBER 13, 1947

Maple Leaf Gardens played host to the first All-Star Game in NHL history. After several rounds of negotiation, the league finally established a players' pension fund, and this game raised $25,685 to benefit the cause. The All-Stars outlasted the Stanley Cup champion Leafs, 4-3.

OCTOBER 10, 1949

Bill Barilko had the lone goal for the Leafs, losers of their third straight All-Star game. Bob Goldham and Doug Bentley of the Black Hawks and Paul Ronty of the Bruins each scored in a 3-1 All-Stars win.

OCTOBER 9, 1951

In a modified format, the First Team, consisting of players from the four American teams, was matched against the Second Team, the roster of which was filled with Leafs and Canadiens. Ted Kennedy had a minor scuffle with Ted Lindsay, while Maurice Richard tangled with Gordie Howe in a brief wrestle. The game ended, 2-2.

OCTOBER 6, 1962

Prior to the game, Chicago owner James Norris made headlines by offering the exorbitant sum of $1 million to buy Leafs winger Frank Mahovlich. The offer was promptly rejected by Toronto executive Stafford Smythe. On the ice, Johnny Bower backstopped the Leafs to a 4-1 win over the All-Stars.

OCTOBER 5, 1963

Mahovlich was far and away the game's best player, scoring two goals and earning most valuable player honours as the teams skated to a 3-3 tie. Ed Litzenberger also found the net for Toronto. The All-Stars scorers were Henri Richard, Bobby Hull, and Marcel Pronovost.

OCTOBER 10, 1964

At a pre-game event, league president Clarence Campbell introduced two new trophies. The Conn Smythe Trophy was created to recognize the most valuable player in the playoffs,

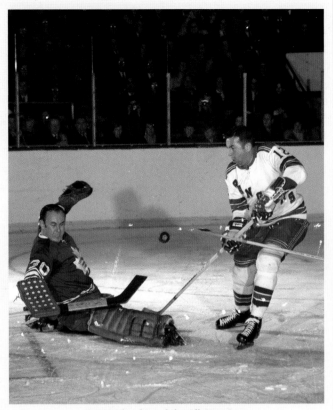

Toronto has hosted the All-Star Game eight times, most recently in 2000.

while the Lester Patrick Award was introduced for outstanding contributions to hockey in the United States. The All-Stars edged the Leafs, 3-2. Jean Beliveau was the MVP of the game and later claimed the first Conn Smythe Trophy at the end of the season.

JANUARY 16, 1968

Two days before the game, Minnesota's Bill Masterton had died after hitting his head on the ice during a game, casting a sombre mood on the festivities. The tragedy fuelled debate over whether helmets should be mandatory. Meanwhile, Bobby Orr suited up for his first of eight All-Star Game competitions, wearing number 5 (Jean Beliveau had number 4). The Leafs came out on top, 4-3, versus the All-Stars.

FEBRUARY 6, 2000

The 50th All-Star Game matched Team World versus Team North America at Air Canada Centre in the first full season of the venue's operation. Pavel Bure had a hat trick and was the game MVP in a Team World 9-4 rout.

Flyers Wear Cooperalls

The Canada Cycle and Motor Co. Ltd.—better known as CCM—was formed in 1899 in the Toronto suburb of Weston. It started as a bicycle manufacturing venture, but within a decade, CCM's focus shifted to hockey equipment, particularly skates. The Tackaberry Boot, a.k.a. "Tacks," helped garner a dominant share of the hockey skate market for the company.

At the start of the 1981-82 season, the Philadelphia Flyers experimented with full-length hockey pants, black with an orange vertical stripe trimmed in white. The pants were officially called "CCM Pro Guard" though they came to be known as Cooperalls.

The pads under the Cooperalls were tight to the body, running from the waist to the ankles, almost custom-fitted. The theory behind the design was to help prevent the pads from moving and leaving the body vulnerable to injury.

Opening night was held at the Spectrum on October 9 against the Detroit Red Wings. Captain Bill Barber led the Flyers onto the ice as the NHL introduced the new apparel for the first time. The game ended in a 2-2 tie.

Philadelphia compiled a respectable 38-31-11 record in the debut season of the Cooperalls, good for third place in the Patrick Division and eighth-best overall. But the team faltered in the first round of the playoffs against the New York Rangers.

The Hartford Whalers followed the Flyers' lead a year later, adopting the long pants as part of their uniform. On December 11, 1982, Philadelphia paid a visit to the Hartford Civic Center, marking the first ever game between two Cooperall-wearing teams. The Whalers won the long pants showcase by a score of 7-4.

Both teams finished at opposite ends of the standings in 1982-83. Philadelphia was the second-best squad with 106 points, while the Whalers—with a paltry 19 wins and 45 points—were second-worst overall. However, for the second straight year, the Flyers lost to the Rangers in their opening playoff series.

Aside from the optics that made the Cooperalls the target of fashion critics, the main indictment against the equipment was its lack of friction. Players who fell wearing the long pants slid along the ice and crashed into the boards at higher speeds. Citing concerns over player safety, the league banned Cooperalls after just two seasons.

Five Hockey Hall of Famers have worn Cooperalls in the NHL: Bill Barber, Bobby Clarke, Mark Howe, and Darryl Sittler with Philadelphia, and Ron Francis with Hartford.

Cooperalls were the most radical innovation to make it to the NHL in decades.

Ottawa's CAPTAINS

Jack Darragh, 1917-19

Eddie Gerard, 1919-23

Cy Denneny, 1923-26

George Boucher, 1926-28

King Clancy, 1928-30

Frank Finnigan, 1930-31, 1932-33

Syd Howe, 1933-34

Laurie Boschman, 1992-93

Brad Shaw, Mark Lamb and Gord Dineen, 1993-94

Randy Cunneyworth, 1994-95 to 1997-98

Alexei Yashin, 1998-99

Daniel Alfredsson, 1999-2000 to 2012-13

Jason Spezza, 2013-14

Erik Karlsson, 2014-15 to present

It was only fitting that Daniel Alfredsson chose to retire as a Senator after playing the 2013-14 season with Detroit. When Alfredsson hung up the skates, in December 2014, he signed a one-day contract with Ottawa, the team with which he spent 17 of his 18 NHL seasons. Three months later, he was given the keys to the city in a ceremony that honoured not only his on-ice accomplishments but also his community service to charities in the nation's capital.

Daniel Alfredsson was Ottawa's most respected and successful captain in the modern era.

Laurie Boschman captained the Jets for one season, 1992-93.

Gretzky Scores 50 in 39

When "Rocket" Richard broke hockey's 50-goal barrier in 1944-45, he accomplished the feat in as many games. Over the years, Bobby Hull and Phil Esposito surpassed Richard's single-season goal total, but no other player scored 50 in 50 until Mike Bossy did so in 1980-81.

After needing two dramatic third period goals in the 50th game to equal the mark, Bossy had less than a year to share the record exclusively with Richard.

Gretzky's 50 goals in 39 games is a record that might well endure for decades.

As the 1981-82 season got under way, Wayne Gretzky—in only his third year in the NHL—was scoring at an unprecedented pace. Already a two-time defending Hart Trophy winner and recently-anointed record holder for most points in one season (164, set the previous year), number 99 was the centrepiece of the Oilers' unstoppable offence.

On November 29, Edmonton demolished Winnipeg, 10-2. By then, the "Great One" had compiled a jaw-dropping 31 goals in 26 games. Then, Gretzky went into a 'slump' in which he didn't find the back of the net in four straight outings. Of course, a slump by Gretzky's standards was still pure excellence by anyone else's. The Oilers' captain had 13 assists in the four-game goalless skein.

Heading into a five-game homestand that would extend into the Christmas holidays, Gretzky had 35 goals in 34 games. It appeared that the benchmark set by Bossy and Richard would be matched or, at best, beaten by Gretzky by one or two games, presumably not until late January.

Instead, Northlands Coliseum seatholders were treated to a spectacle of superhuman talent over the ensuing two weeks. Gretzky notched a hat trick and four assists in a 9-6 firewagon victory over Minnesota on December 19. He scored three times over the next two games.

Then, on December 27, Gretzky had a four-goal outburst in a 10-3 Oilers shellacking of the Los Angeles Kings. His output was now an astounding 45 goals in 38 games heading into a game against the Flyers, three nights later.

Not even the most optimistic of Gretzky lovers could have envisioned from the start of the season that Gretzky would get to 50 goals before the end of the calendar year. But Gretzky got four pucks past Pete Peeters by the six-minute mark of the third period, leaving him one goal short of the magical milestone.

With Philadelphia trailing, 6-5, Peeters left the net for a sixth attacker. As the game neared expiration, the Oilers cleared their zone. Gretzky, with a full head of steam, carried the puck over the Flyers' blue line and deposited it into the open goal for the record-breaker. Fifty goals in…39 games! Incredible.

Best Players Born in
Calgary

BILL GADSBY

Hall of Famer Bill Gadsby earned a remarkable seven career All-Star Team berths on defence, at least once on each of the three teams for which he played: Chicago, New York Rangers, and Detroit. While with the Rangers, Gadsby was twice the runner-up for the Norris Trophy.

MIKE GREEN

An offensive defenceman with blazing speed, Green has electrified fans of the Washington Capitals with his end-to-end rushes. He was named a First Team All-Star in 2008-09 and 2009-10 and was also a Norris Trophy finalist in both years.

HERBIE LEWIS

Lewis was a mainstay with Detroit's NHL franchise from when it was first known as the Cougars, then the Falcons, then the Red Wings. The left winger won two Stanley Cups with the Wings and was inducted into the Hockey Hall of Fame in 1991.

TAYLOR HALL

A junior sensation, Hall won back-to-back Memorial Cups with the Windsor Spitfires. The second championship came in 2010, the year he was chosen first overall at the NHL Entry Draft by the Edmonton Oilers. He registered 263 points in 299 games over his first five seasons, all before the age of 24.

TIM HUNTER

Tim Hunter's mark of 3,146 penalty minutes is the eighth-highest total of all-time. A rugged enforcer, Hunter shared the captaincy with Lanny McDonald and Jim Peplinski in 1988-89 when Calgary won its first Stanley Cup.

FRANK McCOOL

Nicknamed "Ulcers" because of extreme nervousness he suffered on game days, McCool was a replacement in the Maple Leafs net in 1944-45 for Turk Broda, who enlisted in the Army. McCool won the Calder Trophy that year, then led the Leafs to an improbable Stanley Cup win, ousting the heavily-favoured Canadiens in the semi-finals.

CHRIS PHILLIPS

Philips became a mainstay on the blue line of the Ottawa Senators after the team made him the NHL's first-overall draft pick in 1996. Over his first 17 seasons with the club, Phillips played in 1,179 regular-season games and 114 playoff games. He won two World Junior Championship gold medals with Canada in 1996 and 1997.

GARRY UNGER

An iron man with Detroit, St. Louis, and Atlanta, Unger compiled a streak of 914 consecutive games played that stood as the NHL record until it was broken by Doug Jarvis. Unger scored 413 career goals and appeared in seven All-Star Games.

MIKE VERNON

One of the all-time goaltending leaders with 385 career wins, Vernon helped lead Calgary to the 1989 Stanley Cup. Eight seasons later, he was the Conn Smythe Trophy winner as Detroit ended its 42-year championship drought in 1997.

Homegrown Mike Vernon helped Calgary win a Cup in 1989.

High-Scoring Oilers

A tired yet accurate cliché in sports is 'you have to learn how to lose before you can win'. The Edmonton Oilers painfully took the first part of the sage wisdom to heart when they were swept by the New York Islanders in the 1983 Stanley Cup finals.

Led by a 22-year-old Wayne Gretzky, the Oilers expected to overhear triumphant, celebratory cheers as they walked by the champion Islanders' dressing room after the final game. Instead, the young upstart finalists were surprised to see the victors, many of them seasoned veterans, quietly nursing injuries, as if returning from a battlefield.

The highly-skilled, but still not yet Cup-worthy Oilers, realized that they had not expended the requisite energy or commitment to win a championship.

In 1983-84, they took to the ice with a vengeance. Six times they scored ten or more goals in a game. On November 19th, after a 13-4 demolition of New Jersey, Gretzky drew the ire of Devils fans when he referred to the team as a "Mickey Mouse organization."

Gretzky, of course, led the offence. Number 99 recorded a 51-game point streak en route to an easy Art Ross Trophy, registering 205 points. His closest competitor was his teammate, defenceman Paul Coffey with 126 points, 79 fewer than Gretzky's total. This marked the highest margin of victory ever for a scoring title.

For the first time in history, a team boasted three, 50-goal scorers: Gretzky (87), Glenn Anderson (54), and Jarri Kurri (52). With Coffey's 40 goals, the Oilers had four skaters who reached the 40-goal mark, tying their own NHL mark established the previous season.

As well, Edmonton's four, 100-point scorers—Gretzky (205), Coffey (126), Kurri (113), and Mark Messier (101)—equalled the NHL mark that the Oilers shared with the 1970-71 Bruins and the 1982-83 edition of their own team.

The high-flying Oilers scored a record-setting 446 goals in the 80-game campaign. In the Stanley Cup finals, they again faced their nemesis, the Islanders. Motivated by the previous year's sweep, Edmonton exacted revenge against Bryan Trottier, Denis Potvin, and a team that was aiming for its fifth straight championship. Sparked by three-point performances from Gretzky and Kurri in Game Five, the Oilers dethroned the Islanders at Northlands Coliseum, winning their first-ever Stanley Cup.

No team in league history has scored more than the Oilers teams in the mid-1980s.

Edmonton was so dominant on the power play, especially at four-on-four, that the NHL instituted a rule change. Beginning in 1985-86, substitutions were allowed in the event of coincident minor penalties. The change was rescinded seven years later, unsurprisingly after the Oilers' dynasty team had been dismantled.

Of the four teams that joined the NHL as a result of the WHA merger, the Edmonton Oilers became far and away the most successful of the clubs, evolving into an unstoppable scoring machine that rewrote the record books.

The seeds of the dynasty that would rise to glory in the 1980s were first planted in 1978 when owner Peter Pocklington purchased the contract of 17-year-old Wayne Gretzky from Indianapolis of the WHA. Mark Messier was drafted in 1979, followed by Paul Coffey and Jari Kurri in 1980.

The Oilers won the Cup five times in seven years from 1984 to 1990.

With Glen Sather as coach, the Oilers were a veritable offensive powerhouse, using their brand of firewagon hockey to score at will. Edmonton not only became the first NHL team to score 400 or more goals in a season, but it did so with regularity.

The Oilers received their first taste of Stanley Cup glory in 1984. One year after being swept in the finals by the New York Islanders, Gretzky & Co. avenged the defeat, ending the Islanders' bid for a fifth straight title. The Conn Smythe Trophy honours went to Mark Messier, who registered 26 points in 19 games.

Edmonton defended its title the next season, ousting the Philadelphia Flyers in a five-game finals series in 1985. Gretzky had a playoff year for the ages, setting records for assists (30) and points (47) in one post-season. Kurri had 19 goals in 18 games to tie Reggie Leach's playoff mark, set in 1976.

The two teams met again in 1987 in a series that was much more dramatic. After the Oilers jumped to a three games to one lead, the Flyers roared back with two straight wins to set up a decisive match at Northlands Coliseum. Late in Game Seven, Edmonton held a 2-1 lead as Philly looked for the equalizer, but Glenn Anderson fired home the insurance marker for the Oilers en route to their third title in four years.

The 1988 finals series was the Oilers swan song for Gretzky. After a power failure forced the suspension of Game Four in Boston, the series shifted to Edmonton where the Oilers had the chance to complete the sweep on home ice. They did so in convincing fashion, 6-3. Three months later, the Great One was traded to Los Angeles.

Edmonton won its only Cup without Gretzky in 1990. Goaltender Bill Ranford backstopped the team for all 16 playoff wins on the way to winning the Conn Smythe Trophy. Seven players were part of all five Oilers championships: Anderson, Kurri, Messier, Grant Fuhr, Randy Gregg, Charlie Huddy, and Kevin Lowe.

Steve Smith's Own Goal

When the Flames moved from Atlanta to Calgary in 1980, a natural rivalry was forged with their provincial counterparts 300 kilometres to the north, the Edmonton Oilers.

Calgary was a good, but not excellent, team at the time. Edmonton, on the other hand, had the game's greatest player in Wayne Gretzky. Along the way to consecutive appearances in the Stanley Cup finals in 1983 and 1984, the Oilers doused the Flames in the playoffs.

When Edmonton won its second Cup in a row, in 1985, the Flames took a backwards step, bowing out in the first round to the Winnipeg Jets before even having a chance to avenge the previous two post-season defeats.

But in 1986, the third playoff edition of the "Battle of Alberta" was staged in the Smythe Division finals. Calgary shocked the defending champions in their own barn, 4-1, in the opening game of the series. Glenn Anderson's overtime tally in Game Two salvaged a split for the heavily-favoured Oilers.

The teams again split the next two outings in Calgary before the Flames earned yet another road win in the fifth game. Undaunted, the Oilers returned the favour, setting up a decisive Game Seven at Northlands Coliseum on April 30.

Calgary's Hakan Loob opened the scoring in the first period with a short-handed goal. Jim Peplinski then beat Grant Fuhr two minutes into the middle frame to put the Flames up, 2-0. Resilient Edmonton tied the score before the period ended on goals by Anderson and Mark Messier.

But just over five minutes into the third period, disaster struck for the Oilers. Flames forward Perry Berezan harmlessly dumped the puck into the Edmonton zone where it was retrieved by rookie defenceman Steve Smith.

Smith surveyed the ice, looking for a target for a pass out of the zone. Casually, he directed the puck towards his intended recipient—or so he thought. Instead, his pass bounced off the pad of a startled Grant Fuhr and into the Oilers net. Smith slumped to the ice in disbelief as the official scorer credited the go-ahead goal to Berezan.

The Flames held Gretzky, Mark Messier, and the rest of the potent Oilers' offence in check for the remaining minutes of the game. As the final buzzer sounded, a devastated Smith slammed his stick on the bench on the way to the dressing room, obviously in no mood to celebrate his 23rd birthday. The miscue ended Edmonton's bid for a third straight championship.

However, when Gretzky reclaimed the Stanley Cup for the Oilers the following year, the first person to whom he handed the coveted trophy was none other than Smith.

Steve Smith's own goal in 1986 remains a haunting moment in league history.

BEST GAME EVER IN VANCOUVER May 1, 1982

CANUCKS VS. BLACK HAWKS

The late Roger Neilson was not only one of hockey's greatest coaches, he was also a master innovator. He pioneered the use of videotape footage as an instructional tool, earning the nickname "Captain Video."

Neilson also found ways to use the rulebook to his team's advantage. While coaching the junior Peterborough Petes, he once substituted defenceman Ron Stackhouse for the goalie on a penalty shot to knock the shooter off the puck, necessitating an explicit rule change.

In 1981-82, Neilson was an assistant coach to Harry Neale behind the bench of the Vancouver Canucks. Late in the regular season, Neale was suspended for ten games for an altercation with a fan in Quebec City. Neilson was named Neale's replacement and led the Canucks through the postseason even after Neale was eligible to return.

Under Neilson's guidance, Vancouver advanced to the Campbell Conference finals against Chicago. After winning the series opener on the road in double overtime, the Canucks got off to a terrible start in Game Two. With his team trailing, 4-1, late in the third period and the game out of reach, Neilson, believing the officiating to have been biased against Vancouver, staged his personal protest against referee Bob Myers.

Neilson grabbed a white towel and placed it on the stick of Canucks defenceman Jim Nill, as if to wave a white flag in surrender. Vancouver players Stan Smyl and Gerry Minor followed suit. All three were ejected from the game. Neilson was fined $1,000, and the team was fined $10,000 by the NHL.

When the Canucks returned to Vancouver for Game Three, Pacific Coliseum was filled with fans waving white towels in unison in support of the team. Neilson's mock gesture was now a rallying cry around which the Canucks built their momentum.

The Canucks won the third game, 4-3. Smyl, one of the offending protesters from the previous outing, had the game-winning goal. Riding the wave of "towel power," Vancouver won the next two games to take the series and advance to its first Stanley Cup finals in team history.

The magical playoff run came to an end at the hands of the New York Islanders. In the midst of a dynasty, the Islanders swept the finals on the way to their third straight Stanley Cup.

In April 2011, a bronze statue honouring Neilson was unveiled outside of Vancouver's Rogers Arena. The sculpture depicts Neilson holding a stick capped with a white towel, just as he had done to help spark his team nearly three decades earlier.

Roger Neilson was singularly influential on modern coaches.

Six Sutters in the NHL

The agricultural town of Viking, Alberta, was the birthplace of the Sutter clan – six brothers who each had successful careers in the NHL. Characterized by a strong work ethic instilled by their parents, Louis and Grace, the Sutter brothers collectively played almost 5,000 regular-season games and more than 600 playoff games.

Brian Sutter was the elder statesman. He spent his entire 12-year playing career with St. Louis, the team that drafted him in 1976. Darryl, two years younger than Brian, was selected by the Chicago Black Hawks and spent seven seasons in the Windy City.

The only two Sutters to win the Stanley Cup as players were Duane and Brent. Both men were part of the New York Islanders' dynasty of the early 1980s. Duane was a member of all four Islanders championships between 1980 and 1983, earning the latter two Stanley Cup rings alongside Brent.

At the start of the 1982-83 season, the league welcomed twins Ron and Rich Sutter into the league. Both siblings were first-round picks at the 1982 Entry Draft; Ron at fourth overall by Philadelphia and Rich at tenth overall by Pittsburgh.

Incredibly, six brothers were playing in the best professional hockey league in the world simultaneously. Rich stayed with the Penguins for only nine games over two seasons. On October 23, 1983, he was traded to the Flyers, joining Ron. A week later, Philadelphia hosted the four-time defending champion Islanders. With Duane and Brent in the lineup for the visitors, it marked the first time that four brothers played in the same NHL game.

Duane was the first Sutter to get on the scoresheet, poking the puck free out of a goalmouth scramble before teammate Greg Gilbert capitalized, just 72 seconds into the game. Brent led the way with two goals, the second assisted by Duane. Twins Rich and Ron had to surrender family bragging rights as the Flyers fell, 6-2.

For four years, the name Sutter was stitched on six different NHL sweaters. At the end of the 1986-87 season, Darryl was forced to retire because of chronic knee injuries. Later that fall, Brent earned an invitation to play for his country at the Canada Cup. He had only one goal in nine games, but it came in the decisive third game of the finals in which Mario Lemieux had the tournament-winning goal.

Four of the brothers—excluding the twins—have coached in the NHL. Darryl, the most successful sibling behind the bench, guided the Los Angeles Kings to Stanley Cup wins in 2012 and 2014.

The tradition continues. Three of the Sutters have children in the NHL today: Brent's son, Brandon; Darryl's son, Brett; and, Duane's son, Brody.

The Sutter family is hockey's greatest and is now in its second generation.

Montreal's HALL OF FAMERS

Players

Jean Beliveau, 1972
Toe Blake, 1966
Butch Bouchard, 1966
Chris Chelios, 2013
Sprague Cleghorn, 1958
Yvan Cournoyer, 1982
Ken Dryden, 1983
Dick Duff, 2006
Bill Durnan, 1964
Bob Gainey, 1992
Herb Gardiner, 1958
Bernie Geoffrion, 1972
George Hainsworth, 1961
Joe Hall, 1961
Doug Harvey, 1973
Tom Johnson, 1970
Aurele Joliat, 1947
Elmer Lach, 1966
Guy Lafleur, 1988

Newsy Lalonde, 1950
Rod Langway, 2002
Guy Lapointe, 1993
Jacque Lapperiere, 1987
Jack Laviolette, 1962
Jacques Lemaire, 1984
Frank Mahovlich, 1981
Joe Malone, 1950
Sylvio Mantha, 1960
Dickie Moore, 1974
Howie Morenz, 1945
Buddy O'Connor, 1988
Bert Olmstead, 1985
Didier Pitre, 1962
Jacques Plante, 1978
Ken Reardon, 1966
Henri Richard, 1979
Maurice Richard, 1961
Larry Robinson, 1995
Patrick Roy, 2006

Denis Savard, 2000
Serge Savard, 1986
Steve Shutt, 1993
Babe Siebert, 1964
Georges Vezina, 1945
Gump Worsley, 1980

Builders

Scotty Bowman, 1991
Pat Burns, 2014
Joseph Cattarinich, 1977
Leo Dandurand, 1963
Tommy Gorman, 1963
Hon. Hartland Molson, 1973
William Northey, 1945
J. Ambrose O'Brien, 1962
Sam Pollock, 1978
Senator Donat Raymond, 1058
Frank J. Selke, 1960

Toe Blake had a great career as a player and then an equally great one as a coach.

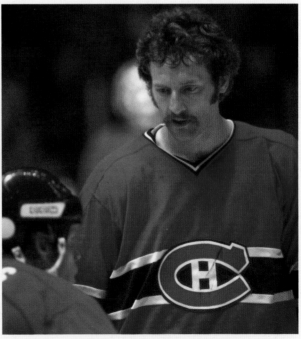

Larry Robinson was one of many Canadiens to make it to the Hockey Hall of Fame.

Smallest Crowd Ever

The 497th game of the 1986-87 schedule looked to be of little consequence. Slated for January 22, the matchup featured two teams – the New Jersey Devils and the Calgary Flames – at opposite ends in the standings. The Flames were competitive, en route to a 95-point season, while the host Devils were in a freefall.

Over 11,000 tickets had been sold for the Thursday night contest, but in the afternoon, the Atlantic coast of the United States from New York all the way to Georgia was walloped by a severe snowstorm. Driving conditions were treacherous throughout New Jersey, including the roads leading to the Devils' home, the Brendan Byrne Arena.

Ironically, the road team, Calgary, had no trouble getting to the rink. The Flames stayed at a hotel close to the arena and had a full complement of players ready for the game, well in advance of the 7:30 pm start time.

The Devils players, hampered by the storm and the ensuing chaos on the streets, were the latecomers. As the home team approached the requisite—but not maximum—number of players to start the game, New Jersey coach Doug Carpenter hid his late arrivals in the medical room. His Calgary counterpart Bob Johnson kept his own meticulous count, all too eager to call the referee's attention at a moment's notice.

The opening faceoff did not take place until 9:22 pm, nearly two hours late. The stands were all but deserted. Only 334 people were able to defeat the havoc created by Mother Nature and use their tickets. The players could hear not only spectators yelling "icing" or "offside," but also intoxicated hecklers voicing their opinions.

Paul Reinhart had two goals for Calgary, the second coming in the final minute of regulation to get the Flames to within a goal at 6-5. But New Jersey's Doug Sulliman iced the game with an empty-netter, making the proceedings all the more worthwhile for the sparse hometown crowd.

The goal was Sulliman's third of the night. Normally the ice surface would have been littered with hats, but as Sulliman told NHL.com years later, headwear was scant.

"I think one of our trainers threw his hat on the ice," Sulliman said. "There were only one or two hats out there, so he threw his baseball cap on the ice just so there was another hat on the ice."

During the game, Devils public relations staff collected the names and addresses of all of the attendees. Days later, the spectators received tickets to a future game, a shirt, and a commemorative badge welcoming them to the "334 Club."

Doug Sulliman (white) had a hat trick before the smallest crowd in NHL history.

Winnipeg's Biggest Trades

TOP TRADE

JUNE 16, 1990 Winnipeg Jets trade Dale Hawerchuk, a 1st-round draft choice in 1990 (Brad May), and future considerations to Buffalo for Phil Housley, Scott Arniel, Jeff Parker, and a 1st-round draft choice in 1990 (Keith Tkachuk)

Dale Hawerchuk was the first-overall draft pick by the Jets in 1981 after the team plummeted to the bottom of the league standings the previous season, winning just nine of a possible 80 games. A standout with the Cornwall Royals in junior hockey, Hawerchuk had the skill set of a veteran, collecting 103 points on the way to a Calder Trophy-winning season in 1981-82.

Over eight seasons in Winnipeg, Hawerchuk established all-time club records with 379 goals and 929 points. But by 1990, the superstar centre asked for a trade after a rift with general manager Mike Smith proved irreconcilable.

Coming to the Jets from the Sabres was offensive-minded blueliner Phil Housley. An effective power-play quarterback, Housley produced at a point-per-game clip in 232 games over three years with Winnipeg.

Although the Jets' position at the 1990 draft dropped by five places as a result of the swap, the team ended up with a more heralded, blue-chip prospect. Buffalo selected Brad May at 14th overall while Winnipeg chose Keith Tkachuk with the 19th selection.

HONOURABLE MENTION

FEBRUARY 11, 2015 Winnipeg trades Evander Kane, Zach Bogosian, and Jason Kasdorf to Buffalo for Tyler Myers, Drew Stafford, Joel Armia, Brendan Lemieux, and a 1st-round draft pick in 2015

After being appointed the Jets' first general manager following the franchise's move from Atlanta, Kevin Cheveldayoff didn't make a player-for-player trade until well into his fourth season on the job.

But he made a splash with his first significant transaction. Evander Kane, a first-round draft pick in 2009 by Atlanta, was superbly talented but also an off-ice distraction. In 2015, an altercation involving teammate Dustin Byfuglien detracted from the team's focus in trying to qualify for a playoff berth. Kane was sent packing within a week.

The blockbuster deal also involved two first-round picks from 2008 as Tyler Myers and Zach Bogosian exchanged sweaters. Myers's move to Winnipeg signified a restart for the career of the one-time Calder Trophy winner. The 6'8" Myers struggled in Buffalo under the lofty expectations of being named the NHL's best rookie in 2010.

Both Myers and Stafford were key contributors down the Jets' regular season stretch run in 2015 as the franchise snapped its eight-year playoff drought, bringing NHL playoff hockey back to Winnipeg for the first time since the old Jets left town, 19 years earlier.

Evander Kane may have been a skilled player, but the Jets needed to get rid of him.

Last Brawl in the NHL

Since the early years of professional hockey, players have been taught that, in some instances, their fists are as much a part of their equipment as their sticks and skates. Conn Smythe coined the phrase, "If you can't beat 'em in the alley, you can't beat 'em on the ice."

The NHL's rulemakers discovered that with proper punishment bench-clearing brawls could be eradicated.

The role of fighting in hockey has changed over time. During the six-team era, from 1942-1967, every team faced each other up to 14 times a year. The frequency of bitter rivals coming together meant that animosity between feuding players escalated as the season progressed.

Generally speaking, every player – from superstar to utility skater – fought his own battles. Gordie Howe infamously pummelled Lou Fontinato. Rocket Richard had a punch-up with Hal Laycoe, then linesman Cliff Thompson, resulting in a season-ending suspension that precipitated the Richard Riot in Montreal.

In the 1960s, teams started employing enforcers, players whose primary role was physical intimidation as opposed to scoring goals. John Ferguson of Montreal and Ted Green of Boston fit the bill for their respective squads.

Then, when the Philadelphia Flyers, the Broad Street Bullies as they were called, introduced their truculent style of play to the league in the 1970s, there was chaos on the ice. Dave "The Hammer" Schultz racked up a record-setting 472 penalty minutes in one year. Aggression surpassed skill as a means to success.

Bench-clearing brawls were commonplace throughout the 1970s and '80s. The last of these occurred on February 26, 1987, at the Boston Garden when the Bruins hosted the Quebec Nordiques. Near the midway point of the game, Boston had already put the game out of reach with a 4-0 lead.

Play was halted at 9:05 of the second period when Nevin Markwart of the Bruins and Randy Moller of the Nordiques engaged in fisticuffs. Meanwhile, Boston's Jay Miller wrestled with Quebec's Basil McRae in one corner of the rink. Two fights turned into five almost instantaneously.

In a split-second, Bob Sweeney led a charge off the Bruins bench, and, of course, the Noridques players followed suit. Mayhem ensued. Referee Terry Gregson, helpless to intervene in twenty separate fights, simply wrote down the names of the most egregious offenders. Altogether, he assessed ten game misconducts, and the NHL fined both teams a total of $32,000.

In the summer of 1987, the league instituted Rule 70.1, providing for an automatic ten-game suspension and $10,000 fine for any player leaving the bench or penalty box for the purpose of starting an altercation. That put an end to brawls.

Toronto's TOP DRAFT CHOICES

1963 – Walt McKechnie, #6, London Jr. B

1968 – Brad Selwood, #10, Niagara Falls

1970 – Darryl Sittler, #8, London

1972 – George Ferguson, #11, Toronto

1973 – Lanny McDonald, #4, Medicine Hat

1973 – Bob Neely, #10, Peterborough

1973 – Ian Turnbull, #15, Ottawa

1974 – Jack Valiquette, #13, Sault Ste. Marie

1975 – Don Ashby, #6, Calgary

1977 – John Anderson, #11, Toronto

1977 – Trevor Johansen, #12, Toronto

1979 – Laurie Boschman, #9, Brandon

1981 – Jim Benning, #6, Portland

1982 – Gary Nylund, #3, Portland

1983 – Russ Courtnall, #7, Victoria

1984 – Al Iafrate, #4, Belleville

1985 – Wendel Clark, #1, Saskatoon

1986 – Vincent Damphousse, #6, Laval

1987 – Luke Richardson, #7, Peterborough

1988 – Scott Pearson, #6, Kingston

1989 – Scott Thornton, #3, Belleville

1989 – Rob Pearson, #12, Belleville

1990 – Drake Berehowsky, #10, Kingston

1992 – Brandon Convery, #8, Sudbury

1992 – Grant Marshall, #23, Ottawa

1993 – Kenny Jonsson, #12, Rogle Angelholm

1993 – Landon Wilson, #19, Dubuque

1994 – Eric Fichaud, #16, Chicoutimi

1995 – Jeff Ware, #15, Oshawa

1998 – Nik Antropov, #10, Torpedo Ust-Kamenogorsk

1999 – Luca Cereda, #24, Ambri-Piotta

2000 – Brad Boyes, #24, Erie

2001 – Carlo Colaicovo, #17, Erie

2002 – Alex Steen, #24, Vastra Frolunda

2005 – Tuukka Rask, #21, Ilves Tampere Jr.

2006 – Jiri Tlusty, #13, Poldi Kladno

2008 – Luke Schenn, #5, Kelowna

2009 – Nazem Kadri, #7, London

2011 – Tyler Biggs, #22, USA U-18

2011 – Stuart Percy, #25, Mississauga St. Michael's

2012 – Morgan Rielly, #5, Moose Jaw

2013 – Fredrik Gauthier, #21, Rimouski

2014 – William Nylander, #8, Modo

Darryl Sittler was a 1st-round draft choice of Toronto…and he didn't disappoint.

1987 Canada Cup Best Ever

For two-and-a-half weeks at the end of the summer of 1987, the hockey world was treated to a spectacular series played at the highest level. The strongest nations at the 1987 Canada Cup were the host country – led by Wayne Gretzky and Mario Lemieux – and the Soviet Union.

At 26, Gretzky was already the game's most offensively-gifted player ever. In each of the previous six seasons, he established points totals that today still rank among the top six single-season outputs ever recorded by one player.

The heir apparent to the "Great One" was Lemieux. Just shy of his 22nd birthday, Lemieux gave every indication that he could be just as dominant as Gretzky. Coach Mike Keenan created a roster that balanced the skill of the Edmonton Oilers—Gretzky, Mark Messier, and Paul Coffey—with the grit of his own squad, the Philadelphia Flyers—Brian Propp, Rick Tocchet, and Doug Crossman.

Canada finished the five-game round robin with a record of three wins and two ties. In the semi-finals, the Canadians rallied from a panic-setting 2-0 deficit to oust Czechoslovakia, 5-3. The best-of-three final series featured, as expected, historic rivals Canada and the Soviet Union.

In Game One at the Montreal Forum, the Soviets jumped to a 4-1 lead before Canada mounted a comeback to even the score. The home side then briefly took the lead. However, CCCP forced overtime, the first extra period in the country's history. Alexander Semak got the better of Grant Fuhr in the extra session to draw first blood for the Soviets.

The series shifted to Hamilton's Copps Coliseum for the final two games. Game Two turned out to be what Gretzky later called the greatest international game he ever played. He registered five assists while linemate Lemieux scored in double overtime – a hat-trick goal – to force a decisive game.

The third game was played at an even higher tempo than the previous two, a fast-paced exchange of end-to-end scoring chances. The Soviets built a 4-2 lead after the first period, but Canada rallied, as it had done so often during the tournament.

Tied at 5-5, the teams appeared headed for overtime to decide the series. But after Dale Hawerchuk won a defensive zone faceoff, he passed over to Gretzky, who fed Lemieux. In one of Canada's most cherished international moments, Lemieux found the top corner of the net, winning the series for his country.

All three exhilarating games ended by a score of 6-5.

Perhaps there was no finer series than the finals of the 1987 Canada Cup.

Winnipeg Jets Who Have Played in the All-Star Game

★ ★ ★

Phil Housley wasn't in Winnipeg long, but his offensive abilities were impressive all the same.

MORRIS LUKOWICH (1980, 1981)

The Jets' scoring leader in 1979-80, Lukowich won an AVCO Cup with the team in the World Hockey Association's final season, the previous year. He played six-and-a-half NHL seasons in Winnipeg before being traded to Boston for Jim Nill.

DALE HAWERCHUCK (1982, 1985, 1986, 1988)

Hawerchuk became the cornerstone of the franchise after being drafted first overall in 1981. The future Hall of Famer recorded at least 100 points in six of his first seven seasons, including his rookie year when he was the runaway Calder Trophy winner.

DAVE BABYCH (1983, 1984)

Winnipeg's first pick, second overall, at the 1980 draft, Babych also played for Hartford, Vancouver, Philadelphia, and Los Angeles over a 19-year career that spanned 1,195 games.

DAVE ELLETT (1989)

A power-play specialist from the blue line, Ellett collected a career-high 22 goals in 1988-89. He was traded to Toronto the following season along with Paul Fenton for Ed Olczyk and Mark Osborne.

DOUG SMAIL (1990)

Smail topped the 20-goal mark four times in his career and also played with Minnesota, Quebec, and Ottawa after a decade in Winnipeg. He played three seasons in Great Britain after his NHL days were over.

PHIL HOUSLEY (1991, 1992)

The all-time scoring leader among American-born defencemen, Housley was named to the Second All-Star Team in 1991-92 and was a Norris Trophy finalist. He played just three seasons in Winnipeg but registered an impressive 259 points in 232 games over that stretch.

TEEMU SELANNE (1993, 1994, 1996)

The "Finnish Flash" entered the NHL with a fury in 1992-93, shattering the all-time mark for goals by a rookie (76). A tenth-overall Jets draft pick in 1988, Selanne enjoyed his greatest team success with Anaheim, winning the Stanley Cup in 2007. He also won four Olympic medals – one silver and three bronze – with Finland.

DUSTIN BYFUGLIEN (2015)

"Big Buff" is a rare commodity who can switch seamlessly between the forward and defence positions. After winning the Stanley Cup with Chicago in 2010, Byfuglien was traded to Atlanta (now Winnipeg) as part of a Blackhawks' overhaul because of salary cap limits.

KEITH TKACHUK*

The power forward was named an All-Star twice in his career, once with Winnipeg, and once in 1997-98 after the franchise moved to Phoenix. He also played for St. Louis and Atlanta, amassing 1,065 points during his NHL career.

ALEXEI ZHAMNOV*

Zhamnov registered 65 points in the 48-game lockout-shortened season to finish third in league scoring. In 1996, after the franchise's first year in Phoenix, he was traded to Chicago with Craig Mills and a first-round draft choice in 1997 (Ty Jones) for Jeremy Roenick.

*Named to All-Star Team in 1994-95, but no game held because of the lockout.

Gretzky Traded

To truly appreciate Wayne Gretzky's status as hockey's most influential player ever, one simply needs to reflect on how the shocking trade that sent the "Great One" south of the border changed the landscape of the sport.

Gretzky and Mark Messier paraded the Stanley Cup in front of delirious Northlands Coliseum fans after completing a sweep of the Boston Bruins in the 1988 Stanley Cup finals. It was Edmonton's fourth championship in five years.

But hidden from the euphoric celebrations was the momentum of a plan set in motion by Oilers' owner Peter Pocklington to sell the game's greatest player. The economics of running a team in the small city of Edmonton made it necessary to prioritize the balance sheet over the scoresheet, in his view.

On August 9, just two-and-a-half months after hoisting another Stanley Cup, and three weeks after marrying actress Janet Jones, Gretzky tearfully addressed reporters at a packed Molson House. Number 99 would wear the colours of the Oilers no more. He had been traded to the Los Angeles Kings.

Accompanying Gretzky to Hollywood were tough guy Marty McSorley and Mike Krushelnyski. Edmonton received prospects Jimmy Carson and Martin Gelinas, three first-round choices (Jason Miller in 1989, Martin Rucinsky in 1991, and Nick Stajduhar in 1993), and, most importantly, $15 million in cash.

Pocklington was vilified, not just in Edmonton where fans were ready to storm the castle, as it were, but throughout Canada. How dare he and NHLPA executive director Alan Eagleson refer to hockey's royal superstar as a mere 'depreciating asset?'

Nevertheless, Gretzky's arrival in California was the catalyst in an exponential increase in hockey's popularity in the United States. The Fabulous Forum hosted a slew of Hollywood celebrities who otherwise visited the venue only for Lakers' basketball games. Young kids watched Gretzky on television, weaving his magic, and said, "I'd like to do that!"

Traumatizing Edmonton fans even further, Gretzky rallied the Kings from a 3-1 deficit in the first round of the playoffs against his former team to take the series in the spring of 1989. The Oilers recovered to win a fifth Stanley Cup in 1990, but Messier and Grant Fuhr were soon traded as well as the dismantling of the dynasty continued.

Gretzky led Los Angeles to its first Stanley Cup finals appearance, in 1993. By then, his presence had drawn so much attention in America that the league had expanded to San Jose and Tampa Bay. Florida and Anaheim soon followed. Nashville came on board in 1998.

The "Great One" not only rewrote the league's record books; he put franchises in places that would otherwise have been indifferent to the game.

The hockey world changed forever in the summer of 1988 when Wayne Gretzky was traded.

Quebec/Colorado CAPTAINS

Marc Tardif, 1979-80, 1980-81

Robbie Ftorek and Andre Dupont, 1981-82

Mario Marois, 1982-83 to 1984-85

Mario Marois and Peter Stastny, 1985-86

Peter Stastny, 1986-87 to 1989-90

Joe Sakic and Steven Finn, 1990-91

Mike Hough, 1991-92

Joe Sakic, 1992-93 to 2008-09

Adam Foote, 2009-10, 2010-11

Milan Hejduk, 2011-12

Gabriel Landeskog, 2012-13 to 2014-15

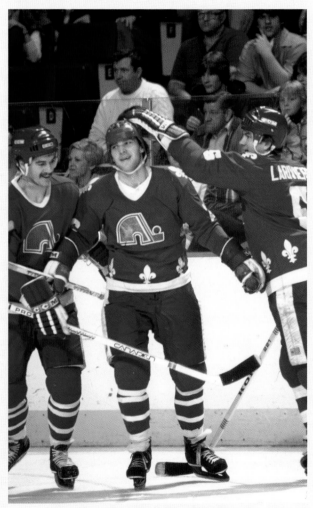

Peter Stastny (middle) captained the Nordiques during their years in Quebec.

Marc Tardif was the Nordiques captain in 1979, when the team joined the NHL.

Lemieux Scores Quintella

How long did take Mario Lemieux to score in his rookie debut? Two minutes and 59 seconds.

The "Magnificent One" was the clear first-overall pick in 1984 after closing out his junior career in Laval with a season that saw him average more than four points a game. The Pittsburgh Penguins wasted no time in selecting their franchise player.

Although Lemieux, at a contract impasse with Pittsburgh, refused to wear the club's sweater at the draft, negotiations were settled in time for the Penguins' season opener against Boston. On his first shift of the game, Lemieux displayed his eventual Hall of Fame greatness, stripping defenceman Ray Bourque of the puck and streaking in on a breakaway. He then fooled goalie Pete Peeters with a backhand deke for the first of his 690 career goals.

The incredible Mario Lemieux scored the NHL's only quintella.

Lemieux was an easy choice for the Calder Trophy, posting 43 goals and 100 points. It quickly became evident that suggestions of his ability to challenge Wayne Gretzky as the sport's next marquee superstar weren't mere hyperbole.

In 1987-88, Lemieux usurped Gretzky for the two most coveted individual awards, the Hart Trophy and the Art Ross Trophy. Gretzky had held strangleholds on the MVP award and scoring title for eight and seven consecutive years, respectively.

Lemieux continued to light the lamp with unmatched frequency throughout the first half of the next season. On New Year's Eve 1988, Pittsburgh's Civic Arena was the venue for a game against the New Jersey Devils. The 16,025 spectators in attendance were treated to a truly historic night.

In the first period, Lemieux's centring pass deflected off Devils defenceman Craig Wolanin's skate into the New Jersey net. He scored that lucky and relatively uneventful goal at even strength, a fact that later proved to be meaningful.

Just over three minutes later, Lemieux deked forward Aaron Broten and goalie Bob Sauve on the way to a short-handed goal. Number 66 completed a first-period hat trick with a one-timer on a five-on-three power play after taking a pass from Paul Coffey.

Chris Terreri replaced Sauve in the Devils net in the second period. After throwing his stick to prevent a scoring chance, Terreri unenviably faced the task of having to deny Lemieux on a penalty shot. But there was no stopping the Penguins' captain. Lemieux scored his fourth marker of the game by shooting between the goalie's pads.

Lemieux rounded out the scoring into an empty net for an 8-6 Pittsburgh win, thus becoming the only player in NHL history to score five different ways in one game.

Vancouver Milestones

MOST SEASONS TREVOR LINDEN (16)

After winning the 1988 Memorial Cup with his hometown Medicine Hat Tigers, Linden was the second-overall pick at that summer's NHL Draft. He immediately earned a place on the Vancouver roster and finished second to the Rangers' Brian Leetch in Calder Trophy balloting in 1988-89.

Linden was appointed the team's full-time captain at age 21, a post that he held for six seasons. He guided the Canucks to an appearance in the 1994 Stanley Cup finals against the Rangers. Linden scored both goals in Vancouver's narrow 3-2 defeat to the Blueshirts in Game Seven.

MOST POINTS HENRIK SEDIN (915, TO 2014-15)

Henrik and Daniel Sedin have been the foundation of Vancouver's offence since 2005-06, the first season following the year-long, NHL lockout. The twins from Ornskoldsvik, Sweden, are the top two scorers in franchise history.

Both players have won an Olympic gold medal (2006) and a scoring title. Henrik posted 112 points in 2009-10 to claim the Art Ross Trophy while also winning Hart Trophy honours that year. Daniel was the scoring champion the following season, registering 104 points.

MOST WINS ROBERTO LUONGO (233)

The fan favourite was acquired by the Canucks from Florida on June 23, 2006, in a trade that involved Todd Bertuzzi going to the Panthers. Luongo won the Jennings Trophy in 2010-11, leading the NHL with 38 wins. In the playoffs, he earned four shutouts en route to an appearance in Game Seven of the Stanley Cup finals. But Vancouver's bid fell short against Boston.

Luongo has flourished on the international stage. He backstopped Team Canada to gold at both the 2004 World Championships and the 2010 Winter Olympics.

MOST PENALTY MINUTES GINO ODJICK (2,127)

A fifth-round selection of the Canucks in 1990, Odjick possessed a belligerent style of play that endeared him to

Vancouver coach and general manager Pat Quinn. The native of Maniwaki, Quebec, led the NHL with 371 penalty minutes in 1996-97.

In June 2014, Odjick wrote a heartfelt letter to fans and teammates after being diagnosed with AL (Primary) amyloidosis, a rare terminal heart illness. His condition improved following months of chemotherapy, and the former Canucks enforcer was on hand to cheer the team during the 2015 playoffs.

Markus Naslund was a cornerstone of the Vancouver franchise after coming to the team in a trade.

MILESTONES AND RECORDS

Entering the 2015 playoffs, the feat of an NHL defenceman scoring a hat trick has been accomplished on eleven occasions. Doug Halward became the first Canuck rearguard – and the fifth defenceman all-time – to score three goals in a post-season game, on April 7, 1984, leading Vancouver to a 7-0 win over Calgary.

Gretzky Passes Howe

After leading the Oilers to four Stanley Cup triumphs, it was only fitting that Edmonton was the city in which Wayne Gretzky surpassed his childhood idol, Gordie Howe, to become the NHL's all-time leading scorer, even as a member of the opposition.

Gretzky had been traded to the Los Angeles Kings in the summer of 1988 in the biggest blockbuster deal in NHL history.

The Kings' sixth game of the 1989-90 season came on October 15, in Edmonton. The "Great One" took the warmups with 1,849 regular-season points to his credit, one shy of matching Howe, whom he had befriended almost two decades earlier by responding to a childhood letter Gretzky had written to his idol.

At 4:32 of the first period, Gretzky earned an assist on the opening goal by Bernie Nicholls. For most of the rest of the evening, he and Howe were on equal footing atop the league's all-time scoring list.

Los Angeles trailed 4-3 late in the third period. With a faceoff in the Edmonton zone, the Kings brought goalie Mario Gosselin to the bench. Six L.A. skaters, including Gretzky, lined up for the draw. Meanwhile, the crowd of 17,503 rose in unison in anticipation of a record-breaking moment. Number 99 consistently had a flare for the dramatic during his Oilers tenure, especially in this building. Why would tonight be any different?

Nicholls lost the draw to Mark Messier, who passed the puck behind him to Kevin Lowe. But Lowe's clearing attempt was picked off by Steve Duchesne at the blue line. Duchesne then found Dave Taylor at the side of the net as a mini-scrum developed in front of Oilers goalie Bill Ranford. While the Edmonton defenders were preoccupied with the

charging L.A. attackers, Gretzky was stationed all by himself in front of the net.

Taylor fed a cross-ice pass to Gretzky. With a simple backhander, number 99 deposited the puck into the net to make history. Leaping into the air, an elated Gretzky – the new all-time leading scorer with 1,851 points – was mobbed by his teammates in celebration.

Their friendship started years earlier, so Gordie Howe was expecting number 99 to pass him at some point.

As if he needed an encore, Gretzky also scored the overtime winner in a 5-4 Kings victory. The accelerated pace at which the "Great One" overtook Howe was phenomenal. Howe compiled his career total in 1,767 games over 26 seasons. It took Gretzky a mere 1,117 games in eleven seasons to eclipse Howe's mark.

After the game, NHL Commissioner Gary Bettman told Gretzky, "You've always been the "Great One," but tonight you've become the greatest."

GREAT RIVALRIES Vancouver vs. Chicago

When Roger Neilson waved his white towel behind the Vancouver bench during the 1982 playoffs, not even he could have envisioned that his Chicago opponents would become the Canucks' most bitter rival almost 30 years later.

After nearly three decades of relative normalcy between the two squads, an incident in a game on March 29, 2009, ignited a long-lasting feud. At the 5:50 mark of the third period, Chicago's Dustin Byfuglien drove towards the net on a scoring chance, but as he did so he hit goaltender Roberto Luongo on the chin with an elbow.

The Canucks players came to their netminder's defence, sparking a melee. Vancouver's Burrows notoriously pulled the hair of Chicago's Duncan Keith during the fighting.

Vancouver and Chicago have developed a heated rivalry in recent years.

A month later, the teams faced each other in the Western Conference semi-finals. Vancouver took a two games to one series lead. However, Andrew Ladd's overtime winner in Game Four sparked the Blackhawks en route to a six-game triumph.

In 2010, they met again in the second round. The end result was identical to the previous year, Chicago prevailing in six games. While the Canucks licked their wounds, the Blackhawks went on to win their first Stanley Cup in 49 years.

For a third straight year, Chicago and Vancouver exchanged hostilities in the playoffs in 2011. The Canucks appeared headed for an easy sweep after taking the first three games of the series. But the Blackhawks stormed back with three consecutive wins.

Fortunately for Vancouver, it avoided disaster in Game Seven. In overtime, Alex Burrows pounced on a turnover by Chris Campoli, firing the puck past goalie Corey Crawford to oust the defending champions.

Things turned nasty again in December 2011 when Chicago forward David Bolland referred to the Sedin twins Daniel and Henrik as "sisters" during a radio interview. Vancouver coach Alain Vigneault retaliated by saying that Bolland "has the IQ the size of bird seed, and a face that only a mother could look at."

On the ice, the jabs were just as vicious. Three months later, 'Hawks defenceman Duncan Keith elbowed Daniel Sedin with a menacing head shot. Keith was suspended for five games for his actions. Sedin, however, was sidelined for the remainder of the regular season and the first three games of the playoffs. His absence was a key factor in Vancouver's first-round exit at the hands of the Los Angeles Kings.

Because of the lockout-shortened season, the teams didn't meet after the Keith hit until a year and a half later, on February 1, 2013. Despite the pre-game speculation about potential payback, the 2-1 Vancouver shootout win was relatively uneventful.

Video Review Established

The breakneck speed at which hockey is played makes it one of the most difficult sports to officiate. The referees not only have to keep a watchful eye on an assortment of infractions, they must also track a rubber disc that can travel in excess of 170 kilometres per hour while keeping out of harm's way and out of the players' way.

It is unreasonable to expect the officials to make the correct call in every situation. However, in 1991-92, the NHL made a major stride in minimizing errors when it introduced video replay as means of settling disputed goals.

The newly-created video-goal judge could decide whether the puck crossed the goal line, or whether time expired at the end of the period before the puck entered the net. But goaltender interference, for example, stayed solely with the discretion of the referees.

In the 1992 playoffs, video review decided a game for the first time. Game Six of the Norris Division semi-finals between Detroit and Minnesota went into overtime. Red Wings goalie Tim Cheveldae and North Stars netminder Jon Casey had kept the game scoreless.

The Red Wings needed a win to stay in the series. At 16:13 of the fourth period, Detroit sniper Sergei Fedorov fired the puck above Casey's shoulder that, at first, appeared to hit the crossbar. Play continued until the next stoppage. As per protocol, referee Rob Shick consulted with video-replay supervisor Wally Harris. They ruled that the puck had indeed entered the net before ricocheting out and back into play. Detroit staved off elimination and forced a seventh game, which it also won.

As the sport has evolved, so has video replay's application. When the shootout was first introduced in 2005, the breakaway tiebreaking format wasn't subject to the cameras. The omission was quickly amended after Los Angeles's Jeremy

Roenick was credited with a shootout-winning goal against Nashville, even though he had clearly scored on a rebound, in violation of shootout rules.

Beginning in 2014-15, the NHL expanded the number of situations subject to video review. Referees could uphold a goal if the puck deflected off a skate while the player was in the process of stopping. Also, pucks entering the net through the outside of the mesh and pucks hitting the protective spectator netting prior to entering the net could also be reviewed.

Today the NHL "war room" in Toronto is where every game is scrutinized in high-definition television by off-ice officials. Telephone lines are available between the room and each NHL rink for instant communication.

"They're going upstairs," entered the game's lexicon with the introduction of video review.

Best Players Born in
Ottawa

CLINT BENEDICT

In the early days of the Ottawa Senators, Benedict backstopped the franchise to two Stanley Cup wins. He led the league in wins for six consecutive years, ending in 1923-24. Benedict also won a Stanley Cup with the Montreal Maroons, twice posting eleven or more shutouts in a season with that team.

ROD BRIND'AMOUR

After displaying his offensive talents in St. Louis and Philadelphia, Brind'Amour achieved his greatest success with Carolina while in the twilight of his career. At age 35, he captained the Carolina Hurricanes to their first Stanley Cup, in 2006. It was also the year that he won the first of two back-to-back Selke Trophies as the best defensive forward.

KING CLANCY

A solid anchor on defence, Clancy won two Stanley Cups with Ottawa before being sold to Toronto during the Great Depression. Clancy received four All-Star Team nominations with the Leafs, adding a third career Stanley Cup in 1932.

ALEC CONNELL

Connell's mark of 81 career shutouts was tied with Tiny Thompson and Dominik Hasek for sixth on the all-time list at the end of the 2014-15 season. A Hockey Hall of Fame inductee, Connell won championships with both Ottawa and the Montreal Maroons.

MIKE GARTNER

One of the fastest skaters ever to lace up the blades, Gartner combined his phenomenal speed with a lethal shot to net 708 career goals. His record of 17 seasons with 30-or-more goals is a benchmark that may stand for decades.

EBBIE GOODFELLOW

Goodfellow is one of only a few defencemen to win the Hart Trophy, taking honours with the Detroit Red Wings in 1939-40. A three-time All-Star Team selection, Goodfellow won two Stanley Cups in the Motor City.

SYD HOWE

Although not related to Gordie Howe, Syd Howe was a standout with the Red Wings. He won three championships in 12 years long before his more famous namesake arrived in Detroit. His greatest single-game output was six goals, which he scored on February 3, 1944, versus the New York Rangers.

DENIS POTVIN

The most decorated defenceman ever to play for the New York Islanders, Potvin was a Calder Trophy winner, three-time Norris Trophy winner, and seven-time selection to the All Star Team. Potvin captained the team for eight seasons, the first of which was 1979-80 – the first season of the Islanders' four-year Stanley Cup dynasty.

DOUG WILSON

Wilson's greatest season was 1981-82 when he won the Norris Trophy as the league's best defenceman while with the Black Hawks. He earned three All-Star Team nominations in a career that spanned 14 seasons in Chicago and an additional two years in San Jose. Wilson became general manager of the Sharks in 2003.

Mike Gartner was known for two things: consistency in scoring and blazing speed.

Manon Plays in the NHL

Goaltender Manon Rheaume famously broke the gender barrier for not only hockey but all of professional sports in 1992, inspiring a generation of young girls to pursue their athletic ambitions to the fullest.

Born in February 1972 in Lac Beauport, Quebec, Rheaume took to the ice in her family's backyard rink at age three. After she decided that goaltending was her forte, she signed on to play with boys' teams. When Rheaume was eleven, she became the first girl to participate in the International Pee Wee Tournament in Quebec City.

Rheaume continued her development, showing that her skill – and not her gender – justified her place on any roster. On November 26, 1991, Rheaume strapped on the pads for the

Manon Rheaume played an NHL exhibition game, the first woman to do so.

Trois-Rivières Draveurs of the Quebec Major Junior Hockey League, becoming the first woman to play major junior hockey.

Five months later, Rheaume backstopped Team Canada to the gold medal at the 1992 Women's World Championships in Tampere, Finland. She surrendered just two goals in three games while posting a goals-against average of 0.67.

Rheaume's play caught the attention of Phil Esposito, the general manager of the Tampa Bay Lightning, one of two new expansion teams that would begin play in the fall of 1992. Esposito extended an invitation to Rheaume for the team's training camp, an offer that was duly accepted.

The tryout with the Lightning was not without its anxious moments. Speaking very little English at the time, Rheaume was under the scrutiny of hordes of reporters. Nevertheless, Rheaume withstood the challenges of the publicity. On September 23, the Lightning played the St. Louis Blues in an exhibition game. Smiling from ear-to-ear, mask in hand, Rheaume skated onto the ice and into the crease as Tampa's starting goaltender.

For twenty minutes, Rheaume stood tall, not looking out of place. She stopped seven of the nine shots she faced. The two players who scored on her were Jeff Brown and Brendan Shanahan, and there was certainly no shame in surrendering a goal to a future Hall of Famer in Shanahan.

Rheaume's foray onto an NHL rink ended with the start of the first intermission. At the conclusion of training camp, she signed a three-year contract with the Lightning's International Hockey League affiliate, the Atlanta Knights.

Rheaume bandied around the minor leagues while also playing for Canada's national women's team before retiring in 2000, but not before her place in history as a pioneer for women's sport was forever cemented.

In the NHL's first season of operation, 1917-18, the Stanley Cup was won by the Toronto Arenas. The franchise repeated the feat again in 1921-22 under the St. Patricks name.

By 1927, Conn Smythe had taken ownership of the team and renamed it the Maple Leafs. Four years later, in the midst of the Great Depression, Smythe oversaw the construction of Maple Leaf Gardens, which opened on November 12, 1931.

The Leafs finished in second place in the Canadian Division that year. With the Kid Line of Busher Jackson, Charlie Conacher, and Joe Primeau leading the Leafs in playoff scoring, Toronto won its first Stanley Cup under the Maple Leafs nickname to close out the 1931-32 season.

The Leafs advanced to the Stanley Cup finals six times in the next eight years but came up empty each time. In the 1942 finals series, Toronto's opponent, the Detroit Red Wings, built up a seemingly insurmountable 3-0 series lead. Coach Hap Day altered his lineup, benching veteran Gordie Drillon for Game Four. Motivated by Day's tactics, the Leafs staged a four-game rally to win the 1942 Cup, the greatest comeback in finals history.

The end of the Second World War coincided with the beginning of a Toronto dynasty. The Leafs won their third Cup in 1945, then proceeded to win the championship in four of the next six seasons. Ted "Teeder" Kennedy inherited the captaincy from retiring Syl Apps and became the team's greatest clutch player, earning 23 career points in the Cup finals.

In 1949, Toronto completed a four-game sweep of Detroit to become the first team in history to win three consecutive Stanley Cups. The 1951 finals series was a closely-matched affair versus Montreal in which every game went into overtime. Game Five is remembered for Bill Barilko's famous diving goal in overtime to win the Cup. Sadly, Barilko died in a plane crash just four months later.

Captain George Armstrong cradles the Stanley Cup during the 1967 celebratory parade, to this day the most recent in Toronto's storied history.

The early 1960s were dominated by the Leafs again, a roster that was stacked with future Hall of Famers at every position. Johnny Bower was the number-one goalie. Tim Horton and Allan Stanley were the foundation on defence, and Dave Keon, Frank Mahovlich, and Red Kelly led the forward unit.

Toronto won three straight Stanley Cups from 1962 to 1964. With aging veterans, the team wasn't expected to contend in the final year before expansion, 1967. But a roster dubbed the "Over the Hill Gang" upset the Canadiens in six games, spoiling Montreal's plans to host the Stanley Cup at their World's Fair in Canada's centennial year.

Habs Win Without Europeans

In 1992-93, hockey's most famous trophy, the Stanley Cup, celebrated its 100th anniversary. It was only fitting that the Cup-winner in this centennial season was the NHL's most storied franchise – the Montreal Canadiens.

The Habs made two significant moves in the off-season. Jacques Demers was hired as coach, replacing Pat Burns, who held the job for four years before jumping to the rival Maple Leafs. And, Vincent Damphousse was acquired in a trade from Edmonton for Shayne Corson, Brent Gilchrist, and Vladimir Vujtek.

Montreal posted a 48-30-6 regular-season record, good enough for sixth-place overall, yet only third-best in a strong Adams Division in which powerhouses Boston and Quebec also played.

The 1993 Habs were the last Canadian team to win the Cup, and they did so without even one European on their roster.

The Canadiens drew the Nordiques in the opening round of the playoffs, setting the stage for another Battle of Quebec. Scott Young scored in overtime in Game One to draw first blood for the Nordiques. From then on, goaltender Patrick Roy was invincible in sudden-death.

Trailing 2-0 in the series and heading back to Montreal, the Habs were boosted by an overtime winner from Damphousse in the third game that may have salvaged their season. Montreal reeled off three more wins in a row – including Game Six in a fourth period – to advance to the next round against Buffalo.

Roy continued to work his overtime magic. The Canadiens swept the Sabres aside in four, one-goal games, the last three needing overtime. From there, the Habs needed only five games – including two more OT wins – to defeat the New York Islanders in the Wales Conference finals.

After losing Game One of the Stanley Cup finals to Wayne Gretzky and the Los Angeles Kings, the Habs saw the series turn on an illegal stick penalty assessed to the Kings' Marty McSorley. Both the tying goal and the game-winning goal, scored in (what else?) overtime, were netted by Eric Desjardins. The Habs' defenceman, having scored prior to tying the game, made history by becoming the only blueliner to score a hat trick in the Stanley Cup finals.

The series shifted to Hollywood for the next two games. An unstoppable Roy winked at a frustrated Tomas Sandstrom. John LeClair ended both games in Los Angeles in sudden-death, helping set an NHL record for the Habs with ten overtime wins in one playoff year.

Montreal closed out the series on home ice in Game Five. Patrick Roy won his second Conn Smythe Trophy as playoff MVP. This was the last Cup-winning roster comprised exclusively of North American-born players.

FLAMES VS. CANUCKS

The Calgary Flames won their second straight Presidents' Trophy in 1988-89 and were the overwhelming favourites against the Vancouver Canucks in the Smythe Division semi-finals. Vancouver – a sub .500 team – finished 43 points arrears of Calgary in the regular season and had only won once in the previous 18 regular-season games between the two clubs.

But when the Canucks' Paul Reinhart scored the overtime winner on the road in Game One, Vancouver served notice that it was not to be taken lightly. Calgary replied with a 5-2 win in the second game before the teams split the next two games in British Columbia.

Mike Vernon recorded a shutout in the fifth game to push the Canucks to the brink of elimination. But the resilient Canucks took Game Six by a score 6-3 thanks to a two-goal performance by Rich Sutter, sending the series back to the Saddledome for a decisive seventh game.

Both goalies were sharp to begin the first period. Vernon and his counterpart, Kirk McLean, kept the game scoreless through nine minutes of play. Calgary's Joe Nieuwendyk and Vancouver's Robert Nordmark opened the scoring for their teams with power-play goals. Before the first period was over, the Flames took the lead when Al MacInnis's wicked point shot deflected off Gary Roberts and under the crossbar. Without the benefit of video replay – still three years away – referee Bill McCreary consulted with the off-ice officials before confirming the goal.

Special teams continued to dominate during the second period. Trevor Linden equalled the score at 2:04 with another Vancouver power-play goal. The Flames regained the lead in the final minute of the middle frame when Joe Mullen's shot glanced off Canucks defenceman Harold Snepsts and into the net on a Calgary man advantage.

Vancouver's Doug Lidster had the only marker of the third period to force overtime.

Jim Peplinski played a pivotal role in Calgary's historic win over Vancouver in 1989.

As they had done over the first 60 minutes of the game, the two teams played with frantic urgency, creating several scoring chances with their attacks off the rush, followed by dangerous counterattacks. Smyl had the best chance to end the game for Vancouver, but he was stoned by Vernon's quick glove hand on a breakaway.

When it appeared that a second overtime period was looming, Jim Peplinski's centring pass bounced off the skate of Joel Otto, in the crease, and into the Vancouver goal. The thrilling Game Seven win clinched the first of four series victories for Calgary on the way to its first Stanley Cup title.

Old Players Get Millions

In the late 1950s, Ted Lindsay and Doug Harvey began their inquiries into the value of the players' pension fund. When NHL owners rebuffed their requests, Lindsay's next move was to attempt to start a players' association.

The plan proved to be futile after the players blinked in a staring match against the anti-union owners. Even after the NHLPA was formed in 1967, the allocation of the pension money was still clandestine information to the players.

In 1991, a group of NHL alumni filed a class-action lawsuit against the league. Seven former players were named plaintiffs: Andy Bathgate, Carl Brewer, Gordie Howe, Bobby Hull, Leo Reise, Eddie Shack, and Allan Stanley. The suit alleged that in the 1980s, the NHL Pension Society misappropriated the surplus pension money--$20 million in 1980 and another $2 million in 1982.

The case went before Justice George Adams of the Ontario Court General Division. On October 23, 1992, Justice Adams issued a ruling in favour of the players. The surplus in the fund, plus interest, amounted to $43 million. The beneficiaries were the approximately 1,000 members who were playing while the surpluses were accumulated.

The NHL appealed Adams's decision, but on February 18, 1994, the Ontario Court of Appeal upheld the initial ruling. "It's about time. The money belongs to us. That's why we won," Bernie Geoffrion told the *Chicago Tribune*. "When you take a guy like Gordie Howe, Mr. Hockey, who played all those years and he's got a pension of about $13,000, that's disgusting."

Two-and-a-half weeks later, NHLPA executive director Alan Eagleson was indicted by a U.S. grand jury on charges of fraud, embezzlement, racketeering, and obstruction of justice. The charges stemmed from a two-year investigation conducted by the FBI into Eagleson's business practices, specifically his handling of disability claims and of funds from international tournaments.

The FBI became suspicious following a series of investigative articles published by Russ Conway in the Lawrence *Eagle-Tribune* that revealed Eagleson's improprieties. In addition to the scathing reports written by Conway, there were also complaints raised to the FBI by several current and former players, including estranged former Eagleson client Bobby Orr.

Eagleson pleaded guilty to three charges of fraud and embezzlement on January 6, 1998. The disgraced hockey czar served six months of an 18-month prison sentence, and his memberships in both the Hockey Hall of Fame and the Order of Canada were revoked.

Ted Lindsay (left) fought tirelessly for players' rights.

Vancouver's HALL OF FAMERS

Players

Mark Messier, 2007

Pavel Bure, 2012

Builders

Frank Griffiths, 1993

The tough-as-nails Mark Messier cried repeatedly when he was inducted into the Hockey Hall of Fame.

Mark Messier played for the Canucks for three years.

Pavel Bure displayed sensational speed and skill in the NHL, and he was duly inducted into the Hockey Hall of Fame as a result.

Messier Guarantees Win

The New York Rangers entered the 1994 playoffs under a burden of expectations. First-year coach Mike Keenan had guided the team to its second Presidents' Trophy in three seasons. But, the Blueshirts were coming off a disappointing 1992-93 season in which they missed the playoffs.

There was also the matter of the longest championship drought in the league. The Rangers hadn't won the Stanley Cup since 1940 and were longing to exorcise those demons. Under the leadership of their captain, Mark Messier, the Rangers lost only once in their opening two playoff rounds, sweeping the Islanders, then ousting the Capitals in five games.

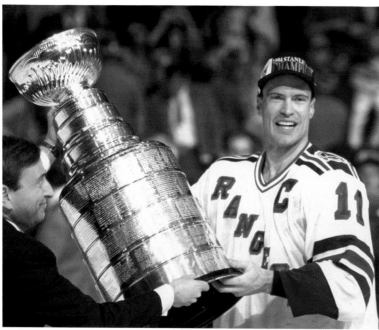

Mark Messier brought the Cup to Manhattan after a drought of 54 years.

In the Eastern Conference finals, New York faced a far more formidable opponent, the Hudson River rival New Jersey Devils. Goaltenders Mike Richter of the Rangers and the Devils' Martin Brodeur battled for every shot. Games One and Three, won by New Jersey and New York, respectively, were both decided in overtime.

Going back to the Meadowlands, the Devils were leading the series three games to two and were looking to eliminate the Rangers in front of the home fans. The day before Game Six, a group of reporters congregated around Messier in his stall at the Rangers' practice facility at Rye Playland.

When asked whether he thought his team would win, Messier said "We're going to go in there and win Game Six. We know we're going to go in and win Game Six and bring it back for Game Seven."

On game day, the back page of the *New York Post* splashed the headline "WE'LL WIN TONIGHT" alongside Messier's picture, and underneath text that read, "Captain Courageous' bold prediction."

"Well, I guess we better win," said Rangers star defenceman Brian Leetch.

Trailing 2-0 after one period, the Rangers were undaunted. Alex Kovalev scored late in the second frame to bring New York to within a goal. Messier used the final twenty minutes to fulfill his prophecy. At 2:45 of the period, his shot between Brodeur's pads on a backhander tied the game. Ten minutes later, "Moose" pounced on a rebound off a Kovalev shot to give his team the lead.

The deafening applause from the scores of fans who had made the trek from across the George Washington Bridge gave the visiting Rangers the feeling of playing at home.

Messier iced the game with an empty net goal to complete his hat trick. Buoyed with the momentum from their captain's guarantee, the Rangers won Game Seven, then defeated Vancouver in the finals to win their first Stanley Cup in 54 years.

Calgary's Biggest Trades

TOP TRADE

DECEMBER 19, 1995 Calgary Flames trade Joe Nieuwendyk to Dallas for Jarome Iginla and Corey Millen

Jarome Iginla was the marquee player on the Flames for 16 years, setting all-time club records for scoring and becoming the unequivocal leader of the franchise.

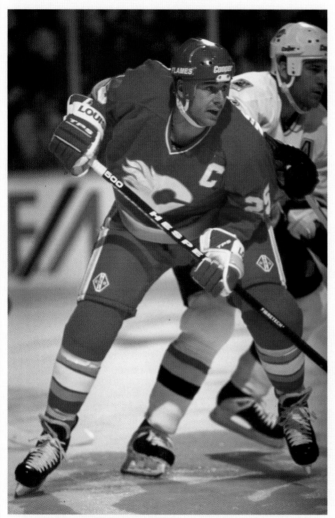

Calgary had to trade Joe Nieuwendyk (pictured) to get Jarome Iginla, a big trade that worked for both teams.

His acquisition didn't come cheaply. General manager Al Coates was forced to part ways with Joe Nieuwendyk, a 51-goal scorer and Calder Trophy winner in 1988. In his second NHL season, Nieuwendyk had ten goals in 22 games during the Flames' march to the Stanley Cup. The future Hall of Famer also enjoyed championship success in Dallas – where he also won playoff MVP honours – and New Jersey.

Iginla achieved stardom despite enduring the disadvantages of playing on a Canadian team that struggled to qualify for, let alone advance in, the playoffs. In 2001-02, he won the "Rocket" Richard Trophy, leading the NHL with 52 goals. He missed out on the Hart Trophy by the slimmest of margins.

Two years later, Iginla led the Flames to a surprise run to the Stanley Cup finals as Calgary lost a heartbreaking seventh game to the Tampa Bay Lightning. Iginla and Nieuwendyk were teammates on Canada's Olympic team that won the gold medal in 2002 in Salt Lake City, ending a 50-year drought for Canada.

HONOURABLE MENTION

NOVEMBER 25, 1981 Calgary Flames trade Don Lever and Bob MacMillan to Colorado Rockies for Lanny McDonald and a 4th-round draft choice in 1983 (Mikko Makela)

McDonald, a native of Hanna, Alberta, turned professional with the Toronto Maple Leafs, where he reached all-star status. But during a period of upheaval in Toronto, McDonald was exiled to the Colorado Rockies, a hapless franchise that later moved to New Jersey.

McDonald scored a career best 66 goals in 1982-83 with Calgary and also won the Bill Masterton Trophy for perseverance and dedication. Six years later, the Flames advanced to the Stanley Cup finals against Montreal. The Forum was historically unkind to visitors. No Canadiens opponents had ever clinched the Stanley Cup in the hallowed arena.

But in Game Six, McDonald exorcised those Forum ghosts. He scored his final career goal, getting the better of Patrick Roy to help lift Calgary to a 4-2 win and the franchise's first championship.

Closing out a 1988-89 campaign during which he had also scored his 500th NHL goal and 1000th point, McDonald retired from the game.

Gretzky's 99 All-Stars Tour Europe

The first NHL lockout in 1994 was an acrimonious staring match between NHL commissioner Gary Bettman and NHLPA executive director Bob Goodenow. With neither man willing to budge on salary cap and revenue-sharing issues, the resulting labour stoppage cancelled the first half of the 1994-95 season.

Wayne Gretzky – a man who had been perennially attached to rinks since his childhood – wasn't about to allow his ice time to be completely abolished. The "Great One," the defending Art Ross Trophy winner, assembled a group of players to tour Europe to not only promote the game but also to raise funds for charity. The team was aptly named the Ninety-Nine All-Stars.

The players included goaltenders Grant Fuhr and Kelly Hrudey; defencemen Rob Blake, Paul Coffey, Todd Gill, Charlie Huddy, Al MacInnis, and Marty McSorley; and, forwards Pat Conacher, Russ Courtnall, Sergei Fedorov, Tony Granato, Brett Hull, Steve Larmer, Kirk Muller, Mark Messier, Rick Tocchet, Steve Yzerman, and, of course, Gretzky.

Recently-retired defenceman Doug Wilson was appointed the head coach. Joining Wilson behind the bench was the world's most famous hockey dad, Walter Gretzky.

The Ninety-Nine All-Stars tour provided the opportunity for the players to take a bit of a travelling vacation and to also maintain their conditioning in the event of an end to the labour dispute and the return of NHL games. The All-Stars' sweaters were red and white, bearing a resemblance to vintage Detroit Red Wings' sweaters. The words "Ninety-Nine" were emblazoned on the front in cursive font.

Before heading overseas, Gretzky's squad visited The Palace of Auburn Hills (Michigan) for a December 1 game against the Detroit Vipers of the International Hockey League. The Vipers prevailed, 4-3.

The European tour kicked off two nights later in Helsinki, Finland. The All-Stars had seven different scorers, including Gretzky himself, in a 7-1 rout of Jokerit. The next day the NHLers fell, 4-3, in overtime to Ilves of Tampere.

From there it was off to Oslo to face the Norwegian Spectrum All-Stars. Gretzky scored in his team's 6-3 win that also featured goals from Kings teammate Tony Granato and former Oilers teammate and current Rangers star Mark Messier.

The All-Stars then faced three Swedish opponents: Djugarden, Vastra Frolundra, and Malmo. They won the first two games, 9-3 and 5-2, before losing the third, 6-5, in overtime. The tour concluded on December 14 with an 8-5 win over the German All-Stars. Gretzky's squad finished with five wins and three losses, and on January 11, 1995, the lockout ended after 103 days of negotiations.

Wayne Gretzky toured Europe in 1994, much to the delight of fans everywhere.

Ottawa's TOP DRAFT CHOICES

1992 – Alexei Yashin, #2, Dynamo Moscow

1993 – Alexandre Daigle, #1, Victoriaville

1994 – Radek Bonk, #3, Las Vegas

1995 – Bryan Berard, #1, Detroit

1996 – Chris Phillips, #1, Prince Albert

1997 – Marian Hossa, #12, Dukla Trencin

1998 – Mathieu Chouinard, #15, Shawinigan

1999 – Martin Havlat, #26, Trinec

2000 – Anton Volchenkov, #21, HK Moscow

2001 – Jason Spezza, #2, Windsor

2001 – Tim Gleason, #23, Windsor

2002 – Jakub Klepis, #16, Portland

2003 – Patrick Eaves, #29, Boston College

2004 – Andrej Meszaros, #23, Dukla Trencin

2005 – Brian Lee, #9, Moorhead

2006 – Nick Foligno, #28, Sudbury

2007 – Jim O'Brien, #29, U. of Minnesota

2008 – Erik Karlsson, #15, Vastra Frolunda Jr.

2009 – Jared Cowen, #9, Spokane

2011 – Mika Zibanejad, #6, Djugarden

2011 – Stefan Noesen, #21, Plymouth

2011 – Matt Puempel, #24, Peterborough

2012 – Cody Ceci, #15, Ottawa

2013 – Curtis Lazar, #17, Edmonton

Chris Phillips was part of Team Canada's gold-medal winning entry at the 1996 World Junior Championship. After the Senators made him the first-overall pick in the June draft, he returned to the Western Hockey League to play his final year as a junior. He won a second straight U20 gold medal, then helped Lethbridge advance to the final game of the Memorial Cup. He was named to the tournament's All-Star Team on defence.

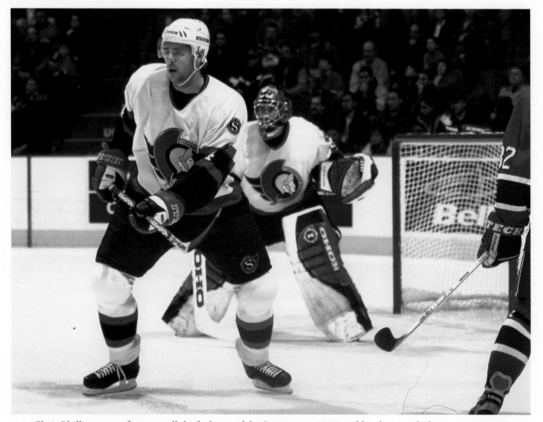

Chris Phillips was a first-overall draft choice of the Senators in 1996 and has been with the team ever since.

Hasek Wins Two Harts

If there were one word to describe Dominik Hasek, it would be unorthodox.

As a kid there was no single style of goaltending that he could emulate, not even that of his idol Jiri Holecek. Nor would any parent or netminding coach in today's game suggest that his protégé try to master Hasek's unconventional manoeuvres.

Drafted by the Chicago Black Hawks in 1983, Hasek continued to play in his native Czechoslovakia. The exodus of Eastern Bloc players to the NHL had not yet begun in earnest. Nevertheless, Hasek was the best at his craft in his home country, earning Czechoslovakian Goaltender of the Year honours in five straight years ending in 1990.

Hasek made his debut with Chicago in the 1990-91 season. But, with Ed Belfour firmly entrenched as the Hawks' starter, Hasek was traded to Buffalo in what is now regarded as one of the most one-sided deals ever made. Chicago received unheralded netminder Stephane Beauregard and a draft pick in return (Eric Daze).

The change of scenery worked wonders. Opportunistically rising to the challenge of becoming a starter, Hasek vaulted into the upper echelon of goaltenders. He won his first Vezina Trophy in 1993-94, posting seven shutouts and a miniscule goals-against average of 1.95. It was the first GAA below 2.00 in twenty years.

Hasek defended his Vezina win in the lockout-shortened season the following year. It was a foreshadowing of even more stellar accomplishments. In 1996-97, Hasek backstopped the Sabres to a 40-win season, earning 37 of those victories in the Buffalo net. Whether he was using his flexibility to flop to make a save, or contorting to stop the puck at the last millisecond with the back of his arm, Hasek simply dominated. He was indeed "The Dominator."

Hasek won not only the Vezina Trophy but the Hart Trophy as the NHL's most valuable player. This latter award marked the first time in 35 years that a goaltender had been so honoured. The last Hart Trophy goalie had been Jacques Plante in 1962.

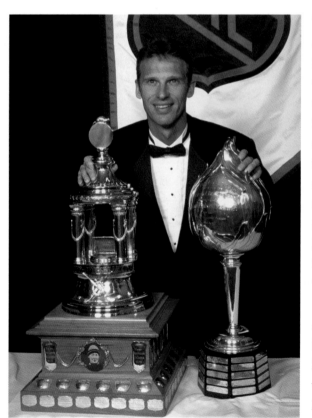

If they call you the "Dominator," you better be good—and Dominik Hasek was very good.

The next season, Hasek was sensational on both sides of the Pacific Ocean. As the Olympics welcomed NHL players for the first time, Hasek led the Czech Republic to the country's first-ever gold medal. His year with the Sabres was also nothing short of sheer brilliance. Hasek recorded 13 shutouts and had a save percentage of .932. For his efforts, Hasek became the first goalie ever to win the Hart Trophy in consecutive years.

Although Hasek won his only Stanley Cup with Detroit, in 2002, the back-to-back MVP wins with Buffalo rank as "The Dominator'"s greatest single-season performances.

The All-Star Game in Ottawa

★ ★ ★

JANUARY 29, 2012

The nation's capital hosted the All-Star Game for the first time in history, and hometown fans had the chance to show their appreciation for team captain Daniel Alfredsson.

Alfredsson, the franchise's all-time leader in games played, goals, assists, and points was voted by the players as one of the two All-Star captains along with Boston defenceman Zdeno Chara, himself a former Senators blueliner.

Daniel Alfredsson was the star in 2012 when Ottawa hosted the All-Star Game.

For the second year in a row, rosters were filled by way of a fantasy draft. Alfredsson selected the three available Ottawa players: forwards Jason Spezza and Milan Michalek, and defenceman Erik Karlsson. Not surprisingly, all four Senators placed at the top of the overall positions in fan balloting.

Team Chara's most dangerous player was New York Rangers winger Marian Gaborik. By the 1:23 mark of the second period, Gaborik had already registered a hat trick in the offence-laden exhibition.

With his team trailing 5-4 in the middle frame, Alfredsson brought the sellout gathering at Scotiabank Place to its feet. The 39-year-old scored twice in a span of 91 seconds, prompting the Ottawa faithful to chant, "Alfie! Alfie!"

However, ex-teammate Chara had the last laugh. The towering defenceman's goal at 12:20 of the third period held up as the game-winner, and Team Chara won the scoring festival, 12-9. Alfredsson, playing on a line with Canucks snipers Daniel and Henrik Sedin, finished the game with two goals and an assist.

While Gaborik claimed the honour of the game's most valuable player, the title would almost certainly have been awarded to Alfredsson had he not missed a hat trick by the width of a goal post.

Spezza and Michalek each had a goal and an assist, and Karlsson was held pointless. The game featured only the second penalty shot in All-Star Game history when Tampa Bay sharpshooter Steven Stamkos was foiled by Montreal goalie Carey Price.

The weekend's festivities were offset by a mini-controversy when Capitals forward Alex Ovechkin declined his invitation. Ovechkin was serving a three-game suspension for a check to the head of Pittsburgh's Zbynek Michalek – Milan's brother – but was eligible to participate in the All-Star Game.

Nevertheless, "Ovi" used the unplanned time off to skip the proceedings altogether. Sidney Crosby also missed the game, having played only eight games in the regular season as a result of ongoing concussion issues. The absence of the game's top two marquee stars, however, didn't deter fans from whisking through the turnstiles. Some 20,510 spectators attended the event.

NHL Goes to Nagano

For many years, international competition in a true best-on-best showcase had been exclusive to the Canada/World Cup tournaments that began in 1976. Such was the inequity in Canada being unable to use professional players that Canada refused to ice a team from 1970 until 1976.

Interestingly, Canada was the sole hockey power objecting to the first ever participation by professionals for the 1998 Olympic Winter Games. However, as discussions progressed regarding the logistics for the Games to be held in Nagano, Japan, Canada relented.

"All of the European countries, along with the U.S., wanted NHL players involved because they really thought it would give better exposure to hockey globally," Hockey Canada president Bob Nicholson said. "We were the odd federation out, so we went on side with it."

To showcase the Olympics, Japan hosted the first-ever regular-season NHL games played outside of North America. Billed as "Game One '97," the two-game mini-series featured the Vancouver Canucks and the Mighty Ducks of Anaheim. Ducks star and Team Canada candidate Paul Kariya – a player of Japanese heritage – was the marquee player of the games. He took his middle name Testuhiko from his father's first name. The teams split the two games on October 3 and 4, 1997.

The long-anticipated tournament arrived in February. To accommodate the participation of its players, the NHL stopped play for two weeks. Unfortunately for Kariya, he missed the once-in-a-lifetime chance to play in Japan. He was suffering from post-concussion syndrome after being crosschecked to the head by San Jose's Gary Suter. Kariya not only missed the Olympics but the remainder of the NHL regular season.

The tournament featured its share of dramatic moments both on and off the ice. When the Americans lost to the Czech Republic in the quarter-finals, a few of their players trashed a hotel room, bringing international embarrassment to the team.

Led by the impenetrable Dominik Hasek in net, the Czechs forced a shootout against Canada in the semi-finals. He stopped Brendan Shanahan on Canada's final attempt, sending the Czechs to the gold-medal game. A disillusioned Wayne Gretzky mourned on the bench, his international career over.

In the deciding matchup against Russia, Petr Svoboda had the game's only goal. Hasek stopped all 20 shots he faced, leading the Czech Republic to its first-ever Olympic gold. Despite the significant time difference to North America, the television ratings for the Games were impressive. Nagano set the hockey standard for future Olympics.

The NHL's participation in Nagano was historic and allowed for the world to see best-on-best hockey.

Edmonton's CAPTAINS

Ron Chipperfield, 1979-80

Blair MacDonald and Lee Fogolin Jr., 1980-81

Lee Fogolin Jr., 1981-82, 1982-83

Wayne Gretzky, 1983-84 to 1987-88

Mark Messier, 1988-89 to 1990-91

Kevin Lowe, 1991-92

Craig MacTavish, 1992-93, 1993-94

Shayne Corson, 1994-95

Kelly Buchberger, 1995-96 to 1998-99

Doug Weight, 1999-2000, 2000-01

Jason Smith, 2001-02 to 2006-07

Ethan Moreau, 2007-08 to 2009-10

Shawn Horcoff, 2010-11 to 2012-13

Andrew Ference, 2013-14 to 2014-15

Blair MacDonald was one of the first captains of the Oilers in the NHL.

Wayne Gretzky captained every team he played for, notably Edmonton.

Gretzky Retires

It was only fitting that the number 99 figured prominently in bookending the career of Wayne Gretzky, the man who trademarked the double digits. After all, it was on his 18th birthday, while with the WHA Edmonton Oilers, that Gretzky signed a 21-year personal-services contract that expired in 1999.

The "Great One" wore the number throughout his prolific career. After re-writing the NHL record books, winning ten scoring titles, nine MVP awards, and four Stanley Cups, Gretzky chose to retire in 1999.

Speculation was rampant regarding Gretzky's future heading into the final weekend of the 1998-99 season. The New York Rangers held a $5 million option on Gretzky's contract for the following season. "I don't think either one of us wants to embarrass the other side. So, that's not a factor," Gretzky told the *New York Times*.

The penultimate game of the Rangers' season was a 2-2 tie in Ottawa on April 15. As if sensing the inevitable, the Senators fans began chanting, "One more year!" as the third period drew to a close. At the end of the game, Gretzky came out for two curtain calls before skating off an NHL rink in Canada for the final time.

Back in New York the next day, Gretzky confirmed his retirement plans to the media. There would be one final chance for the fans to wave goodbye – April 18 at Madison

The last goodbye as Gretzky waves to appreciative fans

Square Garden – when the Rangers would host the Pittsburgh Penguins.

The Big Apple was the centre of the hockey world's attention on that Sunday afternoon. The guests on hand for the pre-game ceremony included Gretzky's wife Janet and their four children, Mario Lemieux (then retired), former teammate and then-Canucks forward Mark Messier, and NHL commissioner Gary Bettman.

"When you take off that sweater, your jersey, after today's game, you will be the last player in the NHL to ever wear 99," Bettman said to Gretzky. Gretzky was held to an assist in a 2-1 Rangers loss. The winning goal was scored in overtime by Pittsburgh's Jaromir Jagr who, at game's end, asked number 99 for his stick.

The spectators rose to their feat in unison. Gretzky skated around the ice along with his Rangers teammates. Then, the "Great One," waving to the raucous, appreciative crowd, took one final lap on his own. He then departed for the Rangers' dressing room to hang up his skates for good.

Not only was the three-year waiting period waived for Gretzky's induction into the Hockey Hall of Fame, but the Hall decided that he would be the last player to be granted such an exemption.

And, of course, his enshrinement came in 1999.

Montreal Milestones

MOST SEASONS HENRI RICHARD (20)

Although Rocket Richard's younger brother played in the shadow of his legendary sibling, Henri Richard forged his own path on the way to a Hall of Fame career. He won the Stanley Cup a record eleven times as a player and played 65 games in the Stanley Cup finals, tying him with Red Kelly for the all-time mark. Richard's total of 1,256 games in a Habs uniform is a franchise high. In two decades of play, he was named to four All-Star Teams and led the league twice in assists during his career.

MOST POINTS GUY LAFLEUR (1,246)

Lafleur's trademark helmetless stride down the right wing was one of the most iconic sights of the 1970s. The NHL's first overall draft pick in 1971, Lafleur was the first player in history to collect 50 goals and 100 points in a season six consecutive times. His most famous goal came in the 1979 semi-finals against Boston in the infamous "too many men on the ice" game. With Montreal trailing late in Game Seven, Lafleur unleashed a slap shot past Bruins goalie Gilles Gilbert to tie the game. The Habs went on to win in overtime.

MOST WINS JACQUES PLANTE (314)

A master innovator at his position, Plante was the first goalie to stop the puck behind the net for his defencemen. Most notably, he pioneered the use of a mask as part of the goaltender's standard equipment. Plante recorded 58 shutouts in a Montreal uniform, second to George Hainsworth's mark of 75.

MOST PENALTY MINUTES CHRIS NILAN (2,248)

The man known as "Knuckles" wasn't taken until the 19th round, 231st overall at the 1978 NHL Amateur Draft. Nilan led the NHL in penalty minutes in 1983-84 (338) and 1984-85 (358). In the 1986 playoffs, he collected 141 penalty minutes to lead all players on the way to a Stanley Cup title. Nilan was the subject of the 2011 documentary "The Last Gladiators," a film that chronicled the life of a hockey enforcer.

MILESTONES AND RECORDS

Rocket Richard was the NHL's first 500-goal scorer. He reached the mark on October 19, 1957, against Chicago's Glenn Hall.

Three players—Jean Beliveau, Frank Mahovlich and Guy Lafleur—each recorded their 500th career goal and 1,000th career point in a Habs uniform. Henri Richard reached the 1,000-point milestone on December 20, 1973, with an assist against Buffalo.

In Game Two of the 1986 Stanley Cup finals, Brian Skrudland scored the fastest playoff overtime goal ever, firing the puck past Calgary's Mike Vernon just nine seconds into the extra period.

Jean Beliveau (left) poses with the Hart Trophy with Gordie Howe.

Stars Win Toe-Goal Cup

Few NHL rule changes created as much controversy as the initiative for zero-tolerance in the goal crease, adopted in 1996-97. Under this strict enforcement, goals were disallowed if any player on the attacking team had any part of his skate or body in the crease.

The crackdown was aimed at protecting goaltenders, a noble cause, to be sure. But the repercussions were immediate, and the backlash swift. Too many goals were being disallowed because an offending player – having no impact on the goalie's ability to make the save – had even a part of his skate in the crease.

The controversy reached new heights in the 1997 playoffs when Chicago's Tony Amonte had a late goal waived off because he was in the crease before the puck. What had made the ruling so ludicrous? It was an empty-netter.

Nevertheless, the toe-in-the-crease policy continued for the next two years. Only after a controversial season-ending goal

Dallas Stars players celebrate their controversial Cup win in 1999.

did the league review its stance. In the 1999 Stanley Cup finals, the Presidents' Trophy-winning Dallas Stars faced the Buffalo Sabres.

There was no weakness in the Dallas lineup. The forwards were led by Brett Hull, Mike Modano, and Joe Nieuwendyk. The defence was anchored by captain Derian Hatcher. Ed Belfour was the dependable starting goalie.

On the other bench, the Sabres' fortunes rested with two-time Hart Trophy winner Dominik Hasek in goal. No Buffalo player averaged a point per game during the regular season, but Hasek gave the team a chance to win on his own merit every night.

Dallas carried a 3-2 series lead into Game Six at Buffalo's Marine Midland Arena. In a defensive showdown, Belfour and Hasek were nearly flawless, allowing only one goal each after sixty minutes of play. The first two overtime periods were indecisive.

Less than five minutes into triple overtime, Hull – at the top of the Sabres' crease – pounced on a rebound off a shot by Modano. As Hull, a right-handed shot, reached behind him for the puck, he parked his left skate in the crease. He easily flung the puck into the net to clinch the game and the Stanley Cup.

To no avail, the Sabres vehemently protested. The league justified the goal by maintaining that Hull maintained possession throughout the entire play, overriding the crease violation. Sabres' coach Lindy Ruff was expectedly dissatisfied. At the team's end of season rally in Buffalo, he ended the ceremonies with two words for the Buffalo fans: "No goal."

The NHL eliminated the crease crackdown by the start of the next season.

GREAT RIVALRIES Calgary vs. Edmonton

After the Flames franchise was relocated from Atlanta to Calgary in 1980, a natural rivalry was created with their often not-so-friendly provincial acquaintances, the Edmonton Oilers. Both teams became Stanley Cup contenders by the middle of the decade and, indeed, Alberta was represented in the Cup finals every year from 1984 to 1990.

By virtue of their placement in the Smythe Division, the bitter enemies were destined to meet in either the first or second round of the playoffs. Their first ever post-season matchup, in 1983, was a blowout in favour of Edmonton. The Oilers' freewheeling offence outscored the Flames, 35-13, in a four games to one series victory.

The year 1984 was supposed to be another cakewalk for Glen Sather's squad. The Oilers were the runaway leaders in the regular season with 119 points, 37 points better than the Flames. But Calgary picked itself off the mat after falling behind 3-1 in the division finals. Lanny McDonald's overtime winner in Game Six helped push the series to the brink. Ultimately, Edmonton won the seventh game, eventually claiming its first Stanley Cup title.

As Wayne Gretzky continuing to shatter scoring records, the Oilers defended their championship. Edmonton sought a Stanley Cup hat trick in 1986 and was again challenged by Calgary. A line brawl ensued in Game Four after the Flames' Tim Hunter charged goaltender Grant Fuhr.

The series needed a seventh game to declare a winner. Infamously, Oilers defenceman Steve Smith accidentally put the puck in his own net for the clinching goal, shockingly eliminating his team.

By 1988, one year after Edmonton won its third Cup, the Flames had usurped the Oilers as Presidents' Trophy winners. But their season came to an abrupt end when they were swept by Edmonton in the second round of the playoffs.

In overtime in Game Two, Gretzky scored arguably the most famous of his 122 career post-season goals. Number 99 streaked down the left wing on a short-handed breakaway and blasted a slap shot to the top corner over the glove of Flames goalie Mike Vernon.

No greater victory did Calgary experience than in 1986 when it defeated Edmonton in seven games.

The teams waged an epic showdown in the 1991 division semi-finals. Theoren Fleury kept the Flames' hopes alive with a Game Six breakaway winner in overtime, punctuating the evening with a sliding celebration that carried him the length of the ice. But Fleury's exuberant exhibition served as motivation for the Oilers.

Trailing 3-0 in the seventh game, Edmonton rallied for a 5-4 overtime win. The series-winning goal came courtesy of Esa Tikkanen, retaining the Oilers' bragging rights.

First European Coaches

Up until the early 1970s, NHL players were entirely developed in North America. By the middle of the decade, professional hockey teams were scouting the two main Scandinavian powers, Sweden and Finland, for talent. A wave of Eastern Bloc defections followed in the 1980s before the fall of the Iron Curtain paved the way for Russian and Czech players.

Yet the men behind the benches were still exclusively Canadian or American. The monopoly on coaching jobs held by North Americans was finally broken in May 2000 when the Chicago Blackhawks hired Alpo Suhonen to replace the fired Lorne Molleken.

In accepting the position, Suhonen, a native of Valkeakoski, Finland, became the first full-time European-born-and-trained coach in NHL history. The first European-born coach, Johnny Gottselig, worked the Chicago bench from 1944-45 to 1947-48, but he was raised in Canada.

Suhonen had close ties with the Blackhawks' manager of hockey operations, Mike Smith, an executive with an affinity for drafting European-born players. The two men had known each other for more than 20 years and worked together in both Winnipeg and Toronto. Suhonen was the Leafs' assistant coach prior to being hired by Chicago.

"I don't do things to be the first at something. I do them because I think they're the right thing for the organization," Smith told the *Chicago Tribune*. "The fact that Suhonen may or may not be the first European coach is irrelevant."

One month later, the Pittsburgh Penguins promoted Ivan Hlinka from associate coach to head coach. Hlinka's greatest achievement behind the bench was leading his native Czech Republic to the gold medal at the 1998 Olympics in Nagano, Japan.

In taking over from interim coach Herb Brooks, Hlinka once again had the opportunity to be the bench boss for superstar Jaromir Jagr – the defending Art Ross trophy winner – who was part of the Olympic championship team.

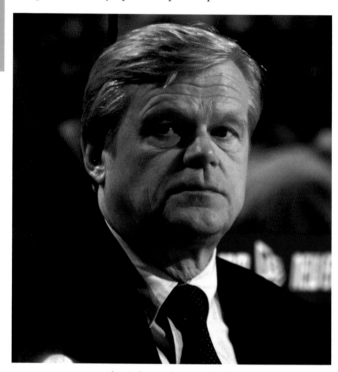

Alpo Suhonen became the first European-trained coach in NHL history.

With an undermanned roster, Suhonen's Blackhawks finished out of the playoffs for a fourth straight year. Their record was a regrettable 29-40-8-5 in 82 games. After just one season as coach, Suhonen resigned.

Hlinka guided the Penguins to the Eastern Conference finals in 2000-01, but the team lost in five games to the New Jersey Devils. The next year, Pittsburgh got off to an horrific start, losing its first four games. The slump cost Hlinka his job.

Since then, no Europeans have been hired to coach in the NHL, leaving Suhonen and Hlinka in a class of their own.

Best Players Born in
Quebec City

MARTY BARRY

A prolific scorer in his era, Barry reached the 20-goal mark for six consecutive years ending in 1935-36 when the NHL season was just 48 games long. The centreman was named to the First All-Star Team in 1936-37 and also won the Lady Byng Trophy that year. He won two Stanley Cups with the Red Wings.

GUY CHOUINARD

Chouinard is the first ever 50-goal scorer in the history of the Flames franchise. He reached the milestone in the second-last game of the 1978-79 season in a win by Atlanta versus the New York Rangers.

KEVIN DINEEN

In 19 seasons with four teams, Dineen collected 760 points in 1,188 career games. He briefly coached the Florida Panthers but saved his greatest achievement behind the bench for the Olympics, guiding the Canadian Women's National Team to the gold medal in Sochi in 2014.

CAMILLE HENRY

One of the more gentlemanly players in history, Henry incurred ten or more penalty minutes in a season only three times in a 16-year career. He was the Calder Trophy winner in 1953-54 and the Lady Byng Trophy winner four years later.

REGGIE LEMELIN

Lemelin patrolled the crease for both the Flames and the Bruins, compiling a 236-162-63 record in 507 appearances. In 1989-90, with Boston, he shared the Jennings Trophy with Andy Moog as the goalie tandem which surrendered the fewest goals in the league.

JOE MALONE

In the NHL's inaugural 1917-18 season, Malone scored an unbelievable 44 goals in just 20 games. He won two Stanley Cups with the Quebec Bulldogs prior to the inception of the NHL. Malone was elected to the Hockey Hall of Fame in 1950.

GERRY McNEIL

McNeil played every minute of every game in the Canadiens net in two consecutive seasons beginning in 1950-51. In 1953, he was named to the Second All-Star Team and also won his only career Stanley Cup.

PATRICK ROY

The legendary goaltender performed at the peak of his game when playing under pressure. Roy is the only player to win three Conn Smythe Trophies as the MVP in the playoffs. His mark of 151 career post-season wins is the best of all-time, and his total of 551 victories in the regular season trails only Martin Brodeur.

Patrick Roy is one of the finest players to have been born in Quebec City.

PAUL STASTNY

A second-round draft pick of the Colorado Avalanche, Stastny had an outstanding rookie season in 2006-07, finishing as the Calder Trophy runner-up to Pittsburgh's Evgeni Malkin. He has represented the United States at three World Championships and also at the 2010 Winter Olympics.

Bowman Wins 9th Cup

William Scott Bowman was simply the greatest coach ever to step behind the bench. Yes, his teams were routinely stocked with Hall of Fame talent. But Bowman was a mastermind at managing and cultivating that talent, while keeping the players sufficiently motivated enough to avoid the so-called Stanley Cup hangover.

Bowman got his first foray into the coaching ranks with the 1967 expansion St. Louis Blues. He guided the team to three straight appearances in the Stanley Cup finals. At the start of the 1971-72 season, he was named coach of the Montreal Canadiens, replacing Al MacNeil. With Jean Beliveau's retirement, the Habs had high expectations for their next potential franchise player, rookie Guy Lafleur.

Montreal built an impregnable dynasty around future Hall of Famers including Lafleur, Jacques Lemaire, Larry Robinson, and Ken Dryden. The team won five championships in eight years under Bowman's guidance, including four Stanley Cups in a row ending in 1979.

The Habs' 1976 dethroning of the Flyers as champions was savoured by hockey fans who loathed Philadelphia's brand of pugilistic hockey. The brutality of the Broad Street Bullies was outdone by skill and speed.

After the 1978-79 season, Bowman moved on to Buffalo to become the Sabres' coach and general manager. He stepped down in 1987, finding work as a television analyst for *Hockey Night In Canada*.

Bowman was inducted into the Hockey Hall of Fame in the Builders' Category in 1991. That fall, he was appointed coach of the defending Stanley Cup champion Pittsburgh Penguins after Bob Johnson passed away. The Penguins, led by the unstoppable duo of Mario Lemieux and Jaromir Jagr, won their second Cup in a row.

After Pittsburgh was upset by the New York Islanders in the 1993 playoffs, Bowman joined the Detroit Red Wings as coach. Throughout his tenure in the Motor City, Bowman was instrumental in assembling a pioneering five-man Russian unit: Sergei Fedorov, Igor Larionov, Vyacheslav Kozlov, Vyacheslav Fetisov, and Vladimir Konstantinov.

Steve Yzerman provided the on-ice leadership as the Red Wings ended a 42-year drought with back-to-back Stanley Cups in 1997 and 1998. The latter victory was Bowman's eighth Stanley Cup, tying him with Toe Blake for top spot on the all-time coaching list.

In Game Five of the 2002 Stanley Cup finals, the Red Wings completed their series victory over the Carolina Hurricanes. Bowman – with his ninth championship – had the record all to himself. Ending his coaching career in style, Bowman strapped on a pair of skates for one final victory lap, raising the Stanley Cup high above his head.

No coach won more Stanley Cups than Scotty Bowman.

The holders of 24 Stanley Cup banners, the Montreal Canadiens stand far and away as hockey's most storied franchise.

The first of the Habs' NHL titles came in 1924, the third-last season that the Stanley Cup was contested between the champions of the NHL and the Western Canada Hockey League. Goaltender Georges Vezina was spectacular in Montreal's two-game sweep over the Calgary Tigers.

Montreal won back-to-back Cups in 1930 and 1931, matching the Ottawa Senators' previously unprecedented feat of repeating as champions. But the Habs suffered through tumul-

Montreal has won the Cup more than any other NHL team.

tuous economic times during the Great Depression and didn't reach the pinnacle of success again until 1944. Led by the Punch Line of Maurice "Rocket" Richard, Elmer Lach, and Toe Blake, the Canadiens swept the Blackhawks in the finals.

Two years later, the Punch Line went head-to-head in the finals against Boston's Kraut Line of Milt Schmidt, Bobby Bauer, and Woody Dumart. Montreal prevailed in five games.

Jacques Plante made his Stanley Cup finals debut in 1953, but coach Dick Irvin replaced Plante with Gerry McNeil in goal

for the last three games of the series. Lach's overtime goal in Game Five was the Cup-winner.

From 1956 to 1960 the Canadiens were the dominant team in the NHL, winning a record five straight Stanley Cups. Legendary players Maurice and Henri Richard, Jean Beliveau, Doug Harvey, and Plante were among the core players of hockey's greatest dynasty. Maurice Richard retired as the game's all-time leading goal scorer after the 1959-60 season.

In 1965, Beliveau became the first-ever winner of the Conn Smythe Trophy as Montreal defeated Chicago for the first of four Stanley Cups within a five-year period. Four years later, after the Habs' sweep of St. Louis in the finals, Serge Savard was the first defenceman ever to be honoured as playoff MVP.

The Habs upset the powerhouse Boston Bruins in the 1971 quarter-finals. With rookie goaltender Ken Dryden having a spectacular play-offs, Montreal won a surprise Stanley Cup, beating Chicago in a seven-game finals series.

Montreal won five more Cups in the decade. The Habs' run of four consecutive championships, ending in 1979, was achieved by a dominant Hall of Fame roster that included Dryden, Guy Lafleur, Jacques Lemaire, Larry Robinson, and Guy Lapointe.

Patrick Roy backstopped the Habs to two more titles. In 1986, the rookie Roy won Conn Smythe honours in a five-game finals win over Calgary. Then, in the 1993 playoffs, Montreal won an incredible ten consecutive games in overtime. Roy was MVP once again as the Canadiens outlasted the Los Angeles Kings for their 24th Stanley Cup.

NHL Adopts 2002 Olympic Rules

The Salt Lake City Olympics resonated differently for hockey fans on both sides of the Canada-United States border.

Canadians rejoiced. Their country won its first gold medal in a half-century. The Americans were dejected. The 5-2 defeat to Canada in the gold-medal game was the first United States Olympic loss at home in 70 years.

However, regardless of international loyalty, fans were at least united in their enjoyment of the 2002 tournament's hurry-up faceoff and line-change rules.

The faceoff procedure provided for the linesman to blow the whistle, then drop the puck within five seconds, whether or not the centremen was ready. If the centre was offside, he was issued a warning. A minor penalty was assessed for any subsequent infractions.

As a result of the hurry-up rules, the games were played at a much higher pace than what NHL fans had been accustomed to seeing. Gone were the obstructions on the faceoffs, or the

The success of certain rules at the 2002 Olympics inspired the NHL to follow IIHF standards.

unnecessary delays caused by players going to the bench for replacement sticks, sometimes legitimately, and sometimes as a stalling tactic.

In their first game of the tournament, Canada seemed unprepared for the faster tempo. The two-line pass, which was also an IIHF rule not seen in the NHL, left Canada unprepared for Sweden's "torpedo" attack using long passes. The result was a 5-2 defeat for the Canadians.

Nevertheless, coach Pat Quinn's squad made the necessary adjustments as the tournament progressed. Their road to the gold-medal game included wins in the quarter-finals and semi-finals versus Finland and Belarus, respectively.

The other nations were also making their way through the new rules. The semi-finals game between long-time rivals the United States and Russia was a classic. Sprinting out to a 3-0 lead, the Americans watched their opponents claw back to within a goal, 3-2. Goalie Mike Richter withstood the onslaught to earn the host country a berth in the gold-medal game. In the final game, Canada had two-goal performances by Joe Sakic and Jarome Iginla to win gold.

The tournament received rave reviews for the expedience at which the games were played. Preliminary round games were finished in two hours, while the medal-round games took only slightly longer. That was a drastic improvement over the pace of NHL games that, at the time, were approaching three hours in length.

Starting in 2002-03, the NHL instituted the hurry-up faceoff rule, while also limiting the length of line changes to five seconds for the visiting team, and eight seconds for the home team. The centre line also vanished for puck movement, allowing two-line passes and opening the game to more offence.

BEST GAME EVER IN QUEBEC CITY April 23, 1985

NORDIQUES VS. CANADIENS

In the 1985 playoffs, the Quebec Nordiques faced the Montreal Canadiens in the Adams Division finals for a second straight year.

The raging bitterness between the combatants in the Battle of Quebec had reached a climax one year earlier. On Good Friday, April 20, 1984, the two teams engaged in two bench-clearing brawls to bookend the second intermission. Montreal eliminated Quebec from the playoffs with a 5-3 win in Game Six.

Seeking to avenge the defeat, the Nordiques kicked off the 1985 series with an overtime win at the Montreal Forum. Mark Kumpel had the game-winner in a 2-1 victory. The Habs took Game Two by a score of 6-4.

Dale Hunter played a vital role in the Nordiques eliminating Montreal in the 1985 playoffs.

As the series shifted to Le Colisee for the next two games, the venue favoured the Canadiens. Quebec had lost all four of its home games against Montreal during the regular season. Nordiques defenceman Brad Maxwell suggested that he and his teammates should have been less focused on the pugilistic side of the game during his team's defeats versus the Habs at home.

"There's a lot of bad blood between these two teams going back to the playoffs last year," Maxwell told the *Associated Press.* "All year, we were trying to beat this guy up or stick that guy, and that maybe didn't help us."

The goals in the third game came fast and furious. Anton Stastny opened the scoring for Quebec in the first period before Montreal replied with two power play goals, courtesy of Mats Naslund and Bobby Smith. Michel Goulet evened the score at 2-2 before the intermission.

After Guy Carbonneau and Goulet, with his second tally, exchanged second-period goals, Bobby Smith notched a controversial, go-ahead marker. The Nordiques protested, to no avail, that the puck entered the net from underneath the goal frame. Immediately after the goal, enforcers Steve Rooney of Montreal and Jimmy Mann of Quebec engaged in a fight and were summarily ejected.

Goulet completed his hat trick in the third period to tie the score. Bruce Bell gave the Nordiques the lead before the Habs' Mike McPhee counted two goals in as many minutes to tilt the game in Montreal's favour. Wilf Paiement scored for Quebec to knot the affair at 6-6 and force overtime.

At the 18:36 mark of the extra session Quebec's Dale Hunter, his face scarred from a first period fight against Chris Nilan, beat goalie Steve Penney with a low shot to win the game. The Nordiques went on to take the series in seven games. Peter Stastny had the winning goal in Game Seven at the Forum.

Heritage Classic in Edmonton

Outdoor hockey dates as far back as the sport's origin in the 19th century when the game developed on frozen ponds and rivers. At the first Winter Olympics in 1924 in Chamonix, France – the second Olympics to feature hockey – the games were played outdoors on natural ice.

The NHL's first outdoor game was played in Edmonton, against Montreal.

In 2001, the "Cold War" game was held at Spartan Stadium, home to Michigan State University. The Spartans hosted the rival University of Michigan Wolverines in front of 74,554 fans who braved the frigid elements.

Impressed, the NHL went beyond the confines of arena walls. On November 22, 2003, the league staged its first regular-season outdoor game. The Heritage Classic was held at Edmonton's Commonwealth Stadium between the Oilers and the Montreal Canadiens.

In the days leading up to the game, the city of Edmonton was pelted with snowstorms, and organizers feared a postponement. Fortunately, by game day, Mother Nature had calmed down, but although there was no falling snow, the thermometer had dipped to -30 degrees Celsius thanks to a nasty wind chill.

Before the NHL game came an exhibition game featuring alumni from both clubs. Undoubtedly the biggest name on the undercard was Wayne Gretzky's. The "Great One" had retired four years earlier and had said shortly afterwards that he would never play in an "oldtimers" game. But for this historic event in Edmonton, he made an exception.

"Back then I said 'never,'" Gretzky told ESPN.com. "Now, I'm saying, 'never say never.'"

The alumni rosters featured a veritable plethora of Hall of Famers including Gretzky, Grant Fuhr, and Jari Kurri for the Oilers, and Guy Lafleur, Steve Shutt, and Larry Robinson for the Habs. Mark Messier, still an active player with the Rangers,

obtained special permission from New York coach Glen Sather to participate. Ken Linesman and Marty McSorley scored, while Fuhr and Bill Ranford combined for the shutout in a 2-0 Oilers win.

From there, the puck dropped on game number 290 of the NHL season. Several players wore balaclavas to fight the biting temperatures. One of the most memorable photos of the game depicts Montreal goaltender Jose Theodore wearing a toque over top of his mask while a foggy cloud emanates from his mouth as he exhales, clear evidence of the numbing conditions.

Richard Zednik of the Habs had two goals including the game-winner, as the Canadiens edged the Oilers, 4-3.

But for 57,167 spectators in Edmonton, the loss was an afterthought. The unforgettable event paved the way for many outdoor games to follow.

Edmonton's **HALL OF FAMERS**

Players

Glenn Anderson, 2008

Paul Coffey, 2004

Grant Fuhr, 2003

Wayne Gretzky, 1999

Jari Kurri, 2001

Mark Messier, 2007

Builders

Glen Sather, 1997

The smooth-skating Paul Coffey was an easy choice for induction into the Hockey Hall of Fame.

A young Jari Kurri joined the Oilers and became the highest scoring European in NHL history.

Steve Moore Attacked

The hockey mentality of frontier justice, often referred to as 'the code,' produced one of the most violent moments in the history of the sport. In the aftermath, a player's career ended.

There was bitter animosity between the Vancouver Canucks and Colorado Avalanche heading into their game on March 8, 2004, at General Motors Place in Vancouver. Three weeks earlier in Denver, controversy arose when Colorado's Steve Moore checked Vancouver captain Markus Naslund. Although no in-game penalty or supplemental discipline was issued to Moore, Naslund missed three games with a concussion.

The outraged Canucks players vowed revenge. Brad May placed a bounty on Moore's head. Amidst much speculation of potential retribution by Vancouver, NHL commissioner Gary Bettman attended the next game between the two clubs on March 3. The incident-free outing ended in a 5-5 draw.

But on March 8, the on-ice war escalated. The Canucks pounded Moore at every turn. Matt Cooke engaged Moore in a fight 6:36 into the game. Meanwhile, the Avalanche were making a rout of the game, further increasing the probability of an ugly incident. Moore was pestered by May and Jarkko Ruutu throughout the evening.

As the eight-minute mark of the third period approached, Colorado had long since put the game out of reach with an 8-2 lead. Vancouver power forward Todd Bertuzzi – who three weeks earlier referred to Moore in derogatory terms – began targeting Moore, shadowing the Avalanche player and trying to goad him into another fight. Moore ignored Bertuzzi, declining the challenge and by so doing, enraging him.

As he released his stick while grabbing Moore's sweater with his left hand, Bertuzzi sucker-punched Moore from behind with a right fist to the face. Both players fell to the ice, Bertuzzi on top of Moore. Colorado's Andrei Nikolishin joined

the pile-up, and a line brawl ensued. But as the players squared off, Moore lay motionless on the ice for nearly ten minutes. A stretcher was summoned to wheel him off the ice.

Bertuzzi was suspended indefinitely, missing the final 13 games of the regular season as well as the playoffs. His ban carried into the 2004-05 season that was eventually cancelled because of the NHL lockout.

The consequences for Moore were far more severe. He had suffered multiple fractures in his vertebrae and incurred a severe concussion. Despite his best efforts to resume his career, Moore was forced to retire.

On August 19, 2014, more than a decade after the attack, Moore reached an out-of-court settlement with Bertuzzi after years of acrimonious litigation.

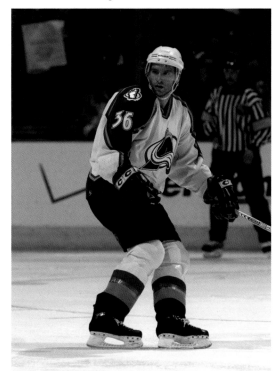

A dark day in the NHL was Todd Bertuzzi's unforgivable attack on Steve Moore.

Vancouver's Biggest Trades

TOP TRADE

JUNE 26, 1999 Vancouver trades its 1st overall draft choice to Atlanta for 2nd overall choice (Daniel Sedin) and a conditional 3rd-round draft choice (Henrik Sedin)

In a masterful series of wheeling and dealing, Canucks general manager Brian Burke orchestrated three separate but related transactions on the draft floor in 1999. The last of these manoeuvres landed Burke in the enviable position of holding the second and third overall selections.

Atlanta had its sights on forward Patrick Stefan, whom the Thrashers chose with the top pick. Burke then approached the draft table with a pair of Canucks sweaters in hand, selecting the highly-touted twins from Ornksoldsvik, Sweden, Daniel and Henrik Sedin.

The brothers had made it clear to all prospective teams that their wish was to play together. Vancouver fans quickly understood their desire after watching the Sedins' mutual understanding of each other's position on the ice, creating highlight-reel goals with tape-to-tape passes that could only come from their innate sibling chemistry.

In 2010 and 2011, the Sedins' made history. Henrik and then Daniel won scoring titles, becoming the first brothers to achieve the feat in consecutive seasons.

Burke had to make preceding deals with Chicago and Tampa Bay to land the coveted selections, trading Bryan McCabe and several high draft picks of his own. But as the Sedins have evolved into the top two scorers in Canucks' history, there's no debate about the success of the grand plan.

HONOURABLE MENTION

MARCH 20, 1996 Pittsburgh Penguins trade Markus Naslund to Vancouver for Alek Stojanov

The late Pat Quinn landed Markus Naslund for the Canucks in one of the most one-sided deals in NHL history. The Vancouver general manager noticed that Naslund was being under-used in Pittsburgh, so he offered Alek Stojanov to the Penguins in exchange.

Naslund represented Sweden at both the World Championships and World Cup of Hockey in 1996 and quickly developed into a consistent scorer. In 1998-99, he had 36 goals and played in his first NHL All-Star Game. Three years later, he was once again wearing the blue and gold colours of Tre Kronor, having been granted the honour of playing in the 2002 Olympics in Salt Lake City.

In 2002-03, Naslund was the runner-up in the scoring race on the way to winning the Lester B. Pearson Award. By the time Naslund signed as a free agent with the Rangers in 2008, he was the Canucks' franchise leader in career points with 756.

The Sedin twins (Henrik is on the left) brought offensive consistency to Vancouver.

Canada's Best World Juniors

The NHL regrettably suffered two lengthy lockouts in ten years. The 1994-95 season was cut nearly in half as a result, while the 2004-05 campaign was cancelled in its entirety.

In both cases, the league's loss was Team Canada's gain. With a windfall of talent available to nations at the World Junior Championship – under-20 stars who would otherwise be playing in the NHL – teams were opportunistic in stacking their rosters. Canada was by far the greatest beneficiary.

The 1995 Canadian junior squad that won gold in Red Deer, Alberta, was one of the best teams ever assembled. The host nation posted a 7-0-0 record, outscoring its opponents, 49-22. Yet as remarkable as it was, the 2005 edition of Team Canada was even more dominant.

Canada was mired in a seven-year gold medal drought, an unprecedented slump for the country since the tournament's

The NHL lockout of 2004-05 gave Canada an awesome roster for the 2005 World Juniors, including Patrice Bergeron (above).

inception in 1977, but in 2005 the team was coached by Red Deer Rebels owner and NHL alumnus Brent Sutter.

Forward Patrice Bergeron was expected to be one of the cornerstones on offence. He had won a gold medal on Canada's senior team the previous year, becoming the first Canadian to play in the World Championships before playing in the under-20 tournament. Bergeron would surely have been playing for his draft team – the Boston Bruins – if not for the lockout.

The 2005 tournament was held in Grand Forks, North Dakota, an hour's drive from the Manitoba border. As thousands of fans draped in red and white made the trek from the Great White North, the U.S. venue was effectively a Canadian "hometown."

Joining Bergeron on the top line was highly-touted junior phenom, Sidney Crosby. Considered a sure-fire first-overall draft pick, the 17-year-old Crosby was part of the Canadian squad that lost a heartbreaking gold-medal game to the United States in 2004.

There was no stopping the Canadians this time, however. Not even young Russian prospect Alex Ovechkin could find an answer for his team in the gold-medal game, a 6-1 pasting by the Canadians. With a perfect 6-0-0 record, Canada – which scored 41 goals compared to a mere seven by the opposition – finally ascended to the top of the junior hockey podium again.

How far ahead were the Canadians of the competition? Consider that the top six forwards—Crosby, Bergeron, Corey Perry, Jeff Carter, Ryan Getzlaf, and Mike Richards—have each gone on to win both a Stanley Cup and an Olympic gold medal. When the lockout ended, 14 of the team's members played in the NHL the next year.

No greater international junior squad has ever been assembled.

The All-Star Game in
Edmonton

★ ★ ★

FEBRUARY 7, 1989

This was Wayne Gretzky's ninth career All-Star appearance and, ironically, he was not representing the Oilers. Instead, the "Great One," having been dealt to Los Angeles the previous summer in a blockbuster trade, was now a member of the Kings.

Once again, Gretzky displayed his unmatched offensive talents before an appreciative, deafening crowd at Northlands Colisuem, the rink that he had called home for nine seasons as he guided Edmonton to four Stanley Cups.

It was Gretzky's second game in Edmonton since the trade. He had made his first visit in a Kings sweater on October 19, 1988, in an 8-6 Oilers victory.

Number 99 was given the "C," and reunited with right-winger Jari Kurri on the Campbell Conference top line created by coach Glen Sather. Gretzky's current linemate Luc Robitaille was on the left wing, and it took just 67 seconds for the dynamic trio to connect. Kurri beat Wales goalie Reggie Lemelin of Boston for the game's opening goal, Gretzky and Robitaille getting the assists.

Five Oilers dressed for the hometown game: forwards Kurri, Mark Messier, and Jimmy Carson, Kevin Lowe on defence, and Grant Fuhr in goal. The Campbells used a balanced attack to roll to a 9-5 victory over the Wales All-Stars. Joe Mullen of Calgary scored twice while each Oilers forward also found the back of the net. The Wales offence was led by Quebec's Walt Poddubny, who had two goals. Their captain, Larry Robinson, chipped in with two assists.

Both honourary captains were Edmonton natives: Hall of Famer Norm Ullman and NHL alumnus Bruce MacGregor, who played 893 career games in 15 seasons with the Detroit Red Wings and New York Rangers.

There was much excitement about the possibility of Mario Lemieux of the Wales being able to keep his torrid pace during the season. Lemieux was not only leading the NHL in scoring but was also on pace to beat Gretzky's single-season record of 215 points, set in 1985-86.

But the showdown between the game's two greatest offensive stars was lop-sided. Lemieux was held to just one assist, while Gretzky scored once and had two helpers on the way to being named the game's most valuable player. The "Great One" was rewarded with a new car for his efforts, which he promptly gave to former teammate Dave Semenko.

Lemieux finished the season with 199 points, his career-best total but one shy of joining Gretzky as the only member of the 200-point club.

*Jari Kurri was one of many Oilers to play in
the All-Star Game in Edmonton in 1989.*

Lockout Cancels 2004-05 Season

The NHL has the ignominious distinction of being the only North American professional sports league to cancel an entire season because of a labour dispute. The long-anticipated and much-maligned standoff between the players and the owners left 30 arenas devoid of professional hockey for over a year and tarnished the sport's reputation.

Even as the Tampa Bay Lightning hoisted the Stanley Cup in June 2004, and the World Cup of Hockey was staged three months later, there was a prevailing pessimism for an immediate start to the season following the expiration of the Collective Bargaining Agreement on September 15, 2004.

The key point of contention was the NHL's intent to impose a salary cap, and the NHLPA's adamant resistance to it. Commissioner Gary Bettman and the owners billed their philosophy as establishing "cost certainty." Bettman was also campaigning for "linkage" between league revenues and player salaries.

U.S. Securities & Exchange chairman Arthur Levitt estimated that the league had lost $273-million during the 2002-03 season. Levitt stated that only eleven teams turned in a profit during that fiscal period. But the NHLPA—led by executive director Bob Goodenow—repeatedly questioned the accuracy of the league's numbers.

"It is clear the Levitt report, commissioned by the League, is fundamentally flawed when the author "elects" to define hockey revenues on the same basis as used in the NBA and NFL for defining revenues in their salary cap systems," Goodenow said in a statement.

Both sides dug in their heels for a long, protracted fight. The NHL had $300-million in its coffers to offset expenses in the event of a cancelled season. Meanwhile, the players were prepared to sit out not only the current season but the next one as well.

Some 400 NHL players went to play hockey in Europe during the stalemate. Their presence overseas only fuelled further controversy as a result of taking roster spots from players in those leagues.

Each passing month reduced the probability of staging a meaningful season. By February, the length of a best-case-scenario was 28 games, hardly a "season" at all. Bettman put forth a "final" offer of a $42.5-million salary cap, with no linkage, and imposed a deadline of 11:00 am on February 16, 2005, but the NHLPA wouldn't come off its $49-million figure that it had most recently presented.

As a result, Bettman announced the cancellation of the entire 2004-05 season. The lockout prevented the awarding of the Stanley Cup for the first time since 1919 when the influenza epidemic prevented the Cup finals from being completed.

"The best deal that was on the table is now gone," said Bettman. "We weren't as close as people were speculating. We were still very far apart."

The Hockey Hall of Fame had no choice but to recognize the absence of a winner of the Stanley Cup in 2004-05.

Winnipeg's CAPTAINS

(1979-80 to 1995-96)

Lars-Erik Sjoberg, 1979-80

Morris Lukowich and Scott Campbell, 1980-81

Dave Christian and Barry Long, 1981-82

Dave Christian and Lucien DeBlois, 1982-83

Lucien DeBlois, 1983-84

Dale Hawerchuk, 1984-85 to 1988-89

Randy Carlyle, Dale Hawerchuk and Thomas Steen
(tri-captains), 1989-90

Randy Carlyle and Thomas Steen
(co-captains), 1990-91

Troy Murray, 1991-92

Troy Murray and Dean Kennedy, 1992-93

Dean Kennedy and Keith Tkachuk, 1993-94

Keith Tkachuk, 1994-95

Kris King, 1995-96

(2011-12 to 2014-15)

Andrew Ladd, 2010-11 to 2014-15

Sweden's Lars-Erik Sjoberg was the first-ever European captain of an NHL team when he was given the "C" by the Winnipeg Jets in 1979.

Shane Doan has been a lifetime member of the Winnipeg/Phoenix/Arizona franchise.

Lockout Ends With Salary Cap

After the cancellation of the 2004-05 season in February 2005, the acrimony between the NHL and the NHLPA was compounded when the league began hinting at the potential use of replacement players.

In March, the league filed an unfair labour practice charge with the National Labour Relations Board in the United States. The NHL's contention was that an NHLPA policy that withheld work-stoppage benefits payable to replacement players was a violation of players' rights.

"The practice of conditioning the receipt of work-stoppage benefits on a player's agreement not to return to the NHL without a new CBA was coercive and in violation of the player's rights under the labour laws," Bill Daly, the NHL's chief legal officer said. The union responded by saying that the league's allegations were 'without merit.'

Negotiations for a new collective bargaining agreement progressed throughout the spring. In mid-April, the league held a Board of Governors' meeting after which it surprisingly retracted its threat of the use of replacement players.

The two sides came to the bargaining table more than thirty times in May and June. Finally, on July 13, the NHL and NHLPA signed a new CBA, ending the longest work stoppage in North American sports history.

A salary cap, which players fought so profoundly to avoid for many years, was now in place. The cap was set at $39-million per team, and no player could earn more than 20 per cent of his team's cap. Additionally, the agreement provided for linkage between league revenues and player salaries; the players were guaranteed to receive 54 per cent of NHL revenues.

All existing contracts were rolled back by 24 per cent, and 2004-05 contract years were nullified. Under the terms of the six-year deal, the NHLPA had the right to either terminate it after four years or extend it to a seventh year.

Although the historic agreement was a clear victory for the owners, the players earned a concession under the revised terms of unrestricted free agency. The age at which a player could move to another team without compensation was lowered from 31 to 27.

With the new deal in place, the economic landscape of the league was completely overhauled. Teams in smaller cities immediately negotiated with big-name players. Columbus and Nashville signed Adam Foote and Paul Kariya, respectively, and Edmonton traded for superstar defenceman Chris Pronger.

The NHLPA extended the agreement to the end of the 2012 season. Unfortunately, for the league and its fans, yet another stoppage cancelled almost half the games the following year.

Bob Goodenow fought to avoid a salary cap. He lost.

Toronto Milestones

MOST SEASONS GEORGE ARMSTRONG (21)

Armstrong played a franchise-high 1,187 career games with the Leafs while wearing the "C" for 12 seasons. He captained the team to four Stanley Cup titles, the last of which came in 1967. No other player in Leafs history has participated in more playoff games than Armstrong, who has 110 post-season appearances to his credit.

Mats Sundin defined the Leafs during his 13 years with the team.

MOST POINTS MATS SUNDIN (987)

Acquired from the Quebec Nordiques in a 1994 blockbuster for Wendel Clark and Sylvain Lefebvre, Sundin proudly held the Leafs' captaincy for ten seasons, ending in 2007-08. Carrying the franchise on his shoulders, he led the team in scoring in all but one of his 13 seasons wearing a Toronto uniform.

Sundin helped lead Sweden to a gold medal at the 2006 Winter Olympics. In 2012, Sundin followed his countryman and idol Borje Salming into the Hockey Hall of Fame. The Leafs legends were the first two Swedes to be inducted.

MOST WINS TURK BRODA (302)

A two-time Vezina Trophy winner and three-time All-Star Team selection, Broda would certainly have achieved even greater statistical totals had he not served for two years in the military during World War II. He played every minute of the regular season and playoffs from 1946-47 to 1948-49 as Toronto became the first team ever to win three consecutive Stanley Cups.

Prior to the 1949 season, Leafs owner Conn Smythe challenged Broda to drop his weight from 197 pounds to 190. The media dubbed the ultimatum as the "Battle of the Bulge." Broda subsisted on a diet of grapefruit and eggs to succeed in the initiative.

MOST PENALTY MINUTES TIE DOMI (2,265)

The long-time Leafs pugilist was the focal point of more than a few infamous altercations. In October, 1995, Domi was suspended for eight games for sucker-punching Ulf Samuelsson of the Rangers. Five-and-a-half years later, Domi landed a vicious elbow to the head of New Jersey's Scott Niedermayer in the 2001 playoffs. He was suspended for the remainder of the post-season.

MILESTONES AND RECORDS

Mats Sundin scored his 500th career goal on October 14, 2006, against the Calgary Flames. The short-handed overtime tally completed a hat trick. Sundin registered his 1,000th NHL point on March 10, 2003, with a goal versus Edmonton.

Five other players have recorded their 1,000th career NHL point while with the Leafs: Norm Ullman, Glenn Anderson, Doug Gilmour, defenceman Larry Murphy, and Alex Mogilny.

Darryl Sittler scored a record ten points in one game, collecting six goals and four assists in an 11-4 Toronto romp over Boston, on February 7, 1976.

Lemieux and Crosby United

There was no question as to who would be the first player selected at the 2005 NHL Entry Draft. However, determining which team would be lucky enough to land the projected franchise star was a complex undertaking.

Sidney Crosby was not only the favourite first-overall pick; he was also heralded as the game's next potential dominant player. The Cole Harbour, Nova Scotia, native registered 168 points in 62 regular-season games in what turned out to be his final junior season, leading the Rimouski Oceanic to the Memorial Cup finals.

Under the terms of the newly-minted collective bargaining agreement that ended the ten-month NHL lockout, all 30 teams had a chance at acquiring the first-overall pick via a lottery. The probabilities were weighted in order of finish to give teams that had missed the most playoff berths in the previous three seasons a greater, proportional chance of winning.

An 18-year-old Sidney Crosby played with team owner and teammate Mario Lemieux.

The draft lottery was conducted in a much-anticipated, made-for-television event on July 22. When the first 28 teams were eliminated from contention, the drama reached its apex. Either Pittsburgh or Anaheim would win the Crosby sweepstakes.

Commissioner Gary Bettman produced the deciding envelope inscribed with the Penguins logo. An elated Pittsburgh CEO Ken Sawyer shook hands with Ducks general manager Brian Burke to conclude the proceedings. The selection of Crosby by the Penguins, eight days later in Ottawa at the Entry Draft itself, was a mere formality.

To no one's surprise, Crosby made the team out of training camp. The rookie took up residence with the family of Mario Lemieux, Pittsburgh's owner and team captain. On October 5, Crosby and Lemieux were in the lineup in a road game against the New Jersey Devils. Pittsburgh lost, 5-1, in its first post-lockout game. Crosby collected his first career NHL point, assisting on a Mark Recchi goal.

Crosby's most celebrated goal in his freshman season came in a shootout versus Montreal. With the game tied, 2-2, Lemieux had already been denied by Habs goalie Jose Theodore in the shootout.

Sporting his number 87, Crosby was summoned to try to end the game. Skating towards the net, Crosby snapped his right leg in the air to distract Theodore, then deked the goaltender, lifting the puck to the top of the net on a backhander. The puck popped Theodore's water bottle off the top of the net, an exclamation mark on a great play.

Crosby and Lemieux played as teammates for 24 games. Lemieux was diagnosed with an irregular heartbeat in December and retired six weeks later. But the torch in Pittsburgh had already been passed to the team's next cornerstone player.

For 15 years, Quebec's two hockey teams were as divisive as the cities that they represented. It was Francophone-based Quebec City versus bilingual Montreal; the fledgling WHA team against the NHL's most storied and historic franchise; the Carling O'Keefe-owned Nordiques against the Molson-owned Canadiens.

When the NHL realigned for the 1981-82 season, the Nordiques and Habs were both placed in the Adams Division. The league also altered its playoff format to bracket the first two rounds within each division, thus intensifying geographic rivalries.

For the first time ever, Quebec and Montreal clashed in the post-season in 1982. The best-of-five, division semi-final went the distance. Game Four featured a first period brawl, a scene re-enacted between the clubs on numerous occasions. In the deciding game, Dale Hunter scored 22 seconds into overtime to win the series for the Nordiques.

Two years later, the teams staged a full-scale exhibition of brutality in what is known as the Good Friday Massacre. In Game Six of division finals, the second period ended in a bench-clearing brawl. Tempers flared when Quebec's Louis Sleigher knocked out Montreal's Jean Hamel with a punch to the face.

Referee Bruce Hood issued a plethora of game misconducts. When the teams returned from the intermission, they were joined by the players who had been ejected, a harbinger of more violence. Inevitably, the teams renewed hostilities before the puck was dropped to start the final 20 minutes. Another brawl erupted, resulting in more mayhem. The ice was littered with an array of sticks and gloves after the fisticuffs had ceased.

Altogether ten players were ejected and 252 penalty minutes were assessed. The game finished with shortened benches as a result of all the expulsions. Montreal eliminated Quebec with a 5-3 victory.

The Nordiques avenged the defeat the following year. Their second round matchup against the Habs again went the full seven games. The hard-fought, decisive game went into overtime where Peter Stastny silenced the Montreal Forum crowd, finding a loose rebound for the series-winner.

Two years later, in 1987, the Quebec rivals duelled once again. A controversial call went against the Nordiques in Game Five when Alain Cote's apparent go-ahead tally was disallowed because of goalie interference. Moments later, Montreal's Ryan Walter notched the game-winner. The Habs took the series in seven games.

In 1993, the Canadiens fell behind two games to none in the first round before reeling off four straight wins. Two of those victories came in overtime, sparking Montreal's miraculous, record-setting run of ten consecutive overtime wins in a single post-season.

No rivalry in sports had more animosity than Montreal's with Quebec.

Shootouts in 2005

Purists have come to loathe the shootout as a means of deciding games. The argument is that reducing the tie-breaker to just a single shooter and goalie while eliminating every other facet of the sport is gimmicky and amounts to nothing more than a skills competition.

Canadians weren't enamoured at losing the 1994 Olympic gold-medal game to Sweden in a shootout, particularly NHL fans who were accustomed to seeing playoff games extended to multiple overtimes.

On the other hand, proponents of the shootout were drawn by the element of excitement inherent in watching a glorified "penalty-shot contest." If the penalty shot is one of the most exciting plays in hockey, then why not create more of those dramatic situations?

Coming out of the 2005 lockout, the NHL sided with the advocates. Beginning in 2005, the NHL instituted the shootout as a tiebreaker for games that were still deadlocked after five-minutes of sudden-death overtime. The winning team still received two points in the standings; the loser one.

Unlike the IIHF's five-shooter standard, the NHL decided to use three skaters each before moving on to a sudden-death format if the shootout was still tied.

The first shootout in league history took place on opening night at Toronto's Air Canada Centre as the Maple Leafs renewed hostilities with their provincial rivals, the Ottawa Senators. The teams battled to a 2-2 tie followed by a scoreless overtime.

Senators captain Daniel Alfredsson was the first player to shoot. Alfredsson shot low to the glove side and beat Leafs goalie Ed Belfour to give Ottawa the edge. The first Toronto player to shoot was Jason Allison. He was denied on a deke attempt against Dominik Hasek. Critics suggested that Allison skated far too slowly on the attempt.

In the second round, Martin Havlat (Ottawa) and Eric Lindros (Toronto) were both unsuccessful. Dany Heatley salted the game away by successfully shooting at Belfour in much the same manner as Alfredsson had. Since the Senators never trailed in the shootout at any point, Alfredsson, whose goal gave Ottawa the lead they never relinquished, earned credit for the shootout winner.

Shootout goals were not credited towards the players' regular-season statistics, nor were goalies' save percentages or goals against-averages affected.

By 2015, however, it had become clear that teams didn't settle very many games in overtime any more, and the shootout had become far too influential in deciding rankings in the standings. The gimmick now had playoff ramifications, and general managers were unhappy. There was talk about doing more to produce overtime wins and even suggestions of abandoning the shootout.

After losing a year to the lockout, the NHL instituted the shootout for 2005-06 in the hopes of entertaining fans.

Small-Town Canadian Heroes

SHEA WEBER, SICAMOUS, BRITISH COLUMBIA

A stalwart on the blue line for both Team Canada and the Nashville Predators, Weber is one of the most feared defenders in the game. He won Olympic gold medals in both 2010 and 2014.

GRANT FUHR, SPRUCE GROVE, ALBERTA

During the Oilers' dynasty of the 1980s Fuhr was the goaltender for four of the team's Stanley Cup titles. He also played in all nine games for Team Canada's winning squad at the 1987 Canada Cup.

MAX BENTLEY, DELISLE, SASKATCHEWAN

Bentley was part of the Blackhawks' Pony Line with his brother Doug and Bill Mosienko. Just one year after winning the 1946 Hart Trophy with Chicago, Max was traded to Toronto in a blockbuster swap for five other players.

ED BELFOUR, CARMAN, MANITOBA

The Hall of Famer won four Jennings Trophies and was a three-time All-Star Team selection over 17 NHL seasons. He backstopped Dallas to a Stanley Cup win in 1999.

CHRIS PRONGER, DRYDEN, ONTARIO

Pronger's best season was in 1999-2000 when he earned both the Hart and Norris Trophies as captain of the St. Louis Blues. By winning a Stanley Cup in 2007 with Anaheim, Pronger completed his membership in the IIHF's Triple Gold Club.

ALEX TANGUAY, STE. JUSTINE, QUEBEC

The NHL's only player to hail from Ste. Justine, Tanguay has a distant bloodline to Roch Carrier, author of "The Hockey Sweater." The children's story has been made into a popular animated story by the National Film Board.

LUC BOURDON, SHIPPAGAN, NEW BRUNSWICK

Bourdon won gold medals with Canada at the World Junior Hockey Championship in 2006 and 2007. Tragically he lost his life in a motorcycle accident on May 29, 2008, at age 21.

AL MacINNIS, PORT HOOD, NOVA SCOTIA

Born in neighbouring Inverness, MacInnis possessed the hardest slap shot in the game, instilling fear into opposing goalies and defenders. The Norris and Conn Smythe Trophy winner was inducted into the Hockey Hall of Fame in 2007.

BRAD RICHARDS, MURRAY HARBOUR, PRINCE EDWARD ISLAND

En route to winning the 2004 Stanley Cup with Tampa Bay, Richards set an NHL record with seven, game-winning goals in one playoff year. He was named playoff MVP for his efforts.

ALEX FAULKNER, BISHOP'S FALLS, NEWFOUNDLAND

Faulkner became the first Newfoundlander to play in the NHL, in 1961. He played one game with Toronto before joining the Red Wings for two seasons.

GEOFF SANDERSON, HAY RIVER, NORTHWEST TERRITORIES

In a career that spanned 16 seasons, Sanderson played 1,104 NHL games. He won two World Championships with Team Canada in 2004 and 2007.

JORDIN TOOTOO, RANKING INLET, NUNAVUT

The Manitoba-born, Nunavut-raised draft pick of the Nashville Predators won a silver medal with Canada's junior team in 2003. Tootoo has battled substance abuse problems on the way to playing over 600 career NHL games.

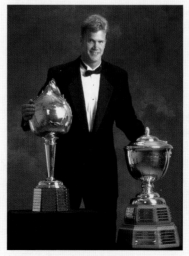

Chris Pronger was a big defenceman who came from a small town and proved victorious wherever he played.

Ovi Scores on His Back

Washington Capitals superstar Alex Ovechkin has electrified hockey fans for a decade with his combination of speed, shot, and skill. The NHL's first-overall draft pick in 2004, Ovechkin had to wait a year before making his professional debut as a result of the league's season-long lockout in 2004-05.

Russia's Alexander Ovechkin has scored many highlight-reel goals, none greater than one in his rookie season.

When league play resumed in the fall of 2005, Ovechkin and Pittsburgh's Sidney Crosby were the early favourites for the Calder Trophy. The two players had duelled in the gold-medal game at the 2005 World Junior Championship, but the game was a mismatch in as much as Canada dominated the game and won handily, 6-1.

However, the 20-year-old Ovechkin had an advantage over Crosby by virtue of being two years older than the Pittsburgh teen. Nevertheless, the two freshmen battled for every vote in the rookie-of-the-year race.

Crosby made his presence felt with the signature goal of his rookie season, a November shootout winner against Montreal that knocked the water bottle off the net. Among Ovechkin's many highlights of the 2005-06 season, one goal resonates as his defining moment. It's a play that is replayed on sports highlights reels even now, a decade later.

In the third period of Washington's game in Phoenix on January 16, 2006, the Capitals built a commanding 5-1 lead over the Coyotes. Ovechkin had already scored once in the first period and had added an assist in the game. His second goal of the night was a performance of pure magic.

Streaking into the Coyotes' zone down the right wing, Ovechkin had his path to the goal blocked by Phoenix defenceman Paul Mara. As Ovechkin cut to the middle of the ice, Mara knocked him down, sending him sprawling on his back.

However, Ovechkin was still able to maintain possession of the puck. As he was sliding towards the corner boards on his back, he extended his stick along the ice just far enough above his head to slide a one-handed backhand shot from an almost impossible angle into the Phoenix net. Coyotes goalie Brian Boucher, along with the spectators at Glendale Arena, could only marvel in awe. And among those in awe was Coyotes coach Wayne Gretzky, who knew a thing or two about great goals.

Ovechkin scored a total of 52 goals and 106 points in his rookie year and went on to an easy Calder Trophy victory. His scoring has yet to abate. On March 31, 2015, Ovechkin became just the sixth player in NHL history to record six seasons of 50 goals or more.

Quebec's Biggest Trades

▶ TOP TRADE

JUNE 30, 1992 Quebec Nordiques trade Eric Lindros to Philadelphia for Peter Forsberg, Steve Duchesne, Kerry Huffman, Mike Ricci, Ron Hextall, a 1st-round draft choice in 1993 (Jocelyn Thibault) a 1st-round draft choice in 1994 (Nolan Baumgartner), future considerations (Chris Simon), and $15 million

Eric Lindros steadfastly refused to wear a Nordiques sweater after the club selected him first overall at the 1991 NHL Entry Draft. The top pick had pleaded with Quebec general manager Pierre Page not to take him, wishing instead to start his career in a larger hockey city and away from Quebec's volatile political landscape.

But Page wasn't about to pass on the opportunity to draft a potential franchise player or trade him away. With neither side budging, Lindros held out of training camp, joining Team Canada's Olympic squad for the 1991-92 season. Canada's entry won a silver medal at the Games in Albertville, France.

Almost a year to the day that he became Nordiques property, Lindros was traded to Philadelphia in a blockbuster trade. Number 88 was a dominant force on the Flyers for eight seasons, winning a Hart Trophy in 1994-95 and leading his club to the Stanley Cup finals in 1997.

Using the many players they received in this trade, the Nordiques assembled a team which won two Stanley Cups, in 1996 and 2001. Forsberg, a 2014 Hockey Hall of Fame inductee, also won two Olympic gold medals and two World Championship golds, the first player in hockey history to earn Triple Gold Club status twice.

HONOURABLE MENTION

JUNE 28, 1994 Quebec trades Mats Sundin, Garth Butcher, Todd Warriner, and a 1st-round draft choice in 1994 (Nolan Baumgartner) to Toronto for Wendel Clark, Sylvain Lefebvre, Landon Wilson, and a 1st-round draft choice in 1994 (Jeff Kealty)

The Nordiques made Mats Sundin the first-overall pick in 1989 and the first European in the history of the draft to be so chosen. The tall Swede compiled a career-best 114 points in 1992-93 but had earned the ire of Quebec coach Pierre Page. The Swede needed a change of scenery.

In Wendel Clark, Quebec received a bruising left-winger with a lethal wrist shot, but whose style of play also left him susceptible to injuries. The Nordiques also obtained reliable, stay-at-home defenceman Sylvain Lefebvre. Clark was subsequently dealt in a three-way trade in which Claude Lemieux ended up in Quebec. Both Lefebvre and Lemieux won a Stanley Cup with the franchise after it transferred to Colorado in 1995-96.

Sundin became Toronto's consummate leader on the way to a Hall of Fame career. In 13 seasons in a Leafs uniform, Sundin set all-time franchise records for goals and points. He led Toronto in scoring twelve times and is the NHL's highest-scoring Swedish-born player of all time.

The best thing that ever happened to the Quebec Nordiques was Eric Lindros's refusal to play for them and the trade that ensued.

Leafs-Wings Take it Outside

An outdoor game between long-time rivals Toronto and Detroit had been scheduled for New Year's Day 2013, but it was postponed because of an NHL lockout.

However, the patience of fans on both sides of the Ambassador Bridge was duly rewarded when the 2014 Winter Classic between the Leafs and Red Wings was finally staged at Michigan Stadium on January 1 of that year.

Despite the accumulating snow and several shovel delays, 105,491 fans cheered from the stands at the Ann Arbor football venue, shivering in their seats as the temperatures plummeted to -12 degrees Celsius.

The continuous snowfall not only obscured the ice markings but made for difficult puck manoeuvring. Indeed, it took over 33 minutes for the game's opening goal to be scored off the stick of Detroit's Daniel Alfredsson, the Leafs' nemesis and former Senators captain.

But Toronto fans who made the border trek gained redemption when James van Riemsdyk tied the score with less than 37 seconds left in the second period, batting the puck out of mid-air for the goal.

Toronto's Tyler Bozak and Detroit's Justin Abdelkader exchanged third-period goals to force overtime. When nothing was decided in the five-minute extra session, Bozak sealed the win for the Leafs in the third round of the shootout.

Leafs goalie Jonathan Bernier – sporting a lucky toque – played spectacularly in a 41-save performance. With point-blank saves off Daniel Cleary and Pavel Datsyuk, Bernier kept the game from getting out of hand and gave the Leafs the chance to gain two points on foreign soil.

The Leafs caught a lucky break thanks to the requirement for teams to switch ends at the midpoint of both the third period and overtime. The rule was instituted to give each side the same amount of time playing with whatever the weather offered. As a result, the buzzer went off at 2:30 of the short fourth period just as Wings sniper Henrik Zetterberg was breaking into the offensive zone for a scoring chance.

The game wasn't hockey at its purest, but the showcase was a ratings success. A CBC record average of 3.57 million viewers tuned in, the largest audience in Canada for a non-playoff game. In the United States, the 2.5 rating tied the 2009 edition of the Winter Classic as the highest-rated NHL regular-season game since 1975.

Toronto and Detroit played outside before a world record crowd.

Vancouver's TOP DRAFT CHOICES

1970 – Dale Tallon, #2, Toronto

1971 – Jocelyn Guevremont, #3, Montreal

1972 – Don Lever, #3, Niagara Falls

1973 – Dennis Ververgaert, #3, London

1977 – Jere Gillis, #4, Sherbrooke

1978 – Bill Derlago, #4, Brandon

1979 – Rick Vaive, #5, Sherbrooke

1980 – Rick Lanz, #7, Oshawa

1981 – Garth Butcher, #10, Regina

1982 – Michel Petit, #11, Sherbrooke

1983 – Cam Neely, #9, Portland

1984 – J.J. Daigneault, #10, Longueil

1985 – Jim Sandlak, #4, London

1986 – Dan Woodley, #7, Portland

1988 – Trevor Linden, #2, Medicine Hat

1989 – Jason Herter, #8, North Dakota

1990 – Petr Nedved, #2, Seattle

1990 – Shawn Antoski, #18, North Bay

1991 – Alek Stojanov, #7, Hailton

1994 – Mattias Ohlund, #13, Pitea

1996 – Josh Holden, #12, Regina

1997 – Brad Ference, #10, Spokane

1998 – Bryan Allen, #4, Oshawa

1999 – Daniel Sedin, #2, MoDo Ornskoldsvik

1999 – Henrik Sedin, #3, MoDo Ornskoldsvik

2000 – Nathan Smith, #23, Swift Current

2001 – R.J. Umberger, #16, Ohio State

2003 – Ryan Kesler, #23, Ohio State

2004 – Cory Schneider, #26, Andover

2005 – Luc Bourdon, #10, Val d'Or

2006 – Michael Grabner, #14, Spokane

2008 – Cody Hodgson, #10, Brampton

2009 – Jordan Schroeder, #22, U. of Minnesota

2011 – Nicklas Jensen, #29, Oshawa

2012 – Brendan Gaunce, #26, Belleville

2013 – Bo Horvat, #9, London

2013 – Hunter Shinkaruk, #24, Medicine Hat

2014 – Jake Virtanen, #6, Calgary

2014 – Jared McCann, #24, Sault Ste. Marie

*Cam Neely was originally a Vancouver draft choice,
but he was eventually traded to Boston.*

Oilers Win McDavid Sweepstakes

Far removed from their dynasty years during which they won five Stanley Cups in seven seasons, the Edmonton Oilers of the 21st century have been in perpetual rebuild mode. After a surprise run to the finals in 2006, the Oilers missed the playoffs in each of the next nine years that followed.

Connor McDavid (#17, red) is expected to bring the Stanley Cup to Edmonton.

The solace in the team's poor play was the benefit of picking first overall in the NHL draft for three straight years. As a result, Edmonton landed top prospects Taylor Hall in 2010, Ryan Nugent-Hopkins in 2011, and Nail Yakupov in 2012.

However, Hall was the only member of the trio to emerge as a point-per-game player in any of his first three seasons. To make matters worse, the Oilers were still lacking depth on defence and in goal and so continued to wallow near the bottom of the standings.

In 2014-15, Edmonton finished with the third-worst record in the league. Heading into the final months of the season, the worst of the non-playoff teams appeared to be engaged in a reverse "race" to finish last overall and have the best chance of acquiring the top overall draft pick.

The top draft-eligible player was Erie Otters sensation Connor McDavid. Blessed with outstanding speed and seemingly infinite skill, McDavid showed all the prowess of a once-in-a-generation franchise superstar even as an 18-year-old junior.

His end-to-end breakaway goals went viral over the Internet. At the 2015 World Junior Championship, McDavid collected eleven points in seven games on the way to a gold medal with Team Canada. Despite missing over a month with a broken hand, McDavid finished third in OHL scoring with 120 points in only 47 games.

With the potential payout of the so-called "McDavid Sweepstakes" so high, fans of the league's worst teams rooted for their favourite squad to lose. The situation reach farcical levels when the league's two worst teams, Buffalo and Arizona, played a game that went to overtime. When the Coyotes scored the game-winner, the hometown Sabres fans cheered.

Going into the April 18 draft lottery, Buffalo – by virtue of its last-overall finish – had the best chance of winning at 20.0%. Arizona was next at 13.5%, followed by Edmonton at 11.5%.

The suspense built to a climax towards the end of the nationally-televised event. Much to the disappointment of the other 13 non-playoff teams, the Oilers were the victors.

Edmonton's draft lottery win kicked off a series of franchise-changing events. Within a month, former Hockey Canada CEO Bob Nicholson took over the same position with the Oilers, while Peter Chiarelli and Todd McLellan were hired as general manager and coach, respectively.

The All-Star Game in
Montreal
★★★

OCTOBER 3, 1953

Rookie Jean Beliveau made his NHL debut after signing a five-year contract earlier in the day. He earned an assist on Rocket Richard's goal in a 3-1 Montreal loss to the All-Stars.

OCTOBER 9, 1956

Fierce rivals Rocket Richard and Ted Lindsay provided all the scoring in a 1-1 tie. After the game, Lindsay called a secret meeting among a select few players to talk about forming a union.

(l-r) Al Langlois, Henri Richard, and Maurice Richard played the All-Star Game when it was Cup champions versus the rest of the league.

OCTOBER 5, 1957

Dean Prentice of the New York Rangers had a goal and two assists to lead the All-Stars to a 5-3 victory over the Habs. Lindsay – who had been dealt to Chicago as punishment for his pro-union efforts – was reunited with Red Wings linemate Gordie Howe.

OCTOBER 4, 1958

The Richard brothers, Maurice and Henri, combined for three goals as the Habs doubled the All-Stars, 6-3. Jacques Plante earned the win in net.

OCTOBER 3, 1959

Montreal cruised to a 6-1 win, breaking the game open with four goals in the third period. The All-Stars were missing several key players including Bobby Hull and Tim Horton because they had not yet signed NHL contracts.

OCTOBER 1, 1960

Rocket Richard was honoured for his service to the sport, having announced his retirement a few months after the Habs had won their fifth straight Stanley Cup. The Rangers' Andy Hebenton had the game-winner in a 2-1 All-Stars win.

OCTOBER 20, 1965

The line of Detroit's Gordie Howe and Norm Ullman and Chicago's Bobby Hull was unstoppable. The trio combined for four goals and four assists as the All-Stars trumped the Habs, 5-2.

JANUARY 18, 1967

Canadiens goalies Charlie Hodge and Gary Bauman combined for the only shutout in All-Star history as Montreal won 3-0. John Ferguson scored twice.

JANUARY 21, 1969

A revised format matched the best players from the East and West Divisions. Guy Larose of the Minnesota North Stars scored late in the third period to salvage a 3-3 tie for the West.

JANUARY 21, 1975

The Wales Conference All-Stars cruised to an easy 7-1 romp over their Campbell Conference opponents. For the Wales team, Bobby Orr had his only All-Star goal in eight career appearances.

FEBRUARY 6, 1993

In an offensive showcase devoid of physical contact, the Wales Conference dominated with a 16-6 destruction of the Campbell All-Stars. Mike Gartner of the Rangers led the way with a hat trick.

JANUARY 25, 2009

Montreal's Alex Kovalev had the shootout winner in a 12-11 triumph by the Eastern Conference over the Western Conference.

World Cup of Hockey Revived

The World Cup of Hockey was the successor to the Canada Cup. First played in 1996, it was supposed to be held every three or four years, but NHL participation in the Olympic changed that. The World Cup has been played only once more, in 2004.

The United States won the inaugural tournament in 1996, taking both games played in Montreal in the best-of-three series and leaving a bitter taste in Canadians' mouths. And Shane Doan's tournament-winning goal for Canada in 2004 is barely even remembered, let alone mythologized as is Darryl Sittler's Canada Cup winner in 1976 or Mario Lemieux's famous tally in 1987.

The NHL is on the lookout for a new trophy for the new World Cup to be played in Toronto in September 2016.

However, as the NHL continued to review its plans on whether to send its players to the 2018 Olympics in South Korea, the league assured fans of at least one more best-on-best showdown among hockey's most competitive nations in the near future. In January 2015, the league announced plans for the third edition of the World Cup of Hockey. The tournament is scheduled to start September 17, 2016.

Eight teams will participate. The big six include Canada, Czech Republic, Finland, Russia, Sweden, and the United States. There will also be two all-star teams: the North American Youngstars featuring Canadians and Americans under 23 years of age, and Team Europe comprised of players not represented by the four main European countries. All games will be played at Toronto's Air Canada Centre, in NHL-sized rinks and under NHL rules.

Previously, the World Cup featured two groups, one playing games in top European cities, the other playing in Canada and the U.S. The centralized concept makes the event feel more like an Olympics, and the NHL and NHLPA hope to organize many off-ice events to entertain fans from all over the world. And, of course, the ACC will be packed for each game, something another North American city could not likely guarantee.

The tournament has some interesting sidebars. Florida Panthers defenceman Aaron Ekblad, a sensational Calder Trophy nominee and member of Canada's World Championship gold medal-winning team in 2015, will be only 20 years old when the tournament starts. Any player on the Youngstars won't be available to the senior Canada and United States teams, so there may be some debate as to the best spot for Ekblad and other young stars of his stature.

Looking forward, Commissioner Gary Bettman alluded to the possibility of a quadrennial event, and possibly even staging a qualifying tournament to determine participation. The World Cup is back!

New Arena in Quebec

After 16 NHL seasons, the Nordiques bid adieu to Quebec City in 1995. Owner Marcel Aubut decided that the costs of operating the small-city franchise were too prohibitive. As a result, he sold the team to COMSAT Video Enterprises. The franchise moved to Denver, Colorado, and was re-christened the Avalanche.

Since then, Quebec City has been without NHL hockey. Yet local hockey fans remain forever hopeful of a return. The city still plays host to the annual Quebec Peewee International Hockey Tournament, the renowned youth hockey event that hosts competitors from as many as 15 countries. And the QMJHL's Quebec Remparts, the 2006 Memorial Cup champions, are always a popular draw.

Aspirations for a return of pro hockey for the region were fuelled in September 2012 when construction began on a new $400-million, 18,000-seat arena in Quebec City. The presence of the facility, slated to open in the fall of 2015, doesn't necessarily guarantee the NHL's return to the city where Hall of Famers Peter Stastny, Michel Goulet, Joe Sakic, and Mats Sundin once played.

But having an NHL-sized arena definitely enhances Quebec's chances. By comparison, the Nordiques' WHA expansion cousins, the Winnipeg Jets, lost their franchise in 1996. Winnipeg's return to the NHL in 2011 would not have been possible without the MTS Centre, the venue that effectively replaced the antiquated Winnipeg Arena.

Colisee Pepsi, the long-time home of the Nordiques and Remparts, is an historic venue that hosted the two-game Rendez-vous '87 series and the semi-finals and finals of the 2008 World Championships. But with a capacity below 16,000 and an aged structure without revenue-generating private boxes, it no longer meets NHL standards.

The arena's management rights are owned by communications company Quebecor. On April 7, 2015, the arena was officially named Videotron Centre, carrying the brand of a cable company that Quebecor owns. The Remparts, which hosted the 2015 Memorial Cup in their final season at Colisee Pepsi, will be the first tenants of the new rink.

Quebec City has some fair competition for the next wave of NHL expansion. Seattle, Las Vegas, and Southern Ontario are all in the mix. Not since 1995 has the league had eight Canadian franchises. That number shrank to six after a weakening Canadian dollar contributed to the relocation of both Quebec and Winnipeg south of the border.

But the league's revenues are at an all-time high, and the disparity between the Canadian and the U.S dollar isn't as great as it once was. As a result, there is an abundance of optimism for the return of an NHL franchise back to the country of hockey's birthplace.

Quebec City rightly hopes that a new arena will ensure the return of NHL hockey to the great hockey hotbed.

APPENDIX

ALL-TIME NHL REGISTER BY BIRTHPLACE

BY COUNTRY (7,269)

CANADA 5,016
UNITED STATES 1,065
SWEDEN 279
CZECH REPUBLIC 213
RUSSIA 206
FINLAND 185
SLOVAKIA 72
GERMANY 30
SWITZERLAND 26
SCOTLAND 21
ENGLAND 21
LATVIA 20
UKRAINE 14
DENMARK 10
AUSTRIA 9
FRANCE 9
BELARUS 8
KAZAKHSTAN 8
NORWAY 8
POLAND 8
IRELAND 6
YUGOSLAVIA 4
ITALY 3
WALES 3
BRAZIL 2
JAPAN 2
LITHUANIA 2
NIGERIA 2
SOUTH KOREA 2
VENEZUELA 2
BELGIUM 1
BORNEO 1
CROATIA 1
HAITI 1
HOLLAND 1
INDONESIA 1
JAMAICA 1
LEBANON 1
PARAGUAY 1
SLOVENIA 1
SOUTH AFRICA 1
TAIWAN, CHINA 1
TANZANIA 1

CANADA

ONTARIO 2,217
QUEBEC 796
ALBERTA 559
SASKATCHEWAN 499
MANITOBA 386
BRITISH COLUMBIA 371
NOVA SCOTIA 71
NEW BRUNSWICK 52
PRINCE EDWARD ISLAND 30
NEWFOUNDLAND 28
NORTHWEST TERRITORIES 5
YUKON 2

ALBERTA 559
Airdrie: 3
Zach Boychuk, Darcy Campbell, Dana Tyrell
Banff: 2
Kevin Smyth, Ryan Smyth
Bankhead: 1
Frank Jerwa
Barrhead: 1
Leland Irving
Bashaw: 2
Brad Berry, Dave Reierson
Bassano: 1
Mark Marquess
Beaumont: 1
Marc Magnan
Beaverlodge: 3
Jerry Holland, Chris Schmidt, Matt Walker
Bentley: 3
Clayton Beddoes, Perry Turnbull, Randy Turnbull
Blackie: 2
Jeremy Colliton, Pat Egan

Blairmore: 1
Doug Houda
Bonnyville: 3
Justin Fontaine, Jim Harrison, Jon Kalinski
Bow Island: 1
Troy Loney
Cadomin: 1
Milan Marcetta
Calahoo: 2
Frank Banham, Craig Berube
Calgary: 114
John Adams, Stewart Adams, Peter Allen, Cody Almond, Mark Astley, Jared Aulin, Scott Bailey, Bob Bassen, Hank Bassen, Nolan Baumgartner, Jay Beagle, George Boothman, Mike Brodeur, Murray Brumwell, Don Cairns, Brian Carlin, Todd Charlesworth, Dean Chynoweth, Braydon Coburn, Joe Colborne, Rob Conn, Mike Connolly, Al Conroy, Ross Cory, Greg Crozier, Les Cunningham, Rob DiMaio, Micki DuPont, Murray Eaves, Patrick Eaves, Brad Ference, Kris Foucault, Bill Gadsby, Dutch Gainor, T.J. Galiardi, Harrison Gray, Mike Green, Taylor Hall, Mike Heidt, Archie Henderson, Fred Hergerts, Thomas Hickey, Alex Hicks, Matt Higgins, Josh Holden, Ron Hudson, Pat Hughes, Jamie Hunt, Tim Hunter, Bill Hutton, Kim Issel, Connor James, Chad Johnson, Nick Johnson, Terry Johnson, Greg Joly, Joey Kocur, Krys Kolanos, Darryl Laplante, Nathan Lawson, Craig Levie, Herbie Lewis, Bob Liddington, Darcy Loewen, Andrew MacWilliam, Ron Martin, Wayne McBean, Frank McCool, Lyle Moffat, Mike Moller, Mike Moore, Glenn Mulvenna, Troy Murray, Dana Murzyn, David Musil, Mike Needham, Steve Nemeth, Robert Nilsson, Baldy Northcott, Lawrence Nycholat, Myles O'Connor, Darryl Olsen, George Pargeter, Brent Peterson (b. 1958), Brent Peterson (b. 1972), Domenic Pittis, Ty Rattie, Mike Rogers, Tony Savage, Kevin Schamehorn, Jeff Schultz, Sean Selmser, Brandy Semchuk, Trevor Sim, Tyler Sloan, Jason Smith, Brent Sopel, Ron Stewart, Ryan Stone, Jeff Tambellini, Bobby Taylor, Brent Thompson, Rocky Thompson, Ryan Tobler, Garry Unger, Shaun Van Allen, Mike Vernon, Wes Walz, Kyle Wanvig, Eddie Wares, Craig Weller, Chris Wells, Jason Widmer, Bob Wilkie
Camrose: 7
Tyler Bouck, Scott Ferguson, Steve Gotaas, Josh Green, Emil Hanson, Oscar Hanson, Karl Stollery
Canmore: 4
Percy Jackson, Alex Kaleta, Art Michaluk, John Michaluk
Caroline: 4
Kris Russell, Ryan Russell, Jim Vandermeer, Peter Vandermeer
Carstairs: 1
Tony Stiles
Castor: 1
Darcy Tucker
Cochrane: 1
Mason Raymond
Cold Lake: 4
Alex Auld, Doug Hicks, Kevin Krook, Dave Shand
Coleman: 1
Rick Rypien
Consort: 1
Riley Nash
Coronation: 2
Travis Brigley, Dwayne Zinger
Crossfield: 1
Don McFadyen
Daysland: 2
Richard Petiot, Matthew Spiller
Drayton Valley: 1
Greg Pankewicz
Drumheller: 2
Andrew Bodnarchuk, Don Campbell
Duchess: 1
Jeff Shantz
Edmonton: 187
Johnathan Aitken, Doug Anderson, Dave Babych, Wayne Babych, Doug Barrie, Shawn Belle, Brian Benning, Jim Benning, Perry Berezan, Mike Berger, Fred Berry, Blair Betts, Larry Bignell, Mike Bishai, Tom Bladon, Jason Botterill, Jay Bouwmeester, Johnny Boychuk, Gary Bromley, Gerry Brown, Gilbert Brule, Johnny Bucyk, Randy Bucyk, Al Cameron, Craig Cameron, Gene Carrigan, Bill Carse, Bob Carse, Jason Chimera, Colin Chisholm, Erik Christensen, Dave Chyzowski, Dean Clark, Mac Colville, Neil Colville, Mike Comrie, Paul Comrie, Pat Conacher, Kevin Connauton, Don Cutts, Napoleon

Dame, Billy Dea, Gerald Diduck, Chris Dingman, Hnat Domenichelli, Dave Donnelly, Steve Dykstra, Deryk Engelland, Jim Ennis, Tyler Ennis, Taylor Fedun, Andrew Ference, Vernon Fiddler, Jeff Finley, Mark Fistric, Brian Ford, Matt Frattin, Kyle Freadrich, Brendan Gallagher, Jamie Gallimore, Bob Geale, Dave Goertz, Randy Gregg, Kevan Guy, Len Haley, Greg Hawgood, Paul Healey, Jay Henderson, Chuck Holmes, Dave Hoyda, Kelly Hrudey, Cale Hulse, Jarome Iginla, Brad Isbister, Rick Jodzio, Mark Kachowski, Matt Kassian, Matt Keith, John Paul Kelly, Dustin Kohn, Dean Kolstad, Russ Kopak, Dan Kordic, John Kordic, Dave Kryskow, Brett Kulak, Stu Kulak, Daymond Langkow, Brian Lavender, Dale Lewis, Bryan Little, Warren Luhning, Jamie Lundmark, Ross Lupaschuk, Joffrey Lupul, Brett Lysak, Bruce MacGregor, Dave MacKay, Jim MacPherson, Kent Manderville, Dave Marcinyshyn, Gordie Mark, Richard Matvichuk, Kevin Maxwell, Darrell May, Ken McAuley, George McAvoy, John McCormack, Bob McGill, Jack McGill, Jack McIlhargey, Ray McKay, Ross McKay, Jamie McLennan, Billy McNeill, Gerry Melnyk, Glenn Merkosky, Mark Messier, Hugh Millar, Brad Miller, Jason Miller, Duncan Milroy, Roy Mitchell, John Mokosak, Derek Morris, Joe Morrow, Kael Mouillierat, Richard Mulhern, Hap Myers, Brantt Myhres, Tyson Nash, Scott Nichol, Scott Niedermayer, Bill Oleschuk, Dave Orleski, Greg Parks, Dave Pasin, Pete Peeters, Perry Pelensky, Alex Petrovic, Matt Pettinger, Dion Phaneuf, Fernando Pisani, Ray Podloski, Kevin Primeau, Brendan Ranford, Steve Regier, Steve Reinprecht, Kyle Rossiter, Paul Runge, Phil Russell, Phil Samis, Terran Sandwith, David Schlemko, Andy Schneider, Wally Schreiber, John Scott, Jim Shires, Gary Shuchuk, Duncan Siemens, Kent Simpson, Colin Smith, Geoff Smith, Mark Smith, Nathan Smith, Harold Snepsts, Doug Soetaert, Lee Sorochan, Jared Spurgeon, Gord Strate, Garret Stroshein, Jason Strudwick, Brian Sutherby, Ken Sutton, Darryl Sydor, Robbie Tallas, Dave Thomlinson, Jim Thomson, Tim Tookey, Garry Valk, Mickey Volcan, Ed Ward, Shane Willis, Gerry Wilson, Gary Yaremchuk, Ken Yaremchuk, Zarley Zalapski
Elk Point: 2
Mark Letestu, Sheldon Souray
Forestburg: 1
Evan Oberg
Fort McMurray: 5
Scott Lehman, Chris Phillips, Justin Pogge, Nolan Pratt, Scottie Upshall
Fort Saskatchewan: 4
Mike Commodore, Carl Mokosak, Allen Pedersen, Ray Whitney
Fort Vermillion: 1
Dan Hodgson
Glendon: 1
Stan Smyl
Grand Cache: 2
Dean McAmmond, Travis Roche
Grand Centre: 1
Garry Howatt
Grande Prairie: 3
Galen Head, Clint Malarchuk, Howard Walker
Grimshaw: 1
Wade Campbell
Halkirk: 1
Shane Doan
Hanna: 2
Lanny McDonald, Jim Nill
Hardisty: 1
Darrel Anholt
High Prairie: 2
Tom Lysiak, Kelly Pratt
High River: 4
Bruce Greig, Mark Greig, John McKenzie, Glen Sather
Hines Creek: 1
Brad Zavisha
Hinton: 1
Dave Scatchard
Hobbema: 1
Ted Hodgson
Hythe: 1
Ken Solheim
Innisfail: 1
Garry Bauman, Dallas Gaume
Jasper: 3
Ian Herbers, John Hilworth, Brian Young
Lac la Biche: 2
Rene Bourque, Darren Reid

Lacombe: 3
Larry Mickey, Darin Sceviour, Randy Wyrozub
Lamont: 1
Gene Achtymichuk
Langdon: 1
Paul Thompson
Leduc: 2
Matt Climie, Dixon Ward
Lethbridge: 16
Doug Barkley, Brandon Davidson, Allan Egeland, Aut Erickson, Len Frig, Patrick Holland, Earl Ingarfield, Rob Klinkhammer, Spencer Machacek, John MacMillan, Harvie Pocza, Jamie Pushor, Stacy Roest, Vic Stasiuk, Kris Versteeg, Robert Wood
Lloydminster: 4
Cory Cross, David Dziurzynski, Clarke MacArthur, Lance Ward
Mannville: 3
Kyle Calder, Mike Rathje, Miles Zaharko
Medicine Hat: 16
Warren Babe, Murray Craven, Eddie Dorohoy, Joe Fisher, Hec Highton, Corey Hirsch, Rick Hodgson, Matt Keetley, Blaine Lacher, Jamie Linden, Trevor Linden, Neil Little, Al McLeod, Stefan Meyer, Paxton Schafer, Doug Young
Milo: 1
Bob Stumpf
Morinville: 2
Jason Holland, Bryce Van Brabant
Myrnam: 1
Rocky Saganiuk
Nanton: 1
Philip Crowe, Orest Kindrachuk
Olds: 2
Jason Jaffray, Jay Rosehill
Onaway: 1
Paxton Schulte
Peace River: 5
Kelly Kisio, Ken Lovsin, Chris Osgood, Alex Ritson, Brian Skrudland
Pincher Creek: 4
Ray Cote, Leigh Verstraete, Darcy Wakaluk, John Wensink
Ponoka: 5
Gregg Boddy, Jim McCrimmon, Greg Smith, Stan Weir, Harry York
Provost: 3
Lance Bouma, John Chad, Norm Ullman
Red Deer: 19
Ron Anderson, Ossie Asmundson, Matt Fraser, Glenn Hicks, Trent Hunter, Brad Leeb, Greg Leeb, Paul Manning, Chris Mason, Randy Moller, Paul Postma, Dave Rochefort, Colton Sceviour, Ray Schultz, Mark Tinordi, Mike Toal, Russ Walker, Blake Wesley, Glen Wesley
Redwater: 1
Todd Fedoruk
Rocky Mountain House: 4
Dean Magee, Butch Paul, Brad Stuart, Nick Tarnasky
Sexsmith: 1
Duke Edmundson
Sherwood Park: 8
Ryan Bach, Cody Kunyk, Scott Langkow, Ben Ondrus, Mark Pysyk, Duncan Siemens, Tony Twist, David Van Drunen
Slave Lake: 1
Gord Kruppke
Spruce Grove: 6
Stu Barnes, Ryan Bast, Nathan Dempsey, Grant Fuhr, Ben Scrivens, Grant Stevenson
St. Albert: 5
Joe Benoit, Nick Holden, Eddie Joyal, Ryan Stanton, Emanuel Viveiros
Stettler: 3
Bob Falkenberg, Justin Hocking, Brian Ogilvie
Stony Plain: 1
Steve Goertzen
St. Paul: 1
Kyle Brodziak
Strathmore: 1
Keaton Ellerby
Swalwell: 1
Brian Tutt
Swan Hills: 1
Alan May
Taber: 1
Devon Setoguchi
Trochu: 1
Kevin Haller

Two Hills: 1
Brad Werenka
Vegreville: 3
Ed Diachuk, Zenith Komarniski, Brent Severyn
Vermilion: 5
Bill Flett, Ron Jones, Ernest Kenny, Grant McNeill, Jeff Woywitka
Viking: 8
Brent Sutter, Brett Sutter, Brian Sutter, Brody Sutter, Darryl Sutter, Duane Sutter, Rich Sutter, Ron Sutter
Wainwright: 1
Doug Lecuyer
Warburg: 1
Lindy Ruff
Westlock: 3
Rollie Boutin, Kyle Chipchura, Greg Polis
Wetaskiwin: 5
Rod Buskas, Val Fonteyne, Gus Marker, Martin Sonnenberg, Allen York
Willingdon: 1
Cody Rudkowsky
Youngstown: 1
Norm Burns

BRITISH COLUMBIA. 371
Abbotsford: 9
Dean Arsene, Ryan Craig, Kyle Cumiskey, Michael Funk, Derek Grant, Nathan Lieuwen, Brad Moran, Mackenzie Skapski, David Van Der Gulik
Aldergrove: 1
Brad Thiessen
Anahim Lake: 1
Carey Price
Brentwood Bay: 1
Matt Irwin
Burnaby: 19
Karl Alzner, Derek Bekar, Ken Berry, Kris Chucko, Chris Joseph, Jason LaBarbera, Dwayne Lowdermilk, Brian Lundberg, Mike MacWilliam, Darren McCarty, Ryan Nugent-Hopkins, Mark Olver, Byron Ritchie, Cliff Ronning, Joe Sakic, Claudio Scremin, Patrick Wiercioch, Tyler Wotherspoon, Greg Zanon
Campbell River: 4
Brett Connolly, Kris Fredheim, Carsen Germyn, Len Lunde
Cassiar: 1
Rob Niedermayer
Castlegar: 6
Travis Green, Dane Jackson, Steve Junker, Doug Kostynski, Darcy Martini, Gord Walker
Chemainus: 2
Robin Bawa, Doug Bodger
Chetwynd: 1
Dody Wood
Chilliwack: 1
Dave Archibald
Christina Lake: 1
Kevin Sawyer
Coal Creek: 1
Stan Smith
Comox: 2
Brett McLean, Cam Neely
Coquitlam: 3
Garrett Burnett, Terry McDonald, Ben Street
Cranbrook: 13
Ray Allison, Greg Andrusak, Glen Cochrane, Ryan Huska, Jon Klemm, Brad Lukowich, Jason Marshall, Ted McAneeley, Bob Murdoch, Don Murdoch, Corey Spring, Frank Spring, Steve Yzerman
Creston: 3
Jamie Huscroft, Darren Jensen, Randy Rota
Dawson Creek: 3
Dan Brennan, Craig Redmond, Phil Sykes
Delta: 1
Ed Patterson
Duncan: 5
Greg C. Adams, Geoff Courtnall, Russ Courtnall, Matt Ellison, Brad Palmer
Fernie: 5
Shane Churla, Frank Hughes, Jason Krog, David Leneveu, Dan Smith
Fort St. James: 4
Bryan Adams, Jim Playfair, Larry Playfair, Brian Spencer
Fort St. John: 4
Brad Fast, Mark Hartigan, Chris Jensen, Allan Stewart
Golden: 2
Doug Barrault, Curtis McKenzie

Grand Forks: 1
Ronald Areshenkoff
Hazelton: 3
Ron Homenuke, Alan Kerr, Brandon Smith
Hope: 1
Jeff Hoggan
Houston: 1
Ryan Stewart
Invermere: 1
Wade Dubielewicz
Kamloops: 10
Don Ashby, Rick Boh, Craig Endean, Stu Grimson, Doug Lidster, Bert Marshall, Brendon Nash, Rudy Poeschek, Mark Recchi, Tim Watters
Kelowna: 7
Steve Bozek, Jonathan Filewich, Josh Gorges, Tom Martin, Jason Ruff, Justin Schultz, Mitch Wilson
Kimberley: 4
Len Barrie, Don Martineau, Mike McBain, Jason Wiemer
Kitimat: 2
Don Nachbaur, Rod Pelley
Lac La Hache: 1
Al Karlander
Ladysmith: 1
Tony Feltrin
Langley: 2
Jordan Krestanovich, Dave Morisset
Maple Ridge: 3
Victor Bartley, Brad Hunt, Andrew Ladd
Marysville: 1
Carter Bancks
Merritt: 4
Eddy Beers, Ron Fischer, Paul Kruse, Matt Underhill
Miskel: 1
Gord Turlick
Murrayville: 2
Robb Gordon, Danny Lorenz
Nakusp: 1
Brad Larsen
Nanaimo: 5
Wayne Bianchin, Gene Carr, Al Hill, Trent Kaese, Mark Rycroft
Nelson: 5
Greg A. Adams, Danny Gare, Geoff Kinrade, Mike Laughton, Pat Price
New Westminster: 13
Doug Berry, Brenden Dillon, Colin Forbes, Brent Hughes, Nathan Lafayette, Mark Lofthouse, Tom McMurchy, Ken Kariya, Jordan Sigalet, Kyle Turris, Ryan Walter, Barry Wilcox, Terry Yake
North Vancouver: 12
Mark Dekanich, Martin Jones, Steve Kariya, George Lyle, Doug Lynch, Ben Maxwell, Griffin Reinhart, Sam Reinhart, Todd Simpson, Colton Sissons, Greg Tebbutt, Dave Tomlinson
Oliver: 1
Corban Knight
100 Mile House: 2
Sandy Moger, Scott Robinson
Osoyoos: 3
Neil Eisenhut, Mitch Fritz, Chuck Kobasew
Penticton: 3
Ross Fitzpatrick, Dave McLelland, Andy Moog
Pitt Meadows: 1
Brendan Morrison
Port Alberni: 6
Ron Andruff, Laurent Brossoit, Paul Cyr, Jim Hiller, John Newberry, Davis Payne
Port Alice: 1
Jason Bowen
Port Hardy: 1
Chris Murray
Port McNeill: 4
Greg Fox, Willie Mitchell, Rob Skrlac, Clayton Stoner
Port Moody: 1
Jeff McLean
Powell River: 5
Micah Aivazoff, Brad Bombardir, Danny Lucas, Gary Lupul, Terry Richardson
Prince George: 10
Murray Baron, Brett Bulmer, Nick Drazenovic, Kerry Ketter, Greg Kuznik, Stewart Malgunas, Brandon Manning, Mark Morrison, Daryl Reaugh, Turner Stevenson
Princeton: 1
Stephen Peat
Quesnel: 6
Rod Dallman, Brett Festerling, Aaron Gagnon, Bob Gassoff, Brad Gassoff, Errol Rausse

Revelstoke: 2
Bruce Holloway, Aaron Volpatti
Richmond: 7
Scott Hannan, David Mackey, Brandon McMillan, Ken Priestlay, Raymond Sawada, Brent Seabrook, Brandon Segal
Rossland: 3
Seth Martin, Derek Mayer, Joe Zanussi
Salmon Arm: 4
Bruce Affleck, Kris Beech, Scott Jackson, Curtis Lazar
Sandon: 1
Tiny Thompson
Sechelt: 1
David Oliver
Shuswap: 1
Ollie Reinikka
Sicamous: 3
Rob Flockhart, Cody Franson, Shea Weber
Smithers: 4
Ron Flockhart, Dan Hamhuis, Jimmy Watson, Joe Watson
Summerland: 1
Larry Hale
Surrey: 10
Mike Brown, Colin Fraser, Andrew Hammond, Colin Hemingway, Mark Janssens, Bill Muckalt, Gary Nylund, Bob Rouse, Joel Savage, Barry Smith
Telkwa: 1
Michael Wall
Terrace: 4
Wade Flaherty, Dale Kushner, Brad Mills, Jeff Sharples
Trail: 19
Ed Cristofoli, Craig Cunningham, Adam Deadmarsh, Butch Deadmarsh, Gary Donaldson, Dallas Drake, Landon Ferraro, Ray Ferraro, Shawn Horcoff, Barret Jackman, Rich Kromm, Tim Lenardon, Cesare Maniago, Mike Matteucci, Steve McCarthy, Don McLeod, Garth Rizzuto, Steve Tambellini, Mike Zanier
Vancouver: 56
Glenn Anderson, Barry Beck, Sebastien Bordeleau, Tim Bothwell, Troy Brouwer, Doug Buhr, James Camazzola, Tony Camazzola, Steve Clippingdale, John Craighead, Brad Dalgarno, Tyler Eckford, Stefan Elliott, John Ferguson, Norm Foster, Link Gaetz, Joaquin Gage, Zach Hamill, Gord Hampson, Rich Healey, Randy Heath, Dave Hindmarch, Chris Holt, Tony Horacek, Paul Houck, Ryan Johansen, Evander Kane, Paul Kariya, Bracken Kearns, Steve Kelly, Mike Kennedy, Dan Kesa, Sasha Lakovic, Milan Lucic, Dean Malkoc, Sean McMorrow, Peter McNab, Steve Montador, Doug Morrison, Shaone Morrisonn, Cam Paddock, Morgan Rielly, Larry Romanchych, Darcy Rota, Mike Santorelli, Macgregor Sharp, Jonathan Sigalet, Larry Skinner, Mark Taylor, Alex Tidey, Steve Tuttle, Wayne Van Dorp, Phil Von Stefenelli, Aaron Voros, Simon Wheeldon, Brandon Yip
Vernon: 9
Eric Brewer, Jarrett Deuling, Andrew Ebbett, Eric Godard, Ken Holland, Larry Kwong, Bruce Major, Jason Podollan, Jerred Smithson
Victoria: 20
Don Barber, Tyson Barrie, Jeff Batters, Jamie Benn, Jordie Benn, Bruce Cowick, Jesse Fibiger, Ron Grahame, Mike Green, Kyle Greentree, Richard Hajdu, Rick Lapointe, Darryl Maggs, Ryan O'Byrne, Lynn Patrick, Muzz Patrick, Joe Reekie, Geordie Robertson, Torrie Robertson, Mike Stutzel
West Vancouver: 2
John Negrin, Max Reinhart
White Rock: 4
Jeff Bandura, Jason Garrison, Colton Gillies, Colton Teubert

MANITOBA. 386
Ashern: 1
Chuck Arnason
Baldur: 1
Tom Johnson
Basswood: 1
Stu Smith
Beausejour: 1
Bob Davie
Binscarth: 1
Cody McLeod
Birtle: 3
Rick Berry, Bill Derlago, Ron Low

Brandon: 35
Dan Bonar, Jack Borotsik, Turk Broda, Hal Brown, Larry Brown, Matt Calvert, Lude Check, Ron Chipperfield, Jimmy Creighton, Kimbi Daniels, Bill Fairbairn, Triston Grant, Glen Hanlon, Ron Hextall, Eddie Johnstone, Gord Lane, Jordan Martinook, Dwight Mathiasen, Brad Maxwell, Carson McMillan, Bernie Morris, Brady Murray, Chris Oddleifson, John Paddock, Alex Plante, Cam Plante, Bill Ranford, Bryce Salvador, Chuck Scherza, Damon Severson, Brett Skinner, Alex Smart, Brock Trotter, Ryan White, Ken Wregget
Carman: 1
Ed Belfour
Carroll: 2
Clem Loughlin, Wilf Loughlin
Churchill: 1
Jordin Tootoo
Cowan: 1
Wally Boyer
Dauphin: 7
Don Caley, Brad Church, Bob Kabel, Mike Korney, Les Kozak, Colby Robak, Pete Slobodian
Deloraine: 4
Ryan Caldwell, Don Dietrich, Don Gibson, Marty Murray
Dugald: 1
Trevor Kidd
Elkhorn: 1
Sheldon Kennedy
Eriksdale: 2
Ted Green, John Stewart
Flin Flon: 17
Ken Baird, Ken Baumgartner, Bobby Clarke, Matt Davidson, Kim Davis, Dean Evason, Al Hamilton, Gerry Hart, Ron Hutchinson, George Konik, Ray Maluta, Dunc McCallum, Eric Nesterenko, Mel Pearson, Reid Simpson, David Struch, Ernie Wakely
Foxwarren: 2
Pat Falloon, Mark Wotton
Gilbert Plains: 1
Blaine Stoughton
Gimli: 1
Greg Carroll
Glenboro: 1
Mel Hill
Gretna: 1
Hal Winkler
Grosse Isle: 1
Bryan Lefley
Hamiota: 4
Bing Juckes, John Marks, Wayne Ramsey, Dallas Smith
Hartney: 3
Jim Agnew, Hugh Conn, Emory Sparrow
Holland: 1
Glen Harmon
Lettelier: 1
Dick Bouchard
Manitou: 1
Ron Huston
Mariapolis: 1
Rene Trudell
McCreary: 1
Kirby Law
Melita: 1
Wayne Hall
Minnedosa: 3
Peter LeBoutillier, Curt Ridley, Butch Stahan
Morweena: 1
James Reimer
Neepawa: 3
Shawn Byram, Shane Hnidy, Bill Mikkelson
Nesbitt: 1
Aaron Rome
Notre Dame de Lourdes: 1
J.P. Vigier
Oakbank: 1
Drew Bagnall
Oak Lake: 1
Ted Taylor
Oakville: 1
Gordon Sherritt
Pilot Mound: 2
Lyle Phair, Jack Stewart
Pine Falls: 1
Bill Watson
Poplar Point: 1
Dennis Hextall

Portage La Prairie: 11
Arron Asham, Gordie Bell, Joe Bell, Lin Bend, Rick Blight, Troy Bodie, Gord Fashoway, Bill Holmes, Ron Lyons, Leo Murray, Alex Singbush
Riverton: 1
Reg Leach
Russell: 2
Brodie Dupont, Red Dutton
St. Boniface: 17
Garry Blaine, Gerry Brisson, Ed Bruneteau, Mud Bruneteau, Rosie Couture, Marcel Dheere, Butch Goring, Howie Hughes, Gord Labossiere, Dan Lambert, Derek Laxdal, Ray Manson, Ray Neufeld, Dave Richardson, Dave Richter, Wilf Starr, Marcel Tremblay
St. Charles: 1
George Johnston
St. James: 2
Cecil Browne, Harry Taylor
St. Lazare: 1
Dave Chartier
St. Malo: 1
Travis Hamonic
St. Vital: 1
Pete Kelly
Selkirk: 11
Terry Ball, Rich Chernomaz, Paul Goodman, Ian MacIntosh, Alfie Michaud, John Morrison, Andrew Murray, Harry Oliver, Joe Simpson, Nick Wasnie, Neil Wilkinson
Sherridon: 1
Steve Andrascik
Snowflake: 2
Justin Falk, Gord McFarlane
Souris: 4
Archie Fraser, Harvey Fraser, Jayson More, Art Townsend
Steinbach: 2
Ken Block, Dale Krentz
Ste. Rose: 1
Burke Henry
Stony Mountain: 3
Moylan McDonnell, Bill Meronek, Babe Pratt
Swan River: 4
Barry Brust, Micheal Ferland, Chay Genoway, Jack McDonald
The Pas: 2
Murray Anderson, Curt Giles
Thompson: 4
Curtis Leschyshyn, Cameron Mann, Chris Minard, Jody Shelley
Transcona: 1
Cal Gardner
Treherne: 1
Florent Robidoux
Virden: 1
Jim Murray
Winkler: 2
Eric Fehr, Dustin Penner
Winnipeg: 193
Reg Abbott, Clint Albright, Bill Allum, John Arundel, Carter Ashton, Doug Baldwin, Cam Barker, Andy Bathgate, Frank Bathgate, Paul Baxter, Bill Benson, Bobby Benson, Frank Bialowas, Andy Blair, Lonny Bohonos, Larry Bolonchuk, Ryan Bonni, Helge Bostrom, Dan Bourbonnais, Ralph Bowman, Jack Bowness, Dustin Boyd, Andy Branigan, George Brown, Al Buchanan, Bill Burega, Al Carr, Art Chapman, Brad Chartrand, Bob Chrystal, Cam Connor, Joe Cooper, Riley Cote, Art Coulter, Tommy Coulter, Joe Crozier, Joe Daley, Nigel Dawes, Ernie Dickens, Jim Dobson, Jordy Douglas, Chris Driedger, Bruce Eakin, Cody Eakin, Gary Emmons, Brian Engblom, Bill Ezinicki, Wilf Field, Tom Fowler, Frank Fredrickson, Karl Friesen, Owen Fussey, Ryan Garbutt, Herb Gardiner, Paul Gauthier, Art Giroux, Scott Glennie, Bill Gooden, Jack Gordon, Lee Goren, Gord Haidy, Slim Halderson, Jim Hargreaves, Ted Harris, Andy Hebenton, Darren Helm, Jim Henry, Phil Hergesheimer, Wally Hergesheimer, Bryan Hextall, Jr., Ike Hildebrand, Kevin Hodson, Cec Hoekstra, Ed Hoekstra, Quinton Howden, Dave Hrechkosy, Lex Hudson, Ted Irvine, Doug Jackson, Paul Jerrard, Al Johnson, Ivan Johnson, Jim Johnson, Bill Juzda, Mike Keane, Duncan Keith, Bill Kendall, Julian Klymkiw, Neil Komadoski, Alex Krol, Aggie Kukulowicz, Arnie Kullman, Eddie Kullman, Justin Kurtz, Max Labovitch, Pete Langelle, Ted Lanyon, Jamie Leach, Mike Leclerc, Grant Ledyard, Chuck Lefley, Barry Legge, Bob Leiter, Doug Lewis, Brian Loney, Ron Loustel, Norm Lowe, Bill MacKenzie, George Maneluk, Mike Maneluk, Jack Mann, Bill Masterton, Frank Mathers, Eddie Mazur, Kevin McCarthy, Johnny McCreedy, Ab McDonald, Dylan McIlrath, Frazer McLaren, Jack McLean, Derek Meech, Nick Mickoski, Al Millar, Craig Millar, Perry Miller, Mike Mitchell, Amby Moran, Bill Mosienko, Bryan Muir, Rick Newell, Colton Orr, James Patrick, Steve Patrick, Johnny Peirson, Jeff Penner, Cliff Pennington, Calvin Pickard, Alf Pike, Nels Podolsky, Geoff Powis, Ken Reardon, Terry Reardon, Ryan Reaves, Billy Reay, Craig Reichert, Ed Reigle, Mike Ridley, Gus Rivers, George Robertson, Russ Romaniuk, Tom Roulston, Church Russell, Terry Sawchuk, Dave Semenko, Joe Shack, Patrick Sharp, Fred Shero, Alex Shibicky, Brendan Shinnimin, Ron Shudra, Al Simmons, Warren Skorodenski, Eddie Slowinski, Vern Smith, Art Somers, Lorne Stamler, Daryl Stanley, Wally Stanowski, Alex Steen, Pete Stemkowski, Blair Stewart, Mark Stone, Mike Stone, Art Stratton, Billy Taylor, Billy Taylor, Jr., Jim Thomson, Joe Thorsteinson, Kevin Todd, Jonathan Toews, Brad Turner, Lindsay Vallis, Dale Weise, Duvie Westcott, Len Wharton, Ian White, Carey Wilson, Cully Wilson, Steve Witiuk, Bob Woytowich, Travis Zajac
Winnipegosis: 1
Danny Johnson

NEW BRUNSWICK 52
Bayfield: 3
George Allen, Viv Allen, Jim Riley
Big Cove: 1
Everett Sanipass
Campbellton: 5
Bill Dickie, Cory Larose, John LeBlanc, Bill Miller, John Stevens
Cape Tormentine: 1
Sherman White
Chatham: 1
Rick Knickle
Dalhousie: 1
Gord Dwyer
Dorchester: 1
Forbes Kennedy
Edmundston: 2
Cedric Desjardins, Roly Rossignol
Fredericton: 6
Jake Allen, Danny Grant, Buster Harvey, Greg Malone, Rollie McLenahan, Willie O'Ree
Grand Falls: 1
Gerry Ouellette
Lakeville Corner: 1
Fred McLean
Miramichi: 1
Brad Malone
Moncton: 10
Ron Anderson, Charlie Bourgeois, Rick Bowness, Patrice Cormier, Gord Drillon, Scott Fraser, Dick Gamble, Gary Geldart, Rollie Melanson, Calvin Pickard
Newcastle: 2
John Keating, Eddie Wiseman
Port Elgin: 1
Bobby Copp
Quispamsis: 1
Randy Jones
Sackville: 1
Bill Stuart
Saint John: 6
Hilliard Graves, Paul Higgins, Bob Joyce, Andrew McKim, Neil Nicholson, Yvon Vautour
Shediac: 1
Scott Pellerin
Shippagan: 1
Luc Bourdon
St. Stephen: 1
Don Sweeney
Sunny Brae: 1
George Carroll
Sussex: 2
Mike Eagles, Joe Lamb
Woodstock: 1
Sid Veysey

NEWFOUNDLAND. 28
Baie Verte: 1
Brad Brown
Bishop's Falls: 1
Alex Faulkner
Bonavista: 1
Adam Pardy

Carbonear: 1
Daniel Cleary
Come-by-Chance: 1
Bob Gladney
Corner Brook: 4
Keith Brown, Doug Grant, Jason King, Joe Lundrigan
Deer Lake: 1
Darren Langdon
Grand Falls: 3
Don Howse, Dave Pichette, Tony White
Labrador City: 3
Dan LaCosta, Pascal Pelletier, Chad Penney
Mt. Pearl: 1
Darryl Williams
St. John's: 11
Luke Adam, Ryane Clowe, Harold Druken, Colin Greening, Jason Morgan, Dwayne Norris, Doug O'Brien, Teddy Purcell, Terry Ryan, Michael Ryder, John Slaney

NORTHWEST TERRITORIES 5
Hay River: 2
Rob McVicar, Geoff Sanderson
Inuvik: 1
Zac Boyer
Yellowknife: 2
Vic Mercerdi, Greg Vaydik

NOVA SCOTIA 71
Amherst: 3
Stan Jackson, Craig Martin, Bill Riley
Antigonish: 7
Frank Beaton, Dennis Bonvie, Charles Fraser, Alex Grant, Craig MacDonald, Irv McGibbon, Dean Melanson
Bedford: 1
Shawn MacKenzie
Berwick: 1
Wally Wilson
Glace Bay: 3
Dave Amadio, Sandy Snow, Doug Sulliman
Green Bay: 1
Doug Doull
Guysborough: 1
John McKinnon
Halifax: 21
Mike Backman, Eric Boulton, Sidney Crosby, Ryan Flinn, Andrew Gordon, Bert Hirschfeld, Jack Ingram, Andrew Joudrey, Alex Killorn, David Ling, Nathan MacKinnon, Ian MacNeil, Brad Marchand, Peter Marsh, Wayne Maxner, Glen Murray, Liam O'Brien, Pokey Reddick, Cam Russell, James Sheppard, Wendell Young
Inverness: 1
Al MacInnis
Judique: 1
Andrew MacDonald
Kentville: 1
Jerry Byers
Lockport: 1
Mal Davis
Middleton: 1
Bob Hess
New Glasgow: 6
Troy Gamble, Lowell MacDonald, Jon Sim, Ted Stackhouse, Derrick Walser, Colin White
New Waterford: 1
Trevor Fahey
North Sydney: 3
Paul Andrea, Flash Hollett, Bobby Smith
Oxford: 1
Claude Bourque
Pictou: 1
Joey MacDonald
Port Hawkesbury: 1
Aaron Johnson
Sydney: 10
Paul Boutilier, Nelson Burton, Norm Ferguson, John Hanna, Parker MacDonald, Don MacLean, Al MacNeil, Mike McPhee, Kevin Morrison, Dan Poliziani
Sydney Mines: 1
Tony Currie
Truro: 4
David Brine, Lyle Carter, Gordon Kuhn, Zach Sill

ONTARIO 2,217
Agincourt: 1
Bob Babcock
Ajax: 2
Jeff Beukeboom, Brent Burns

Alfred: 1
Benoit Pouliot
Alliston: 1
Larry Gould
Amherstburg: 1
Kevin Westgarth
Arnprior: 2
Dan Fridgen, Randy Pierce
Atikokan: 1
Gary Sampson
Aurora: 4
Norm Dennis, Harry "Hap" Holmes, Ryan Murphy, Keith Wright
Ayr: 2
Kyle Clifford, Bud Maracle
Bancroft: 2
Rod Schutt, Bryan Watson
Barrie: 22
Perry Anderson, Steve Chiasson, Shayne Corson, Joe DiPenta, Hap Emms, Bruce Gardiner, Jim Hamilton, Mike Hoffman, Michael Hutchinson, Greg Johnston, Brian Kinsella, John Madden, Dan Maloney, Terry Martin, Garry Monahan, Hugh Plaxton, Glen Richardson, Darren Rumble, Wayne Rutledge, Darrin Shannon, Darryl Shannon, Garrett Wilson
Barriefield: 1
Mickey Blake
Barry's Bay: 1
Larry Trader
Bayfield: 1
Jeremy Welsh
Beamsville: 2
Ryan Christie, Paul Laus
Beaverton: 2
Basil McRae, Chris McRae
Beeton: 3
John Gould, Warren Holmes, Jim Rutherford
Belle River: 2
Aaron Ekblad, Mike Natyshak
Belleville: 23
Drew Bannister, Bill Boyd, Dale Clarke, Matt Cooke, Nick Cousins, Bob Crawford, Lou Crawford, Marc Crawford, Bob Dillabough, John Doran, Gerry Goyer, Rick Green, Brett Hull, Jack Laviolette, Norm Maracle, Rick Meagher, Andrew Raycroft, Brad Richardson, Andrew Shaw, Derek Smith, Chris Valentine, Ed Westfall, Ty Wishart
Blackburn: 1
Hec Kilrea
Blenheim: 1
Todd Warriner
Blind River: 2
Tom Cassidy, Claude Julien
Blyth: 1
Justin Peters
Bolton: 1
Lorne Duguid
Bothwell: 1
Brett MacDonald
Bourget: 2
Joe Matte, Roland "Joe" Matte
Bowmanville: 4
Josh Bailey, Bryan Bickell, Buck Davies, Brent Hughes
Bracebridge: 5
Ace Bailey, Bill Carson, Frank Carson, Roger Crozier, Kris King
Bradford: 2
Norm Collings, Brandon Mashinter
Bramalea: 3
Andrew Cassels, Chris Felix, Mike Weaver
Brampton: 17
Mike Danton, Mike Dwyer, Todd Elik, Mike Forbes, Tyler Graovac, Justin Hodgman, Randy Johnston, Sheldon Keefe, Mark Kolesar, Tom Laidlaw, Sean Monahan, Rick Nash, Kris Newbury, Tyler Seguin, Jamie Storr, Chris Terry, Mike Wilson
Brantford: 30
Shawn Antoski, Bill Cook, Murray Davison, Bryan Fogarty, Dave Gans, Chris Gratton, Dan Gratton, Gerry Gray, Brent Gretzky, Wayne Gretzky, Len Hachborn, Adam Henrique, Pat Hickey, Fred Hunt, Jim Jamieson, Doug Jarvis, Keith Jones, Barry Long, Paul MacKinnon, Dan Mandich, Jack Marks, Tom McGratton, Mike Posavad, Chris Pusey, Jeff Reese, Len Ronson, Jack Shewchuck, Greg Stefan, Herb Stuart, Paul Szczechura
Bright's Grove: 1
Brad Staubitz

Brockville: 9
Brian Chapman, Herb Foster, Randy Ladouceur, Hank Lammens, Alyn McCauley, Mike McMahon, Noel Price, Cully Simon, Thain Simon

Bromley Township: 1
Lloyd Andrews

Brussels: 1
Jack McIntyre

Burke's Falls: 1
Dave Downie

Burlington: 13
Josh Anderson, Jeff Christian, Cory Conacher, Adam Creighton, Dan Currie, Josh Jooris, Mark Lawrence, Scott McKay, Mark Reeds, Ron Sedlbauer, Jordan Szwarz, Mark Visheau, Chad Wiseman

Byron: 1
Rob Ramage

Cache Bay: 2
Carl Smith, Nakina Smith

Caledonia: 2
Andrew Campbell, Cam Talbot

Callander: 1
Bill Barber

Cambridge: 6
Tim Brent, Louie DeBrusk, Trevor Gillies, Brad Shaw, John Tanner, Scott Walker

Campbellford: 2
Chuck Shannon, Gerry Shannon

Campbellville: 1
Michael Sgarbossa

Capreol: 3
Joffre Desilets, Jim Mayer, Doug Mohns

Cardinal: 2
Rusty Crawford, Todd Gill

Carleton Place: 2
Batt Phillips, Charles Stewart

Carlisle: 1
Jeff Daw

Carp: 2
Calvin de Haan, Kurtis Foster

Cayuga: 3
Ray Emery, Jim Herbert, Frank Martin

Cedar Springs: 1
Harold Jackson

Chapleau: 4
Floyd Curry, Adie Lafrance, Ron Schock, Jason Ward

Charletone: 1
Lorrain Thibeault

Chatham: 12
Chris Allen, T.J. Brodie, Rick Chinnick, Dave Gagner, Lee Giffin, Bob Gryp, Ryan Jones, Dave Kelly, Dennis McCord, Randy Murray, Don Willson, Brian Wiseman

Chesley: 5
Paul MacDermid, Mickey Mackay, Bert McCaffery, Charles Pletsch, Percy Traub

Chesterville: 1
John Sorrell

Clinton: 2
Fred Elliot, Ryan O'Reilly

Cobalt: 3
Max Bennett, Kent Douglas, Joe Levandoski

Cobourg: 4
Gord Brooks, Dean Hopkins, Randy MacGregor, Justin Williams

Cochenour: 1
Mark Vermette

Cochrane: 1
Tim Horton

Collingwood: 10
Claire Alexander, Jason Arnott, Bernie Brophy, Roy Burmister, Eddie Bush, Lindsay Middlebrook, Reg Noble, Randy Osburn, Paul Shakes, Darryl Sly

Coniston: 3
Andy Barbe, Randy Boyd, Jim Fox

Cooksville: 1
Barry Salovaara

Copper Cliff: 4
Sam Bettio, John Sleaver, Jerry Toppazzini, Zellio Toppazzini

Cornwall: 19
Billy Carter, Bob Charlebois, Alain Chevrier, Carson Cooper, Corrie D'Alessio, Corb Denneny, Farrand Gillie, Tony Joseph, Chad Kilger, Newsy Lalonde, Blair MacDonald, John Markell, Scott Pearson, Steve Poapst, Bruce Racine, Steve Seguin, Don Smith, Orval Tessier, Ron Ward

Courtice: 1
Greg Nemisz

Creighton Mines: 2
Bill Regan, Brian Smith

Delhi: 1
Barry Boughner

Deloro: 1
Wayne Brown

Deseronto: 1
Tom O'Neill

Dorchester: 1
Boone Jenner

Downeyville: 1
Dave Lucas

Dresden: 2
Ken Houston, Jeff Jackson

Dryden: 4
Wayne Muloin, Dennis Owchar, Chris Pronger, Sean Pronger

Dublin: 1
Jack Crawford

Dunnville: 3
Ryan Barnes, Dave Fenyves, Ernie Parkes

Durham: 2
Martin Lauder, Jeff MacMillan

Duro: 1
Jack Coughlin

Earlton: 2
Rosie Paiement, Wilf Paiement

Eganville: 3
Gord Byers, Shawn Heins, Dale McTavish

Elgin: 1
Vic Ripley

Elliot Lake: 2
Alex Henry, Zack Stortini

Elmira: 2
Ric Seiling, Dan Snyder

Espanola: 5
Art Gauthier, Tim Jacobs, Bob Jones, Jim Jones, Leo Lamoureux

Essex: 2
Bruce Crowder, Rick Heinz

Exeter: 1
Paul Pooley

Falconbridge: 1
Dale McCourt

Farran's Point: 1
Cy Denneny

Fergus: 5
Ed Chadwick, Bucko McDonald, Jamie McGinn, Tyler McGinn, Doug Rombough

Forest: 1
Bill Lochead

Forks of the Credit: 1
Aldo Guidolin

Fort Erie: 5
John Brenneman, Randy Burridge, John Cullen, Tom Reid, Brian Stapleton

Fort Frances: 9
Dave Allison, Mike Allison, Murray Bannerman, Ray Frederick, Earl Johnson, Ed Kryzanowski, Chris Lindberg, Neil Sheehy, Tim Sheehy

Fort William: 31
Jack Adams, Pete Backor, Steve Black, Gus Bodnar, Bart Bradley, Ron Busniuk, Larry Cahan, Tommy Cook, Alex Delvecchio, Lee Fogolin, Dave Gatherum, Pete Goegan, Bud Jarvis, Ed Kachur, Bob Kelly, Danny Lewicki, Murdo Mackay, Lou Marcon, Rudy Migay, Bud Poile, Don Poile, Charlie Sands, Wayne Stephenson, Gaye Stewart, Ralph Stewart, Joe Szura, Ted Tucker, Gary Veneruzzo, Jimmy Ward, Benny Woit, Steve Wojciechowski

Galt: 9
Lex Chisholm, Joe Contini, Alex Forsyth, Ray Getliffe, Normie Himes, Don Laurence, Mike Moffat, Jim Schoenfeld, Bill Wylie

Garafraxa County: 1
Bert Lindsay

Georgetown: 2
Adam Bennett, Bob Goldham

Geraldton: 2
Bo Elik, John Grisdale

Gloucester: 2
Grant Clitsome, Steve Guenette

Goderich: 4
Al Dewsbury, Gary Doak, Larry Jeffrey, Jack Price

Gravenhurst: 1
Mickey McGuire

Grimsby: 3
Kevin Bieksa, Bob Warner, Cy Wentworth

Guelph: 21
Art Brooks, Paul Brydges, Tony Cassolato, Logan Couture, Lloyd Finkbeiner, Lou Fontinato, Yip Foster, Michael Haley, Mike Hudson, Al Hughes, Greg

Jacina, David Jones, Brian MacLellan, Kirk Maltby, Doug McCaig, George McPhee, Gord McTavish, Rich Peverley, Doug Risebrough, Ron Scott, Bill Sweeney

Hagersville: 1
Brian Watts

Haileybury: 3
Jim Culhane, Leo Labine, Gord Spence

Haliburton: 3
Matt Duchene, Bernie Nicholls, Ron Stackhouse

Hamilton: 57
Spencer Abbott, Dave Andreychuk, Walt Atanas, Krys Barch, Bob Barlow, Paul Beraldo, Allan Bester, Andy Brown, Frank Caprice, Matt Carey, Ben Chiarot, Joe Cirella, Ian Cushenan, Herb Dickenson, Dave Dryden, Ken Dryden, Blake Dunlop, Babe Dye, Don Edwards, Darren Eliot, Ryan Ellis, Nelson Emerson, Tyler Gaudet, Ed Gilbert, Todd Harvey, John Holota, Harry Howell, Ron Howell, Dick Irvin, Al Jensen, Jay Johnston, Stan Kemp, Derek King, Peter Leblanc, Blair MacKasey, Adam Mair, Ken Mann, Jay Mazur, Rick McCann, Tom McCarthy, Al McDonough, Brian McGrattan, Doug McKay, Marty McSorley, Ron Murphy, Ric Nattress, Darnell Nurse, Murray Oliver, George Owen, Pat Quinn, Wayne Rivers, Nick Smith, Steve Staios, Joey Tenute, Scott Timmins, Dennis Ververgaert, Mark Visentin

Hawkesbury: 6
Lionel Bouvrette, Yvan Joly, Rick Laferriere, Denis Larocque, Ralph MacSweyn, Dan McGillis

Hearst: 2
Claude Giroux, Claude Larose

Heathcote: 1
Bobby Rowe

Hespeler: 2
Dolly Dolson, Paul Woods

Highland Creek: 1
Brock Tredway

Hillbrough: 1
Tex White

Holland Landing: 1
Darrin Madeley

Hornepayne: 1
Mike McEwen

Humberstone: 1
Ted Kennedy

Humber Summit: 1
Ron Attwell

Huntsville: 3
Jack Bionda, Ethan Moreau, Norm Shay

Ilderton: 1
Matt Read

Innisfil: 1
Josh Leivo

Iroquois Falls: 3
Paul Gagne, Roger Lemelin, Gerry Rioux

Kanata: 3
Cory Murphy, Travis Scott, Todd White

Kapuskasing: 4
Mitch Babin, Curt Brackenbury, Ted McCaskill, Dave Pulkkinen

Kemptville: 1
Des Roche

Kenora: 12
Bob Bailey, Gary Bergman, Tim Coulis, John Gallagher, Henry Harris, Charley McVeigh, Dennis Olson, Don Raleigh, Mike Richards, Rick St. Croix, Neil Strain, Aubrey Webster

Kerr Lake: 1
Harry Frost

Keswick: 3
Ernie Godden, Curtis Joseph, Chris Tierney

Kincardine: 6
Paul Henderson, Dennis Riggin, Pat Riggin, Jordan Willis, Johnny Wilson, Larry Wilson

King City: 3
Daniel Carcillo, Rick Hampton, Alex Pietrangelo

Kingston: 56
Bryan Allen, Jamie Arniel, Scott Arniel, Cam Botting, Kip Brennan, Fred Brown, Rob Brown, Jack Caffery, Wayne Cashman, Dick Cherry, Don Cherry, Tony Cimellaro, Chris Clifford, Brandon Convery, Bud Cook, Bun Cook, Bob Dailey, Peter Dineen, Jim Dorey, Peter Driscoll, John Erskine, Shawn Evans, Doug Gilmour, Hank Goldup, Scott Harrington, Hugh Harvey, Todd Hawkins, John Hendrickson, Dennis Kearns, Nick Knott, Guy Leveque, Ken Linseman, Jay McClement, Jay McKee, Mike Meeker, Kirk Muller, Mike Murphy, Bob Murray, Mike Murray, Fred O'Donnell, Don O'Donoghue, Rick Paterson, George Patterson, Rob Plumb, Ron Plumb, Ken Randall, Mike

Rowe, Brit Selby, Mike Smith, Rick Smith, Trevor Stienburg, Andy Sutton, Tom Thurlby, John Tripp, Flat Walsh, Brian Young

Kirkland Lake: 22
Ralph Backstrom, Don Blackburn, Buddy Boone, Dick Duff, Murray Hall, Chuck Hamilton, Earl Heiskala, Larry Hillman, Wayne Hillman, Willie Marshall, Kurtis McLean, Bob Murdoch, Claude Noel, Barclay Plager, Bill Plager, Bob Plager, Daren Puppa, Dick Redmond, Mickey Redmond, Mike Walton, Dave Watson, Tom Webster

Kitchener: 58
Don Awrey, Dick Behling, Mike Blake, Brian Bradley, Evan Brophey, Eric Calder, Mike Card, Rob Collins, Dave Cressman, Gary Dornhoefer, Woody Dumart, Lloyd Gross, Ott Heller, Art Herchenratter, Dutch Hiller, Mike Hoffman, Larry Johnston, Bingo Kampman, Jack Keating, Kevin Klein, Jim Krulicki, Gary Kurt, Michael Latta, Howie Mackie, Dave Maloney, Joe McDonnell, Howie Meeker, Harry Meeking, Kevin Miehm, Jim Mikol, Tom Miller, Adam Payerl, Tanner Pearson, Kyle Quincey, Earl Reibel, Paul Reinhart, Steven Rice, Jim Sandlak, Mark Scheifele, Brad Schlegel, Milt Schmidt, Werner Schnarr, Steve Seftel, Earl Seibert, Brad Selwood, Darryl Sittler, Nick Stajduhar, Ed Stankiewicz, Myron Stankiewicz, Mike Stevens, Scott Stevens, Cam Stewart, Greg Stewart, Dennis Wideman, Bennett Wolf, Jamie Wright, Bryan Young

Kleinburg: 1
Andrew Agozzino

Lambeth: 1
Reg Thomas

LaSalle: 3
Andy Delmore, Dalton Prout, Marc Reaume

Leamington: 6
Kirk Bowman, Tim Hrynewich, Kris Manery, Randy Manery, Pat Ribble, Brad Selwood

Levack: 2
Frank St. Marseille, Dave Taylor

Lindsay: 9
Jamie Allison, Ron Ellis, Joe Junkin, Rick MacLeish, Don Maloney, Joe Primeau, Dave Roche, Bill Speer, Tom Thornbury

Listowel: 5
Jeff Bloemberg, George Hay, Larry Huras, Darwin McCutcheon, Paul McIntosh

Little Current: 1
Danny Cox

Lively: 1
Andrew Desjardins

London: 47
Bill Armstrong, Craig Billington, Mike Boland, Colin Campbell, Gregory Campbell, Jeff Carter, Neal Coulter, Abbie Cox, Drew Doughty, Sam Gagner, Rod Graham, Jeff Hackett, Matt Hackett, Dwayne Hay, Bo Horvat, Greg Hotham, Jack Howard, Dave Hutchison, Doug Jarrett, Nazem Kadri, Mike Lenarduzzi, Brett Lindros, Eric Lindros, Don Luce, Craig MacTavish, Mark Mancari, Brad Marsh, Cody McCormick, Curtis McElhinney, Walt McKechnie, Murray McLachlan, Barrie Moore, Joe Murphy, Paul Nicholson, Jeff Paul, Goldie Prodgers, Brandon Prust, Bryan Rodney, Craig Simpson, Andy Spruce, Charlie Stephens, Steve Stoyanovich, Joe Thornton, Scott Thornton, Mike Van Ryn, Jason Williams, Brian Willsie

Long Sault: 1
Jesse Winchester

Lucknow: 1
Murray Murdoch

Lynden: 2
Lloyd Cook, Red Horner

Manitoulin Island: 1
Bobby Burns

Manitouwadge: 1
Mike Moher

Manotick: 1
Ed Lowrey

Maple: 2
Justin Dibenedetto, Lucas Lessio

Markdale: 2
Chris Neil, Brad Tiley

Markham: 2
Sam Carrick, Steven Stamkos

Marmora: 1
Greg Terrion

Massey: 1
Pete Horeck

Matheson: 1
Bob McCord

Mattawa: 1
Ed Rodden

Meaford: 3
Herb Mitchell, Darren Pang, Melville Vail

Midland: 4
Herb Drury, Wayne King, Alex McKendry, Mike Robitaille

Millbank: 1
Jim Nahrgang

Millgrove: 1
Danny Syvret

Milton: 4
Mike Kaszycki, Pete McDuffe, Enio Sclisizzi, John Tonelli

Mimico: 3
Ed Harrison, Ed Sandford, Brendan Shanahan

Mine Centre: 1
Edgar Laprade

Minesing: 1
Frank Foyston

Mississauga: 24
Don Biggs, Brad Boyes, David Broll, Michael Caruso, Matt Corrente, Jamie Devane, Greg Gilbert, Cody Goloubef, Tom Kostopoulos, Manny Malhotra, Grant Marshall, Shawn Matthias, Bill McDougall, Steve Pinizzotto, John Ramage, Zac Rinaldo, Allan Rourke, Mike Sands, Jeff Shevalier, Jason Spezza, Ryan Sproul, Matt Stajan, Ryan Strome, John Tavares

Mitchell: 1
Howie Morenz

Moose Factory: 1
Jonathan Cheechoo

Morrisburg: 2
Mike Casselman, Joe Miller

Mount Albert: 1
Gord Reid

Mount Dennis: 1
Don Head

Nanticoke: 1
Baldy Cotton

Naughton: 1
Art Ross

Nepean: 2
Dan Ratushny, Jason York

New Hamburg: 2
Herb Hamel, Walter Kalbfleisch

New Liskeard: 6
Hal Cooper, Jack Dyte, Marc Lamothe, Lonnie Loach, Gus Mortson, Rod Willard

Newmarket: 14
Darren Archibald, Dutch Cain, Herb Cain, Dit Clapper, Steve Downie, Brian Elliott, Hobie Kitchen, Mike Kitchen, Randy Legge, Jamie Macoun, Geoff Sarjeant, Shayne Stevenson, Bill Thoms, Rob Zepp

Newton Robinson: 1
Bob Pulford

Niagara Falls: 25
John Arbour, Jim Bedard, Bill Cupolo, Kevin Dallman, Marty Dallman, Hank Damore, Nick Damore, Peter Fiorentino, Rick Foley, Mike Glumac, Orville Heximer, Max Kaminsky, Zenon Konopka, Larry Landon, Gus Mancuso, Bob Manno, Don McLean, Terry O'Reilly, Frank Pietrangelo, Nick Ricci, Phil Roberto, Derek Sanderson, Justin Shugg, Jarrod Skalde, Frank Steele

Nobleton: 1
Nick Boynton

North Bay: 23
Clarence Boucher, Stan Brown, Billy Coutu, Brandon DeFazio, Ab Demarco, Bob Dupuis, Pierre Gagne, Ray Giroux, Bob Gracie, Gord Kannegiesser, Sheldon Kannegiesser, Larry Keenan, Pep Kelly, Hec Lalande, Bryan Maxwell, Graeme Nicolson, Pete Palangio, Tony Poeta, Larry Regan, Ken Richardson, Craig Rivet, Brent Tremblay, Ken Wharram

North Gower: 1
Morley Bruce

Norwood: 1
Fred Doherty

Oakville: 16
Eric Cairns, Bruce Dowie, Matt Foy, Vic Hadfield, Ron Hoover, Bob Kelly, Kellan Lain, Scott Laughton, Steve Mason, David McIntyre, John Mitchell, Stuart Percy, Greg Smyth, Kyle Wilson, Scott Wilson, Rob Zamuner

Ohsweken: 1
Stan Jonathan

Orangeville: 2
Brett Ritchie, Bert Wilson

Orillia: 3
Nobby Clark, Rick Ley, Richard Scott

Orleans: 1
Jason Akeson

Osgoode: 1
Todd Flichel

Oshawa: 27
Scott Barney, Frank Bathe, Arnie Brown, Sean Brown, Les Colvin, Jeff Daniels, Dale DeGray, Dave Duerden, Craig Fisher, Dave Gorman, Brent Grieve, Ryan Hamilton, Jay Harrison, Larry Hopkins, Charlie Huddy, Jim Jackson, Ross Lowe, John MacLean, Jeff Madill, Kevin McClelland, Shawn McCosh, Joe Nieuwendyk, Hank Nowak, Rob Pearson, Shawn Thornton, Pete Vipond, Sean Williams

Ottawa: 160
Derek Armstrong, Adrian Aucoin, Philippe Audet, Jamie Baker, Matthew Barnaby, Fred Barrett, John Barrett, Eric Beaudoin, Brendan Bell, Clint Benedict, Bill Beveridge, Mike Bloom, Mark Borowiecki, Billy Boucher, Bobby Boucher, Frank Boucher, George Boucher, Dan Boyle, Fred Brathwaite, Archie Briden, Rod Brind'Amour, Harry Broadbent, Jeff Brown, Gordie Bruce, Mike Bullard, Paul Byron, Leo Carbol, Bruce Cassidy, Cody Ceci, Andre Champagne, Gene Chouinard, King Clancy, Terry Clancy, Bill Collins, Alec Connell, Harry Connor, David Cooper, Mike Corrigan, Barry Cullen, Brian Cullen, Ray Cullen, Harry Darragh, Jack Darragh, John Davidson, Dean Defazio, Jack Duggan, Frank Dunlap, Jerome Dupont, Ben Eager, Mike Eastwood, Stew Evans, Corey Foster, Mark Fraser, Art Gagne, Mike Gartner, Stew Gavin, Eddie Gerard, Ebbie Goodfellow, Leth Graham, Len Grosvenor, Erik Gudbranson, Milt Halliday, Sammy Hebert, Harry Helman, Tim Higgins, Syd Howe, Rolly Huard, Kent Huskins, Bill Inglis, Lloyd Jackson, Ryan Jardine, Aurele Joliat, Rene Joliat, Pat Kavanagh, Kevin Kemp, Brian Kilrea, Ken Kilrea, Wally Kilrea, Ray Kinsella, Murray Kuntz, Jim Kyte, Roland Lafleur, Pete Laframboise, Shawn Lalonde, Mitch Lamoureux, Charles Larose, Gary Laskoski, Tony Licari, Claude Loiselle, Fred Lowrey, Gerry Lowrey, Kilby MacDonald, Jack Mackell, Reg Mackey, Phil Maloney, Renison Manners, Jon Matsumoto, Wally Maxwell, Gilles Mayer, Stan McCabe, Jack McGill, Jim McKenny, Bryan McSheffrey, Horace Merrill, Marc Methot, Tyler Moss, John Newman, Eric O'Dell, Sean O'Donnell, John Ogrodnick, Eddie Ouellette, Jean-Gabriel Pageau, Justin Papineau, Mark Paterson, Denis Potvin, Jean Potvin, Marc Potvin, John Quilty, Dan Quinn, Yip Radley, Brad Ralph, Luke Richardson, Rip Riopelle, Jamie Rivers, Shawn Rivers, Randy Robitaille, Harvey Rockburn, Skene Ronan, Derek Roy, David Saunders, Ted Saunders, Andre Savage, Marc Savard, Andy Schliebener, Al Shields, Hamby Shore, Brian D. Smith, Des Smith, Doug Smith, Gary Smith, Rodger Smith, Tommy Smith, Trevor Smith, Brad Smyth, Ted Snell, Ryan Spooner, Harold Starr, Martin St. Pierre, Chris Therien, Wayne Thomas, Bill Touhey, Connie Tudin, Rick Vaive, Bobby Walton, Steve Washburn, John Wilkinson, Doug Wilson, Hub Wilson, Stephane Yelle, Rod Zaine

Owen Sound: 18
Norm Armstrong, Cody Bass, Les Binkley, Hap Day, Ted Graham, Benny Grant, Gord Henry, Buck Jones, Butch Keeling, Norm Locking, Stan Long, Harry Lumley, Steve McLaren, Pat McReavy, Mike Minard, Nathan Perrott, Gerry Reid, Curtis Sanford

Paisley: 1
Barney Stanley

Palmerston: 2
Lorne Ferguson, Nick Spaling

Paris: 4
Syl Apps, Jr., Zac Dalpe, Ken Ellacott, Jay Wells

Parry Sound: 7
Neil Belland, Fred Bergdinon, John Brackenborough, Gerry Carson, Terry Crisp, Bobby Orr, Gary Sabourin

Pembroke: 13
Jim Anderson, Bert Anslow, Harry Cameron, Gord Fraser, Randy Holt, Doug Keans, Hugh Lehman, Frank Nighbor, Clare Raglan, Leo Reise, Ray Sheppard, Bob Trapp, Dave Trottier

Penetanguishene: 6
Andy Bellemer, Bert Corbeau, Patrick DesRochers, Howard McNamara, Brian McReynolds, Don Tannahill

Perth: 5
Les Douglas, Carl Liscombe, Billy Smith, Floyd Smith, Gord Smith

Petawawa: 2
Gus Giesebrecht, Lloyd Mohns

Peterborough: 38
Zac Bierk, Hank Blade, Doug Brennan, Norm Calladine, Doug Crossman, Paul Curtis, John Druce, Doug Evans, Kevin Evans, Paul Evans, Mike Fisher, Larry Floyd, Mark Freer, Bob Gainey, Doug Gibson, Del Hall, Frank Heffernan, Kerry Huffman, Joey Johnston, Jeff Larmer, Steve Larmer, Dean Morton, Bob Murray, Mickey Murray, Cam Newton, Dennis Patterson, Corey Perry, Steve Peters, Herb Raglan, Ryan Ready, George Redding, Glen Seabrooke, Steve Self, Cory Stillman, Red Sullivan, Greg Theberge, Steve Webb, Brian Wesenberg

Petersburg: 1
Glen Cressman

Petrolia: 10
Todd Bidner, Brian Dobbin, Bobby Gould, Terry Holbrook, Jody Hull, Dale Hunter, Dave Hunter, Mark Hunter, Mike Leighton, John Van Boxmeer

Pickering: 2
Andy Andreoff, Glenn Healy

Plattsville: 1
Babe Siebert

Point Anne: 2
Bobby Hull, Dennis Hull

Point of the Pines: 1
Alex McKinnon

Porcupine: 1
Mark Katic

Port Arthur: 20
John Adams, Stan Baluik, Ken Brown, Ray Ceresino, Dave Creighton, Frank Daley, Bruce Gamble, Jim Haggarty, Fred "Smokey" Harris, Steve Hrymnak, Dick Kotanen, Connie Madigan, Jim McLeod, Stu McNeill, Nelson Pyatt, John Schella, Red Spooner, Ken Stewart, Alex Wellington, Gord Wilson

Port Colborne: 6
Harry Dick, Don Gallinger, Scott Gruhl, Bronco Horvath, Dan Olesevich, Don Simmons

Port Credit: 2
Ken Hammond, Bert Peer

Port Dalhousie: 1
Bill Mitchell

Port Elgin: 2
Kevin Czuczman, Brett MacLean

Port Hope: 4
Dennis O'Brien, Shane O'Brien, Ron Smith, Paul Terbenche

Port Perry: 1
John Ross Roach

Portsmouth: 1
Eddie Nicholson

Prescott: 3
Leo Boivin, Kevin MacDonald, Earl Roche

Preston: 2
Vern Kaiser, Ganton Scott, Barry Sullivan, Bob Wren

Ravenswood: 1
John McIntyre

Red Lake: 1
Mitch Molloy

Renfrew: 6
Lorne Anderson, Bill Brydge, Alan Letang, Ted Lindsay, Jack McVicar, Jim Peplinski

Richmond Hill: 12
Sam Bennett, Luciano Borsato, Mike Cammalleri, Stefan Della Rovere, Jamie Doornbosch, Derek Joslin, Julian Melchiori, Frank Nigro, Jeff O'Neill, Theo Peckham, Keith Redmond, Bob Wall

Ridgeway: 1
Skip Teal

Rockland: 3
Sam Godin, Evariste Payer, Serge Payer

Ruthven: 1
Floyd Hillman

St. Albert: 1
Andre Benoit

St. Catharines: 30
Taylor Beck, Roger Belanger, Brian Bellows, Bill Berg, Gerry Cheevers, Hank Ciesla, David Cullen, Rob Davison, Marv Edwards, Doug Favell, Bob Froese, John Gibson, Glenn Goldup, Mike Iggulden, Jason Lafreniere, Garry Lariviere, Jack Martin, Bryan McCabe, Brian McKenzie, Mike Millar, Jordan Nolan, Ellard O'Brien, Andrew Peters, Mark Plantery, Doug Robinson, Rob Robinson, Andy Rymsha, Riley Sheahan, Vic Teal, Rick Vasko

St. David's: 1
Johnny Mowers

St. George: 2
Don Johns, Adam Munro

St. Isidore: 1
Francis Wathier

St. Lambert: 1
Phil Stevens

St. Marys: 2
Mike Craig, Dan McCarthy

St. Paul's: 1
Mark Bell

St. Thomas: 6
Cory Emmerton, Dave Hudson, Greg McKegg, Bill McKenzie, David Shaw, Jack Valiquette

Sarnia: 28
Tim Bernhardt, Shawn Burr, Jerry Butler, Dino Ciccarelli, Mike Crombeen, Michael Dark, Jamie Fraser, Lloyd Haddon, Gary Holt, Dustin Jeffrey, Henry Lehvonen, John McCahill, Ian McKegney, Wayne Merrick, Robbie Moore, Bob Neely, Kraig Nienhuis, Rob Palmer, Jason Simon, Mike Stapleton, Pat Stapleton, Pat Verbeek, Don Ward, Joe Ward, Paul Ysebaert

Sault Ste. Marie: 38
Ken Belanger, Mike Buchanan, Matt D'Agostini, Paul Di Pietro, Babe Donnelly, Art Duncan, Phil Esposito, Tony Esposito, Drew Fata, Rico Fata, Brian Finley, Alvin Fisher, Ron Francis, Sean Gagnon, Don Grosso, Bryan Helmer, Cole Jarrett, Tyler Kennedy, Joe Klukay, Jerry Korab, Bob LaForest, Chico Maki, Wayne Maki, Jim McBurney, Gerry Munro, Lou Nanne, Brandon Nolan, Ted Nolan, Marty Pavelich, Fred Perlini, Matt Ravlich, Norm Schmidt, Chris Thorburn, Marty Turco, Gene Ubriaco, Dennis Vial, Jim Wiley, Mike Zuke

Schomberg: 1
Bill Kitchen

Schumacher: 6
Norman Defelice, Gord Hannigan, Ray Hannigan, Jim Mair, Dean Prentice, Eric Prentice

Seaforth: 4
Boyd Devereaux, Charley Mason, Dave McIlwain, Reg Reid, Mike Watt, Cooney Weiland

Seneca Township: 1
Roy Edwards

Sharon: 1
Matt Ryan

Shelburne: 1
Aaron Downey

Silver Mountain: 1
Jack Walker

Simcoe: 7
Rob Blake, Jassen Cullimore, Red Kelly, Geordie Kinnear, Dwayne Roloson, Ryan Vandenbussche, Rick Wamsley

Skead: 1
George Armstrong

Smiths Falls: 4
Terry Carkner, Robert Dopson, Gary McAdam, Don McKenney

Smooth Rock Falls: 3
Grant Martin, Dick Mattiussi, J.P.Parise

South Porcupine: 9
Dan Belisle, George Blair, Les Costello, Murray Costello, Lloyd Doran, Don Lever, John McLellan, Bob Nevin, Bud Stefanski

South River: 1
Laurie Scott

Spencerville: 1
Eric Selleck

Stirling: 2
Eric Manlow, Rob Ray

Stittsville: 2
Matt Bradley, Ken Doraty

Stoney Creek: 4
Tyrone Garner, Mark Popovic, Leo Reise, Jr., Jack Stoddard

Stouffville: 2
Keith Acton, Michael Del Zotto

Stratford: 17
Bill Chalmers, Gord Davidson, George Gee, Dan Gloor, Craig Hartsburg, Joey Hishon, Red Kane, Nick Libett, Jud McAtee, Norm McAtee, Bob McCulley, Hank Monteith, Al Murray, Pat Murray, Rem Murray, Chris Taylor, Tim Taylor

Strathroy: 5
Nathan Beaulieu, Brian Campbell, Darryl Edestrand, Andy McDonald, Steve McKichan

Sturgeon Falls: 4
Leo Bourgeault, Dan Frawley, Shep Mayer, Gerry McNamara

APPENDIX

Sudbury: 65
Al Arbour, Larry Aurie, John Baby, Todd Bertuzzi, Fred Boimistruck, Andrew Brunette, Cummy Burton, Bryan Campbell, Wayne Carleton, Randy Carlyle, Marc Chorney, Bob Cook, D'Arcy Coulson, Gary Croteau, Troy Crowder, Marc D'Amour, Gerry Desjardins, Ron Duguay, Craig Duncanson, Jack Egers, Bob Fitchner, John Flesch, Mike Foligno, Dave Fortier, Cameron Gaunce, Sean Gauthier, Aaron Gavey, Ed Giacomin, Mike Gillis, Red Green, Shorty Green, Dave Hannan, Shawn Heaphy, Jim Hofford, George Horne, Joe Ironstone, Yvon Labre, Marc Laforge, Kevin LaVallee, Dave Lowry, Derek MacKenzie, Bernie MacNeil, Troy Mallette, Grant Mulvey, Paul Mulvey, Jim Pappin, Joel Prpic, Sam Rothschild, Bob Sabourin, Brian Savage, Al Secord, Dan Seguin, Eddie Shack, Richard Shulmistra, Irv Spencer, Bob Sykes, Don Sylvestri, Dave Tataryn, Floyd Thomson, Jean-Guy Trudel, Kay Whitmore, Sean Whyte, Jim Wiemer, Bob Wilson, Roger Wilson
Sundridge: 3
Greg de Vries, Bill McCreary, Keith McCreary
Sutton West: 1
Larry Molyneaux
Swansea: 1
Glenn Brydson
Sydenham: 1
George Abbott
Tecumseh: 1
Warren Rychel
Terrace Bay: 3
Aaron MacKenzie, Danny Schock, Charlie Simmer
Thamesford: 1
Tommy Filmore
Thessalon: 1
Jack Markle
Thornhill: 1
Dominic Moore
Thorold: 4
Sean Bentivoglio, Bep Guidolin, Ryan Savoia, Fred Speck
Thunder Bay: 41
Rick Adduono, Pete Bakovic, John Bednarski, Bob Bodak, Danny Bois, Robert Bortuzzo, Rick Bragnalo, David Bruce, Mike Busniuk, Taylor Chorney, Danny Gruen, Jeff Heerema, Mike Hordy, Bill Houlder, Tony Hrkac, Carter Hutton, Jason Jaspers, Trevor Johansen, Greg Johnson, Ryan Johnson, Scott King, David Latta, Trevor Letowski, Norm MacIver, Jeff McDill, Lou Nistico, Steve Passmore, Walt Poddubny, Taylor Pyatt, Tom Pyatt, Steve Rucchin, Eric Staal, Jared Staal, Jordan Staal, Marc Staal, Vern Stenlund, Ron Talakoski, Mike Tomlak, Vic Venasky, Rob Whistle, Murray Wing
Tillsonburg: 3
Bill Anderson, Stan Crossett, Russell Oatman
Timmins: 23
Bill Barilko, Baz Bastien, Billy Cameron, Real Chevrefils, Larry Courville, Armand Delmonte, Shean Donovan, Tony Graboski, Pat Hannigan, Paul Harrison, Al LeBrun, Rick Lessard, Frank Mahovlich, Peter Mahovlich, Hector Marini, Hillary Menard, Howie Menard, Dave Poulin, Ray Powell, Dale Rolfe, Allan Stanley, Steve Sullivan, Eric Vail
Tinturn: 1
Steve Kraftcheck
Toronto: 471
Doug Acomb, Doug Adam, Brad Aitken, Jeff Allan, Jason Allison, Peter Ambroziak, Mike Amodeo, John Anderson, Lou Angotti, Syl Apps, Bob Armstrong, Tim Armstrong, Fred Arthur, Steve Atkinson, Sean Avery, Vern Ayres, Reid Bailey, Earl Balfour, Steve Bancroft, Darren Banks, Norm Barnes, Dave Barr, Kyle Baun, Chris Beckford-Tseu, Bruce Bell, Frank Bennett, Drake Berehowsky, Adam Berti, Nick Beverley, Jesse Blacker, Michael Blunden, Dave Bolland, Hugh Bolton, Darryl Bootland, Mark Botell, Bruce Boudreau, Rick Bourbonnais, Bill Bowler, Carl Brewer, Ken Broderick, Len Broderick, Ross Brooks, Gord Brydson, Bruce Bullock, Eddie Burke, Marty Burke, Dave Burrows, Bert Burry, Mike Byers, Terry Caffery, Brett Callighen, Patsy Callighen, Scott Campbell, Chris Campoli, Luca Caputi, Steve Cardwell, Billy Carroll, Anson Carter, Gino Cavallini, Paul Cavallini, Andy Chiodo, Rob Cimetta, Jason Cirone, Casey Cizikas, Dan Clark, David Clarkson, Rich Clune, Wally Clune, Gary Coalter, Steve Coates, Andrew Cogliano, Carlo Colaiacovo, Tom Colley, Gary Collins, Brian Conacher, Charlie Conacher, Lionel Conacher, Pete Conacher, Roy Conacher, Eddie Convey, Mike Corbett, Norm Corcoran, Frank Corrado, Charlie Cotch, Jeff Cowan, Rob Cowie, Wayne Cowley, Dale Craigwell, Bart Crashley, Tyler Cuma, Randy Cunneyworth, Brian Curran, Doug Dadswell, Trevor Daley, Bob Davidson, Jason Dawe, Rob DeCourcy, Val Delory, Gerry Denoird, Kevin Devine, Gary Dillon, Wayne Dillon, Chuck Dinsmore, Peter Douris, Bruce Draper, Kris Draper, Bruce Driver, Jim Drummond, Mike Duco, Rick Dudley, Ken Duggan, Steve Durbano, Bill Durnan, Chris Durno, Jeff Eatough, Tim Ecclestone, Tom Edur, Gary Edwards, John English, Bob Essensa, Chris Evans, Daryl Evans, J. Paul Evans, Randy Exelby, Rocky Farr, Walt Farrant, Glen Featherstone, Tony Featherstone, Manny Fernandez, Mark Fitzpatrick, Pat Flatley, Adam Foote, Jake Forbes, Dwight Foster, Mike Fountain, Jimmy Fowler, Bob Frampton, Lou Franceschetti, Iain Fraser, Bob Fryday, Larry Fullan, Jody Gage, Percy Galbraith, Bill Gardner, Dave Gardner, Paul Gardner, Ray Gariepy, Red Garrett, Steve Gatzos, Luke Gazdic, Jack Gelineau, Mario Giallonardo, Paul Gillis, Mark Giordano, Kenny Girard, Brian Glennie, Fred Glover, Howie Glover, Warren Godfrey, Larry Goodenough, Barclay Goodrow, Chris Govedaris, David Goverde, Pat Graham, Josh Gratton, Adam Graves, Jeff Greenlaw, Stephen Guolla, David Haas, George Hainsworth, Matt Halischuk, Bob Halkidis, Steven Halko, Doug Halward, Red Hamill, Dougie Hamilton, Freddie Hamilton, Reg Hamilton, Ron Handy, Jeff Harding, David Harlock, Bill Harris, Billy Harris, Hugh Harris, Dale Hawerchuk, Darren Haydar, Brian Hayward, John Henderson, Kevin Henderson, Murray Henderson, Red Heron, Greg Hickey, Andre Hidi, Randy Hillier, Dan Hinton, Lionel Hitchman, Todd Hlushko, Cody Hodgson, Paul Hoganson, Peter Holland, Toots Holway, Scott Howson, Al Huggins, Bob Hurlburt, Ron Hurst, Peter Ing, Johnny Ingoldsby, Ron Ingram, Gary Inness, Ralph Intranuovo, Robbie Irons, Brayden Irwin, Ric Jackman, Art Jackson, Harvey Jackson, John Jakopin, Gary Jarrett, Wes Jarvis, Bill Jennings, Mike Johnson, Bernie Johnston, Ed Kastelic, Mike Keating, Don Keenan, Chris Kelly, Dave Kerr, Rick Kessell, Frank King, Bill Knibbs, Paul Knox, Mike Knuble, Greg Koehler, Steve Konroyd, Chris Kontos, Mike Kostka, Chris Kotsopoulos, Joe Kowal, Alan Kuntz, Ken Kuzyk, Nick Kypreos, Neil Labatte, Ron Lalonde, Steve Langdon, Craig Laughlin, Paul Lawless, Danny Lawson, Gary Leeman, Manny Legace, Corey Locke, Ken Lockett, Howie Lockhart, Bob Lorimer, Darren Lowe, Steve Ludzik, Chuck Luksa, Dave Lumley, Jack Lynch, Steve Lyon, Calum Mackay, Barry MacKenzie, Kevin Maguire, Mark Major, Bryan Marchment, Nevin Markwart, Gary Marsh, Paul Marshall, Mike Marson, Tom Martin, Dennis Maruk, Jamie Masters, Brad May, Jamal Mayers, Kenndal McArdle, Andrew McBain, Cliff McBride, Sandy McCarthy, Tom McCarthy, Tom P. McCarthy, Duke McCurry, Brian McCutcheon, Bob McDonald, Brian McDonald, Sandy McGregor, Mike McKee, Steve McKenna, Kirk McLean, Scott McLellan, Sid McNabney, Gerry Meehan, Brent Meeke, Greg Meredith, Scott Metcalfe, Glen Metropolit, Rick Middleton, Greg Millen, Norm Milley, Craig Mills, Red Mitchell, Alfie Moore, Angelo Moretto, Gavin Morgan, Marc Moro, Elwin Morris, Dave Morrison, George Morrison, Matt Moulson, Jim Moxey, Craig Muni, Brian Murphy, Gord Murphy, Larry Murphy, Mike Murphy, Ken Murray, Rob Murray, Jason Muzzatti, Mark Napier, David Nemirovsky, Lance Nethery, Mike Neville, Mike Nykoluk, Peanuts O'Flaherty, Jamie Oleksiak, Cal O'Reilly, Phil Oreskovic, Keith Osborne, Mark Osborne, Danny O'Shea, Kevin O'Shea, Patrick O'Sullivan, Mike Palmateer, Brad Park, George Parsons, Joe Paterson, Doug Patey, Larry Patey, Colin Patterson, Steve Payne, Michael Peca, Matt Pelech, Anthony Peluso, Mike Pelyk, Jim Pettie, Charlie Phillips, Merlyn Phillips, Harry Pidhirny, Brandon Pirri, Alex Pirus, Geoff Platt, Tom Polanic, Chris Porter, Tom Price, Keith Primeau, Wayne Primeau, Ellie Pringle, Mike Prokopec, John Purves, Bill Quackenbush, Max Quackenbush, Jamie Ram, George Ranieri, Liam Reddox, Greg Redquest, Dave Reid, David Reid, Mike Ricci, Mike Richard, Gary Roberts, Jim Roberts, Jimmy Roberts, Nathan Robinson, Paul Ronty, Bill Root, Mike Rosati, Rolly Roulston, Ron Rowe, Kent Ruhnke, Ken Sabourin, Dave Salvian, Peter Sarno, Howard Scruton, Luke Sellars, George Servinis, Sean Shanahan, Steve Shields, Bill Shill, Jack Shill, Steve Shutt, Mike Siltala, Wayne Simmonds, Todd Simon, Cliff Simpson, Al Sims, Alf Skinner, Jeff Skinner, Don Smillie, Al Smith, Art Smith, Brendan Smith, Derrick Smith, Hooley Smith, Normie Smith, Reilly Smith, Sid Smith, Stu G. Smith, Devante Smith-Pelly, Rod Smylie, Chris Speyer, George Standing, Fred Stanfield, Jack Stanfield, Jim Stanfield, Phil Stein, Bill Stewart, Chris Stewart, John C. Stewart, Karl Stewart, Steve Stone, Mike Stothers, Ken Strong, Malcolm Subban, P.K. Subban, Frank Sullivan, Peter Sullivan, Bill Summerhill, Rick Tabaracci, Chris Tanev, Tony Tanti, Brad Tapper, Ralph Taylor, Bill Terry, Christian Thomas, Rhys Thomson, Morris Titanic, Daniel Tkaczuk, Rick Tocchet, Tyler Toffoli, Kirk Tomlinson, Mike Torchia, Raffi Torres, Ron Tugnutt, Steve Valiquette, Mike Veisor, Mike Vernace, Steve Vickers, Terry Virtue, Joel Ward, Jeff Ware, Don Webster, John Webster, Kevin Weekes, Steve Weeks, Stephen Weiss, Bill White, Barry Wilkins, Brian Wilks, Behn Wilson, Dunc Wilson, Lefty Wilson, Murray Wilson, Ron Wilson, Tom Wilson, Daniel Winnik, Jim Witherspoon, Jason Woolley, Roy Worters, John Wright, Howie Young, Tim Young, Warren Young, Ron Zanussi, Peter Zezel, Mike Zigomanis, Harry Zolnierczyk
Trenton: 7
Mel Bridgman, George Ferguson, John Garrett, Steve Graves, Jack Hamilton, Steve Smith, Tom Tilley
Trout Creek: 1
Gerry Odrowski
Unionville: 1
Bob Beckett
Uxbridge: 1
Chris Breen
Vanier: 1
Eric Gelinas
Vankleek Hill: 1
Connie Brown
Varney: 1
Eddie McCalmon
Vaughan: 1
Philip Varone
Victoria Mines: 1
Toe Blake
Walkerton: 1
Doug Brindley
Wallaceburg: 2
Seth Griffith, Doug Shedden
Waterford: 1
George Massecar
Waterloo: 6
Bobby Bauer, Don Beaupre, Bill Goldsworthy, Mike Halmo, Jim Lorentz, Clare Martin
Waubaushene: 4
Amos Arbour, Jack Arbour, Ty Arbour, Jack Portland
Wawa: 2
Denny Lambert, Chris Simon
Webbwood: 1
James Hughes
Welland: 16
Paul Bissonnette, Ken Breitenbach, Cal Clutterbuck, Yvon Corriveau, Bob Cunningham, Andre Deveaux, Matt Ellis, Dan Girardi, Wayne Groulx, Nathan Horton, Bill Huard, Matt Johnson, Mark LaForest, Daniel Paille, Garry Swain, Jamie Tardif
Weston: 7
Barry Ashbee, Paul Coffey, Iain Duncan, Rob Garner, Mike Liut, Adam Oates, Craig Ramsay
Wheatley: 1
Glen Skov
Whitby: 3
James Neal, Victor Oreskovich, Paul Ranger
White River: 1
Trevor Halverson
Williamstown: 1
Kent McDonell
Winchester: 5
Matt Carkner, Slater Koekkoek, Ken McRae, Larry Robinson, Moe Robinson
Windsor: 51
Russ Adam, Blair Barnes, Matt Beleskey, Brett Bellemore, Bob Boughner, Pat Boutette, Ted Bulley, Sean Burke, Keith Crowder, Ken Daneyko, Tie Domi, Clare Drouillard, Cam Fowler, Ron Friest, David Gagnon, Ken Hodge, Jr., Jack Jackson, Dan Jancevski, Ed Jovanovski, Zack Kassian, Rick Kehoe, Tim Kerr, David Liffiton, Ray Markham, Matt Martin, Ed Mio, Steve Moore, Dan Newman, Wes O'Neill, Bob Parent, Barry Potomski, Bob Probert, Matt Puempel, Joel Quenneville, Mark Renaud, Bruce Shoebottom, Brad Smith, D.J. Smith, Alek Stojanov, Mark Suzor, Harvey Teno, Ray Timgren, Tim Trimper, John Tucker, Joe Turner, Aaron Ward, Eric Wellwood, Kyle Wellwood, Tom Williams, Ron Wilson, Ryan Wilson
Wingham: 1
Dave Farrish
Woodbridge: 4
Mike Angelidis, Mark Cundari, Steve Eminger, Jimmy Jones
Woodstock: 4
Jake Muzzin, Doug Shelton, Glenn Smith, Jeff Zehr
York: 2
Glen Sharpley, Mike Ware

PRINCE EDWARD ISLAND 30
Charlottetown: 18
Dave Cameron, Mark Flood, John Hughes, Tyler Larter, Al MacAdam, Jason MacDonald, Shane MacEachern, Garth MacGuigan, Drew MacIntyre, Billy MacMillan, Bob MacMillan, Adam McQuaid, Hickey Nicholson, Paddy Nolan, Gary Simmons, Bob Stewart, Wes Trainor, Bob Whitlock
Montague: 1
Brad Richards
Murray River: 1
Brandon Gormley
Summerdale: 3
Darryl Boyce, Brett Gallant, Maynard Schurman
Summerside: 7
Chuck Cahill, John Chabot, Gerard Gallant, Nathan McIver, Steve Ott, Kent Paynter, Errol Thompson

QUEBEC 796
Acton Vale: 1
Francis Breault
Alexis-des-monts: 1
Jean-Francois Damphousse
Allomette: 1
Leo Lafrance
Alma: 1
Guillaume Desbiens
Amos: 1
Guillaume Lefebvre
Amqui: 1
Sebastien Caron
Ancienne-Lorette: 1
Patrice Bergeron
Angegardien: 1
Michel Bolduc
Anjou: 3
Martin Brochu, Eric Fichaud, Felix Potvin
Arvida: 3
Bill Dineen, Steve Maltais, Sam St. Laurent
Asbestos: 4
Gilles Hamel, Jean Hamel, Don Marcotte, Sean McKenna
Aylmer: 1
Leo Gravelle
Bagotville: 1
J.C. Tremblay
Baie Comeau: 3
Yves Belanger, Pierre-Cedric Labrie, Dave Morissette
Beaconsfield: 1
Ben Walter
Beauceville: 1
Stephane Veilleux
Beauport: 3
Maxime Ouellet, Michel Picard, Christian Tanguay
Bellefeuille: 1
Francis Belanger
Beloeil: 1
Olivier Michaud
Blainville: 1
Pierre Dagenais
Boucherville: 3
Gilbert Delorme, Kevin Marshall, Stephane Quintal
Bout De L'Isle: 1
Bucky Buchanan
Bristol: 1
Bill Cowley
Brownsburg: 2
Dave Campbell, Pierre Giroux
Buckingham: 5
Billy Cameron, Earl Campbell, Ed Gorman, Claude Lemieux, Rod Lorrain
Cap-de-la-Madelaine: 3
Pierre Aubry, Leon Rochefort, Jean-Guy Talbot
Cap Rouge: 1
Jon Audy-Marchessault
Caughnawaga: 1
Bobby Simpson
Causapscal: 1
Jean-Guy Morissette

APPENDIX

Chambly: 1
Denis Herron

Chambly Basin: 2
Tony Demers, Fern Perreault

Chandler: 1
Mathieu Garon

Charlemagne: 1
Daniel Gauthier

Charlesbourg: 2
Marc Chouinard, Jean-Philippe Cote

Chicoutimi: 9
Michel Bergeron, Luc Dufour, Germain Gagnon, Johnny Gagnon, Leo Gaudreault, Fern Gauthier, Alain Langlais, John Smrke, Georges Vezina

Cowansville: 2
Stephane Beauregard, Bob Richer

Delson: 1
Marcel Cousineau

Dolbeau: 1
Alain Caron

Donnaconna: 3
Eddy Godin, Gaetan Royer, Remi Royer

Dorval: 1
Jason Demers

Drummondville: 15
Serge Boisvert, Sebastien Charpentier, Yvan Cournoyer, Gilbert Dionne, Marcel Dionne, Ray Fortin, Alan Haworth, Gord Haworth, Claude Houde, Yvon Lambert, Eric Messier, Lester Patrick, Marcel Pelletier, Mathieu Perreault, Leo Thiffault

Duparquet: 1
Elmer Vasko

Eardley: 1
Hib Milks

East Broughton: 1
Mario Lessard

Ferme-Neuve: 2
Jose Charbonneau, Daniel Dore

Gaspe: 3
George McNaughton, Cedric Paquette, Pascal Trepanier

Gaspesie: 1
Fern Leblanc

Gatineau: 7
Daniel Briere, Mathieu Carle, Francois Guay, Eric Landry, Steve Martins, Alexandre Picard, Christian Soucy

Granby: 4
Nicolas Blanchard, Michel Dion, Marc Tardif, Fred Thurier

Grande Baie: 1
Jeannot Gilbert

Grand'Mere: 3
Russ Blinco, Andre Corriveau, Fern Rivard

Greenfield Park: 4
Sylvain Couturier, Torrey Mitchell, Jerome Samson, Frederic St. Denis

Harve St. Pierre: 1
Jean-Francois Jomphe

Hauterive: 1
Jean-Claude Bergeron

Herbertville-Station: 1
Frederic Chabot

Hull: 10
Jeff Allan, Derick Brassard, Michel Larocque, Guy Larose, Christian Matte, Rob Murphy, Pierre Parenteau, Stephane J.G. Richer, Dominic Roussel, Guy Trottier

Ile Bizard: 1
Vincent Lecavalier

Ile Perrot: 1
Rich Leduc

Joliette: 3
Lucien Deblois, Andre Faust, Jonathan Girard

Jonquiere: 1
Denis Dupere

Kenogami: 2
Joe Hardy, Pierre Pilote

Kirkland: 1
Brandon Reid

Knowlton: 1
Nels Crutchfield

Labelle: 1
Bobby Guindon

L'Abord a Plouffe: 1
Jean-Guy Lagace

Lachine: 14
Billy Bell, Kelly Burnett, Bob Davis, Frank Eddolls, George Gardner, Mike Gaul, Phil Goyette, Charlie Hodge, Claude Lapointe, Frank Mailley, Georges

Mantha, Pete Morin, Reg Sinclair, Claude Verret

Lachute: 4
Denis Hamel, Kevin Lowe, Gilles Lupien, Glenn Tomalty

Lac la Tortue: 1
Marcel Pronovost

Lac St. Charles: 2
Martin Biron, Mathieu Biron

Lac St. Jean: 2
Armand Gaudreault, Jean Ratelle

Lafontaine: 1
Yann Danis

L'Annonciation: 1
Roger Leger

LaSalle: 11
Jeff Chychrun, Patrick Cote, Nicolas Deschamps, Nicolas Deslauriers, Gilles Gratton, Norm Gratton, Daniel Guerard, Jacques Lemaire, Mike O'Neill, Anthony Stewart, Derek Wilkinson

La Sarre: 1
Bob Mongrain

Laurier Station: 1
David Desharnais

Lauzon: 1
Andre Lacroix

Laval: 14
Donald Audette, Jonathan Bernier, Mathieu Chouinard, Simon Despres, Pascal Dupuis, Philippe Dupuis, Steven Finn, Jean-Francois Fortin, Martin Grenier, Patrick Labrecque, Daniel Laperriere, Maxime Macenauer, Martin St. Louis, Jose Theodore

Laverlochere: 1
Bob Ritchie

Lemoyne: 1
Maxime Talbot

Les Saulles: 2
Gaetan Duchesne, Alexandre Picard

Levis: 2
David Gosselin, Pierre-Luc Letourneau Leblond

Longueuil: 7
Daniel Berthiaume, Richard Brodeur, Claude Evans, Maxime Fortunus, Luc Gauthier, Bruno Gervais, Francois Groleau

Lotbiniere: 1
Charlie Langlois

Magog: 1
Albert Langlois

Malartic: 3
Yves Bergeron, Lucien Grenier, Jim A. Watson

Maniwaki: 2
Marc Labelle, Gino Odjick

Masham: 1
Jocelyn Gauvreau

Mason: 1
Herb Rheaume

Massawippi: 1
Bruce Cline

Matane: 4
Alain Cote, Jacques Lemieux, Yves Racine, Nils Tremblay

Mayo: 1
Hazen McAndrew

Mont Laurier: 4
Sebastien Bisaillon, Dan Cloutier, Sylvain Cloutier, Jocelyn Lemieux

Mont Louis: 1
Jude Drouin

Montmagny: 1
Alain G. Cote

Montmorency: 1
Gilles Tremblay

Montreal: 265
Ramzi Abid, Shawn Anderson, Jean-Sebastien Aubin, Mark Barberio, Marco Baron, Serge Beaudoin, Marc Bergevin, Bob Berry, John Bethel, Paul Bibeault, Alex Biega, Danny Biega, Andre Binette, Dan Blackburn, Sylvain Blouin, Patrick Boileau, Mike A. Boland, Alexandre Bolduc, Marcel Bonin, Patrick Bordeleau, Mike Bossy, Butch Bouchard, Joel Bouchard, Pierre Bouchard, Andre Boudrias, Conrad Bourcier, Jean Bourcier, Ray Bourque, Neil Brady, Patrice Brisebois, Connie Broden, Martin Brodeur, Steve Brule, Ron Buchanan, Hy Buller, Fred Burchell, Robin Burns, Walt Buswell, Larry Carriere, Ron Carter, Sebastien Centomo, Lorne Chabot, Michael Chaput, Denis Chasse, Alex Chiasson, Enrico Ciccone, Odie Cleghorn, Sprague Cleghorn, Rey Comeau, Bert Connelly, Roger Cormier, Mark Cornforth, Jim Corsi, Daniel Corso, Yves Courteau, Corey Crawford, Moe Croghan, Glen Currie, Claude Cyr, Alexandre Daigle,

J.J. Daigneault, Vincent Damphousse, Dan Daoust, Eric Daze, Jean-Paul Denis, Marc Denis, Jacques Deslauriers, Gary Dineen, Jason Doig, Bobby Dollas, Gord Donnelly, Andre Dore, Steve Dubinsky, Anthony Duclair, Jean-Pierre Dumont, Norm Dupont, Yanick Dupre, Eddie Emberg, Bob Errey, Stephane Fiset, Gerry Fleming, Reggie Fleming, Steve Fletcher, Peter Folco, Dave Forbes, Connie Forey, Steve Gainey, Michel Galarneau, Gary Galley, Denis Gauthier, Jean Gauthier, Jean-Guy Gendron, Bernie Geoffrion, Danny Geoffrion, Jean-Sebastien Giguere, Rod Gilbert, Bob Girard, Daniel Goneau, Benoit Gosselin, Marc-Andre Gragnani, Jean-Luc Grand-Pierre, Benoit Gratton, Terry Gray, Richard Grenier, Jocelyn Guevremont, Ben Guite, Pierre Hamel, Walter Harnott, Doug Harvey, Paul Haynes, Gerry Heffernan, Robbie Holland, Gord Hollingworth, Greg Holst, Eric Houde, Mike Hough, Martin Houle, Jim Hrivnak, Ryan Hughes, Harry Hyland, Gord Hynes, Paul Jacobs, Pierre Jarry, Brian Johnson, Eddie Johnston, Ross Johnstone, Steve Kasper, Duke Keats, Mike Krushelnyski, Moe L'Abbe, Francois Lacombe, Daniel Lacroix, Eric Lacroix, Ernie Laforce, Roger Lafreniere, Serge Lajeunesse, Bobby Lalonde, Chris Langevin, Jean-Marc Lanthier, Ian Laperriere, Guy Lapointe, Georges Laraque, Mario Larocque, Phil Latreille, Dominic Lavoie, Gord Laxton, Patrice Lefebvre, Yanick Lehoux, Alain Lemieux, Bob Lemieux, Mario Lemieux, Gaston Leroux, Jean-Yves Leroux, Francis Lessard, Kris Letang, Normand Leveille, Charles Linglet, Dave Logan, Robert Logan, Matt Lombardi, Roberto Luongo, Don MacIver, Fleming Mackell, John Mahaffy, Tom Manastersky, Jimmy Mann, Sylvio Mantha, Daniel Marois, Gilles Marotte, Don Marshall, Randy McKay, Tony McKegney, Ron Meighan, Scott Mellanby, Eric Meloche, Gilles Meloche, Corrado Micalef, Sergio Momesso, Hartland Monahan, Michel Mongeau, Jim Montgomery, Dickie Moore, Stephane Morin, Joey Mormina, Jim Morrison, Ken Mosdell, Hal Murphy, Alain Nasreddine, Maxim Noreau, Buddy O'Connor, George O'Grady, Gates Orlando, Jimmy Orlando, Paul Pageau, Bernie Parent, Rich Parent, Michel Parizeau, Rollie Paulhus, Roger Pelletier, Joel Perrault, Eric Perrin, Jimmy Peters, Jimmy Peters, Jr., Noel Picard, Robert Picard, Roger Picard, Michel Plasse, Adrien Plavsic, Emile Poirier, Kevin Poulin, Yves Preston, Claude Provost, Jean Pusie, Jonathan Racine, Paul-Marcel Raymond, Mel Read, Mike Ribeiro, Henri Richard, Maurice Richard, Dave Ritchie, Claude Robert, Earl Robinson, Louis Robitaille, Luc Robitaille, Ernie Roche, Roberto Romano, Bobby Rousseau, Guy Rousseau, Roland Rousseau, Bernie Saunders, Yann Sauve, Reggie Savage, Serge Savard, Marco Scandella, Richard Sevigny, Daniel Shank, Scott Sharples, Frank Sheppard, Johnny Sheppard, Martin Simard, Bob Sirois, Bob Sneddon, Martin St. Amour, Bruno St. Jacques, Nels Stewart, Gaston Therrien, Gilles Thibeadeau, Jocelyn Thibault, Mario Thyer, Josh Tordjman, Patrick Traverse, Mario Tremblay, Ian Turnbull, Nick Vachon, Carol Vadnais, Randy Velischek, Marc-Edouard Vlasic, Phil Watson, Peter White, Archie Wilcox, Bernie Wolfe, Gump Worsley, Ross Yates, Matthew Yeats, Larry Zeidel

Noranda: 13
Christain Bordeleau, J.P. Bordeleau, Paulin Bordeleau, Jacques Caron, Jacques Cloutier, Dave Keon, Jean Lemieux, Jean-Louis Levasseur, Pit Martin, Ted Ouimet, Bob Sullivan, Dale Tallon, Sylvain Turgeon

Notre Dame de la Salette: 1
Richard David

Nouvelle: 1
Louis Sleigher

Outremont: 1
Tom Draper

Padoue: 1
Serge Bernier

Palmarolle: 1
Rogie Vachon

Papineau: 1
Louis Berlinquette

Peribonka: 1
Michel Goulet

Pierrefonds: 3
Paul Brosseau, Normand Lacombe, Peter Worrell

Pierreville: 1
Matthieu Descoteaux

Pointe-aux-trembles: 3
Yves Beaudoin, Jacques Locas, Yannick Tremblay

Pointe Claire: 4
Marc Boileau, Rene Boileau, Alexandre Burrows, Louis Leblanc

Pointe Gatineau: 1
Denis Savard

Pontiac: 1
Tod Sloan

Pont-Rouge: 1
Joe Juneau

Quebec City: 47
Joel Baillargeon, Marty Barry, Steve Bernier, Frank Brophy, Mario Brunetta, Guy Chouinard, Sylvain Cote, Maurice Courteau, Xavier Delisle, Gord Dineen, Kevin Dineen, Mario Doyon, Rene Drolet, Donald Dufresne, Jonathan Ferland, Len Fontaine, Eric Germain, Alexandre Giroux, Camille Henry, Brent Imlach, Michel Lachance, Pierre Lacroix, Simon Lajeunesse, Jackie Leclair, Reggie Lemelin, Cliff Malone, Joe Malone, Jean Marois, Mario Marois, Jack McDonald, Bert McInenly, Mike McMahon, Jr., Gerry McNeil, Jame Pollock, Marc-Antoine Pouliot, Pascal Rheaume, Jacques Richard, Pierre Rioux, Mario Roberge, Serge Roberge, Jean-Marc Routhier, Patrick Roy, Derek Smith, Paul Stastny, Yan Stastny, Vince Tremblay, Alain Vigneault

Repentigny: 4
Benoit Hogue, Pascal Leclaire, Richard Nantais, Jason Pominville

Richmond: 1
Sylvain Lefebvre

Rimouski: 3
Gabriel Bourque, Michel Ouellet, Alain Raymond

Ripon: 1
Stephane Richer

Robertsville: 1
Dan Poulin

Rosemere: 1
Jean-Yves Roy

Rouyn: 11
Bob Blackburn, Roland Cloutier, Wayne Connelly, Jacques Cossette, Eric Desjardins, Chris Hayes, Rejean Houle, Jacques Lapperriere, Steve Larouche, Bill McDonagh, Pierre Turgeon

Rouyn-Noranda: 4
Marc-Andre Cliche, Stephane Matteau, Andre Racicot, Andre St. Laurent

Ste. Adele: 2
Stephane Charbonneau, Francois Leroux

St. Agapit: 1
Antoine Vermette

Ste. Agathe: 2
Jonathan Drouin, Ron Stern

St. Anicet: 1
Leo Quenneville

Ste. Anne de Bellevue: 4
Benoit Brunet, Hec Lepine, Pit Lepine, Phil Myre

Ste. Anne de la Perad: 1
Benoit Dusablon

Ste. Anne-des-Plaines: 1
Jonathan Delisle

St. Antoine-de-Pontbriand: 1
Michel Dumas

St. Apollinaire: 1
Philippe Boucher

St. Bonaventure: 1
Patrick Lalime

Ste. Catherine: 1
Guillaume Latendresse

St. Charles: 1
Christian Laflamme

St. Charles Bellechasse: 1
Guy Labrie

Ste. Elizabeth: 1
Stephane Guerard

St. Emile: 1
Real Cloutier

St. Ephrem: 1
Eric Bertrand

St. Esprit: 2
Julien Brouillette, Gilles Gilbert

St. Etienne: 1
Edmond Bouchard

St. Fabien: 1
Patrick Coulombe

Ste. Foy: 4
Claude Boivin, Simon Gagne, Steve Penney, Stephane Roy

St. Francis D'Assisi: 1
Mike Labadie

APPENDIX

St. Gabriel de Brandon: 1
Dick Sarrazin
Ste. Genevieuve: 2
Bob Sauve, Jean-Francois Sauve
St. Georges: 1
Mathieu Roy
St. Georges de Beauce: 1
Jesse Belanger
St. Hilaire: 1
Bob Champoux
St. Hyacinthe: 8
Michel Archambault, Oscar Aubuchon, Marc-Andre Bourdon, Denis DeJordy, Louis Domingue, Jean-Paul Gladu, Vincent Riendeau, David Savard
St. Janvier: 1
Alain Belanger
St. Jean: 3
Art Alexandre, Claude Larose, Jean-Francois Quintin
St. Jean-sur-Richelieu: 2
Jeff Deslauriers, David Laliberte
St. Jerome: 4
Tod Campeau, Jonathan Huberdeau, Patrick Lebeau, Stephane Lebeau
St. Joseph de Beauce: 1
Junior Lessard
Ste. Justine: 1
Alex Tanguay
St. Lambert: 1
P.C. Drouin
St. Laurent: 1
Mathieu Darche
St. Leonard: 2
Norm Aubin, Maxim Lapierre
St. Louis-de-France: 1
Marc-Andre Bergeron
St. Malo: 1
Michel Petit
St. Odilon: 1
Simon Nolet
St. Prime: 1
Gilles Bilodeau
St. Raymond: 1
Jean-Marc Richard
St. Remi de Rinqwick: 1
Connie Dion
Ste. Rose: 1
Martin Desjardins
Sayabec: 1
Jordan Caron
Sept-Iles: 4
Guy Carbonneau, Steve Duchesne, Karl Dykhuis, Rob Zettler
Shawinigan: 3
Michael Bournival, Martin Gelinas, Jacques Mailhot
Shawinigan Falls: 9
Michel Briere, Gerry Desaulniers, Jean-Paul Lamirande, Marcel Paille, Jacques Plante, Andre Pronovost, Claude Pronovost, Jean Pronovost, Gino Rozzini
Shawville: 5
Murph Chamberlain, Ed Finnigan, Frank Finnigan, Terry Murray, Marc Rodgers
Sherbrooke: 20
Eric Belanger, Stephane Brochu, Pierre-Marc Bouchard, Dan Chicoine, Mathieu Dandenault, Christian Dube, Gilles Dube, Norm Dube, Bill Heindl, Jean-Francois Labbe, Olivier Magnan, Gord McRae, Yanic Perreault, David Perron, Gerry Plamandon, Christian Proulx, Bob Rivard, Stephane Robidas, Claude St. Saveur, Jimmy Waite
Sillery: 1
Henry Hicks
Sorel: 10
Francois Beauchemin, Michel Belhumeur, Claude Cardin, Frederic Cassivi, Michel Deziel, Marc-Andre Fleury, Andre Gill, Claude Laforge, Wildor Larochelle, Pierre Mondou
South Durham: 1
J-P Leblanc
Taschereau: 1
Pierre Larouche
Temiscamingue: 4
Gaston Gingras, Richard Lemieux, Jake Rathwell, Andre Savard
Terrebonne: 3
Yves Heroux, Jean-Francois Jacques, Xavier Ouellet
Thetford Mines: 6
Bob Fillion, Marcel Fillion, Simon Gamache, Mario Gosselin, Daniel Poudrier, Patrice Tardif

Thurso: 2
Bill Clement, Guy Lafleur
Trois-Rivieres: 16
Steve Begin, Jean Beliveau, Pete Bellefeuille, Gilles Boisvert, Marc Bureau, Alain Daigle, Marc Dufour, Andre Dupont, Red Goupille, Andre Hinse, Bob Perreault, Rene Robert, Normand Rochefort, Pierre Sevigny, Jacques Toupin, Gilles Villemure
Val d'Or: 3
Serge Aubin, Dan Bouchard, Dany Sabourin
Valleyfield: 7
Mario Faubert, Martin Gendron, Rosario Joanette, Albert Leduc, Didier Pitre, Pierre Plante, Yves Sarault
Val-Senneville: 1
Philippe Cornet
Vanier: 1
Patrick Poulin
Verdun: 19
Normand Baron, Jim Bartlett, Eric Charron, Guy Charron, Ed Courtenay, Jean Cusson, Denis Cyr, Polly Drouin, Ron Harris, Bobby Lee, Claude Legris, Fern Majeau, Rick Martin, Les Ramsay, Jean Savard, Dollard St. Laurent, Dan Vincelette, Wally Weir, Moe White
Victoriaville: 7
Rene Corbet, Phillip Danault, Philippe DeRouville, Eric Lavigne, Real Lemieux, Gilbert Perreault, P.J. Stock
Ville Degelis: 1
Gabriel Dumont
Ville de Vanier: 1
Rene Leclerc
Ville St. Pierre: 1
Martin Lapointe
Windsor: 2
Rejean Cloutier, Marc Fortier
Yamaska: 1
Armond Mondou

SASKATCHEWAN 499
Admiral: 1
Jim Bedard
Allan: 1
Willie Brossart
Aneroid: 1
Patrick Marleau
Arcola: 1
Prestin Ryan
Asquith: 1
Hal Picketts
Assiniboia: 2
Doug MacDonald, Clint Smith
Aylesbury: 1
Matt Watkins
Aylsham: 1
Greg Classen
Balcarres: 1
Doug Trapp
Bengough: 1
Earl Robertson
Big River: 3
Hub Macey, Jim Neilson, Barry Pederson
Birch Hills: 1
Marshall Johnston
Blaine Lake: 1
Hugh Coflin
Borden: 1
Bill Hajt
Brock: 1
Steve MacIntyre
Canora: 3
Cliff Korroll, Cam Severson, Tyler Wright
Carlyle: 1
Brenden Morrow
Central Butte: 2
Blair Jones, Clarke Wilm
Churchbridge: 2
Lionel Heinrich, Kevin Kaminski
Climax: 2
Gord Kluzak, Rocky Trottier
Cralk: 3
Jim Archibald, Garnet Exelby, Jeremy Reich
Craven: 1
Frank Ingram
Creelman: 1
Morris Mott
Cudworth: 3
Gerry Ehman, Orland Kurtenbach, Paul Shmyr

Cupar: 1
Rob Tudor
Delisle: 5
Doug Bentley, Max Bentley, Reg Bentley, Dick Butler, Jack Miller
Dinsmore: 1
Jim Leavins
Diwide: 1
Les Colwill
Dodsland: 3
Don Gillen, Bob Hoffmeyer, Brad McCrimmon
Drake: 1
Robin Bartel
Dunblane: 1
Steve Buzinski
Dysart: 3
Fern Flaman, Bill Kyle, Gus Kyle
Edington: 1
Harvey Bennett
Esterhazy: 2
Chris Herperger, Frank Mario
Estevan: 4
Blair Atcheynum, Al Nicholson, Derrick Pouliot, Trent Whitfield
Fairlight: 1
Vic Myles
Fielding: 1
Neil Hawryliw
Filmore: 1
Buzz Boll
Fleming: 1
Fred Gordon
Floral: 1
Gordie Howe
Foam Lake: 3
Pat Elynuik, Bernie Federko, Dennis Polonich
Fort Qu'Appelle: 2
Eddie Shore, Frank Waite
Frobisher: 1
Tom Dewar
Gainsborough: 2
Lew Morrison, Ralph Nattrass
Goodsoil: 1
Ron Greschner
Gravelbourg: 1
Gord Sherven
Grenfell: 2
Bryan Hextall, Max Sutherland
Gull Lake: 1
Jim McKenzie
Hafford: 2
Jason Herter, Roger Kortko
Herbert: 1
Henry Dyck
Hudson Bay: 3
Grant Jennings, Larry Lozinski, Trent Yawney
Humboldt: 10
Jerry Engele, Glenn Hall, Ralph Klassen, Brad Lauer, Tony Leswick, Ross Lonsberry, Kyle McLaren, Nathan Paetsch, Brendan Witt, Brendan Woods
Indian Head: 1
Jeff Lank
Jansen: 1
Ken Schinkel
Kamsack: 4
Jack Church, Darcy Hordichuk, Harold Phillipoff, Wayne Smith
Kelvington: 2
Wendel Clark, Barry Melrose
Kerrobert: 1
Curtis Murphy
Kindersley: 10
Bob Bourne, Derek Dorsett, Curtis Glencross, Lorry Gloeckner, Joel Kwiatkowski, Dave Lewis, Jim Mathieson, Barrie Meissner, Dick Meissner, Greg Paslawski
Kinistino: 2
Gord Nelson, Gord Redahl
Lac La Ronge: 1
Glenn Johannesen
Lac Pelletier: 1
Lloyd Ailsby
Landis: 2
Tony Hemmerling, Ed Zeniuk
Lang: 2
Dennis Sobchuk, Gene Sobchuk
Langenburg: 1
Kelly Buchberger

Lanigan: 5
Bob Baun, Sheldon Brookbank, Wade Brookbank, Brian Propp, Todd Strueby
Lashburn: 1
Dwight Carruthers
Lloydminster: 11
Colby Armstrong, Garnet Bailey, Lyle Bradley, Blair Chapman, Barry Gibbs, Bob Hassard, Braden Holtby, Larry Leach, Justin Mapletoft, Wade Redden, Spence Tatchell
Loon Lake: 1
Ed Cooper
Lucky Lake: 2
Darin Kimble, Glen Smith
Lumsden: 3
Bill Hay, Earl Miller, Beattie Ramsay
MacNutt: 1
Duane Rupp
Major: 1
Laurie Boschman
Manor: 1
Murray Armstrong
Maple Creek: 3
Barry Dean, Gordie Poirier, Zack Smith
Maryfield: 1
Lynn Powis
Meadow Lake: 7
Blake Comeau, Len Esau, Jeff Friesen, D.J. King, Dwight King, Mike Siklenka, Jeremy Yablonski
Melfort: 5
Lorne Henning, Lane Lambert, Pat MacLeod, Jaden Schwartz, Tyson Strachan
Melville: 9
Sid Abel, Phil Besler, Tim Cheveldae, Jim Franks, Shaun Heshka, Todd McLellan, Alex Motter, Jarret Stoll, Arch Wilder
Milestone: 1
Garth Boesch
Montmartre: 1
Norm Beaudin
Moose Jaw: 21
Frank Ashworth, Mike Blaisdell, Brent Gilchrist, Clark Gillies, Norm Johnson, Norm Larson, Bill Lecaine, Bill Lesuk, Reed Low, Butch McDonald, Larry McIntyre, John Miner, Glenn Resch, Don Saleski, Doug Smail, Kenny Smith, Glen Sonmor, Ed Staniowski, George Swarbrick, Jim Wiste, Marty Zoborosky
Moosomin: 5
Dennis Abgrall, Brett Clark, Chuck Corrigan, Dave Dunn, Dave Tippett
Naicam: 1
Lynn Loyns
Neudorf: 1
Ed Litzenberger
Nipawin: 2
Dane Byers, Lyndon Byers
Nokomis: 3
Jordan Hendry, Doug Horbul, Elmer Lach
Norquay: 2
Lloyd Gronsdahl, Ed Panagabko
North Battleford: 13
Ron Delorme, Brennan Evans, Bobby Francis, Emile Francis, Bruce Hoffort, Dale Hoganson, Bernie Lukowich, Merlin Malinowski, Corey Schwab, Gregg Sheppard, Morris Stefaniw, Allan Tuer, Layne Ulmer
Odessa: 2
Jackie Schmidt, Joe "Otto" Schmidt
Outlook: 1
Shay Stephenson
Oxbow: 3
Lindsay Carson, Theo Fleury, Reg Kerr
Paddockwood: 1
Shayne Toporowski
Paradise Hills: 1
John Rogers
Pierceland: 1
Grant Erickson
Ponteix: 1
Mark Lamb
Porcupine Plain: 1
Kelly Chase
Prelate: 1
Mark Pederson
Prince Albert: 20
Mike Bales, Todd Bergen, Johnny Bower, Scotty Cameron, Adam Cracknell, Scott Daniels, Guy Del-parte, Tavis Hansen, Dale Henry, Dave Manson, Josh Manson, Ryan McGill, Jerry Mrazek, Jeff Nelson, Todd Nelson, Ryan Parent, Denis Pederson, Terry Ruskowski, Joey Tetarenko, Rick Wilson

APPENDIX

Punnicht: 1
Nolan Yonkman
Quill Lake: 3
Lyle Odelein, Selmar Odelein, Ed Vokes
Rabbit Lake: 1
Skip Krake
Radville: 1
Darcy Verot
Rama: 1
Barry Nieckar
Redvers: 1
Dean Kennedy
Regina: 88
Dale Anderson, Chris Armstrong, Murray Balfour, Sandy Beadle, Harry Bell, Curt Bennett, Red Berenson, Dwight Bialowas, James Black, Tyler Bozak, Tyler Bunz, Glen Burdon, Garth Butcher, Gord Buttrey, Drew Callander, John Callander, Brett Carson, Joe Carveth, Barry Cummins, Kevin Dahl, Lorne Davis, Don Deacon, Robert Dirk, Devan Dubnyk, Duke Dukowski, Mathew Dumba, Rocky Dundas, Jordan Eberle, Mark Ferner, Dunc Fisher, Dan Focht, Bill Folk, Scott Garland, Ryan Getzlaf, Tanner Glass, Dirk Graham, Taylor Hall, Josh Harding, Terry Harper, Scott Hartnell, Jamie Heward, Bill Hicke, Ernie Hicke, Brian Hill, Terry Hollinger, Fran Huck, Gerry James, Lou Jankowski, David Karpa, Bob Kirkpatrick, Mark Kirton, Terry Kleisinger, Chris Kunitz, Robbie Laird, Jack Lancien, Kim MacDougall, Paul Masnick, Walt McCartney, Jim McGeough, Jackie McLeod, Joby Messier, Mitch Messier, Brendan Mikkelson, Gerry Minor, Garth Murray, Ryan Murray, Bill Orban, Nathan Oystrick, Garry Peters, Rich Preston, Alan Rittinger, Nick Schultz, Mike Sillinger, Don Smith, Chris Snell, Ron Snell, Al Staley, Doug Stevenson, Art Strobel, Bill Sutherland, Bob Turner, Norm Tustin, Gord Wappel, Bill Warwick, Grant Warwick, Doug Wickenheiser, Jeremy Williams, Larry Wright
Rosetown: 2
Randy Ireland, Quintin Laing
Rosthern: 2
Jim Hrycuik, Art Wiebe
Rouleau: 1
Keith Aulie
Sandy Lake Reserve: 1
Fred Sasakamoose
Saskatoon: 79
Keith Allen, Red Almas, Mel Angelstad, Riley Armstrong, Brent Ashton, Ryan Bayda, Wade Belak, Byron Bitz, Ron Boehm, Derek Boogaard, Russ Brayshaw, Cam Brown, Dave Brown, Kim Clackson, Sean Collins, Gerry Couture, Jared Cowen, Hugh Currie, Bobby Dawes, Kevin Doell, Dan Ellis, Shane Endicott, Todd Ewen, Hec Fowler, Perry Ganchar, Bert Gardiner, Michael Garnett, Eric Gryba, Chris Hajt, John Harms, Jim Hay, Vic Howe, Ryan Keller, Lloyd Klein, Dieter Kochan, Don Kozak, Darcy Kuemper, Moe Lemay, Jack Leswick, Pete Leswick, Pat Lundy, Vic Lynn, Keith Magnuson, Chris McAllister, Brayden McNabb, Larry Melnyk, Don Morrison, Rod Morrison, Jack Norris, Rod Norrish, Dave Parro, George Pesut, Warren Peters, Rich Pilon, Gerry Pinder, Darroll Powe, Gary Rissling, Larry Sacharuk, Cory Sarich, Brayden Schenn, Luke Schenn, Bobby Schmautz, Cliff Schmautz, Scott Scissons, George Senick, Randy Smith, Bob Stephenson, Darren Van Impe, Ed Van Impe, Darren Veitch, Mick Vukota, Jesse Wallin, Cam Ward, Harry Watson, Tyler Weiman, Fred Williams, Gord Williams, James Wright, Ralph Wycherley
Sceptre: 1
Bert Olmstead
Semans: 1
Jim O'Neil
Shaunavon: 2
Gary Aldcorn, Rhett Warrener
Silton: 1
Mush March
Speers: 1
Morris Lukowich
Spy Hill: 1
Jeff Odgers
Star City: 1
Bob Solinger
Stewart Valley: 1
Travis Moen
Strasbourg: 2
Greg Hubick, Jesse Schultz
Stoughton: 1
Lorne Carr
Sutherland: 2
Hal Laycoe, Charlie Rayner
Swift Current: 9
Jeff Buchanan, Jack Forsey, Marc Habscheid, Bill Hogaboam, Boyd Kane, Trent McCleary, Darcy Regier, Darrel Scoville, Jeff Toms
Togo: 1
Ted Hampson
Tubrose: 1
Fred Hucul
Unity: 2
Curtis Brown, Boyd Gordon
Val Marie: 1
Bryan Trottier
Vanguard: 1
Al Rollins
Vonda: 1
Lulu Denis
Wakaw: 4
Dave Balon, James Latos, Dave Michayluk, Linden Vey
Waldheim: 1
Dave Schultz
Warman: 1
Ed Dyck
Watrous: 1
Paul Meger
Watson: 2
Max McNab, Dustin Tokarski
Wawota: 1
Brooks Laich
Weyburn: 9
Rene Chapdelaine, Larry Giroux, Wilf Hart, Larry Hornung, Walt Ledingham, Brian Marchinko, Jim McTaggart, Rick Shinske, Tiger Williams
Wilcox: 3
Don Metz, Nick Metz, Jeff Ulmer
Wilkie: 1
Ralph Keller
Wynyard: 2
Wade Skolney, Richard Zemlak
Yellow Grass: 2
Nolan Schaefer, Peter Schaefer
Yorkton: 7
Mike Chernoff, Brent Fedyk, Mervin Kuryluk, Clayton Pachal, Larry Popein, Metro Prystai, Matt Zaba

YUKON.................... 2
Whitehorse: 2
Bryon Baltimore, Peter Sturgeon

UNITED STATES (1,065)

Alabama.................. 2
Jared Ross, Aut Tuten

Alaska.................... 12
Casey Bailey, Matt Carle, Ty Conklin, Joey Crabb, Brandon Dubinsky, Scott Gomez, Barrett Heisten, Jason Ryznar, Brian Swanson, Nate Thompson, Tim Wallace, B.J. Young

Arizona................... 2
Jim Brown , Sean Couturier

California.................. 39
Chris Ahrens, Ralph Barahona, Beau Bennett, John Blue, Jonathon Blum, Mitch Callahan, Noah Clarke, Craig Coxe, John Emmons, Emerson Etem, Craig Ferguson, Tim Friday, Gabe Gauthier, Rocco Grimaldi, Matt Hervey, Ryan Hollweg, Matthew Konan, Brandon Kozun, Mike Lampman, Ray Macias, Kevan Miller, Matthew Nieto, Lee Norwood, Brooks Orpik, Scott Parker, Rhett Rakhshani, Dave Roberts, Chad Ruhwedel, Kerby Rychel, Brian Salcido, Roy Sommer, Garrett Stafford, Brett Sterling, Jeremy Stevenson, Matt Tennyson, Stephen Tepper, Casey Wellman, Rik Wilson, Jason Zucker

Colorado.................. 11
Ben Bishop, Mat Clark, B.J. Crombeen, Parris Duffus, Mike Eaves, John Grahame, David Hale, Ben Holmstrom, Joe Noris, Drew Shore, Nick Shore

Connecticut................ 30
Mark Arcobello, Cam Atkinson, Frank Beisler, Richard Bittner, Eric Boguniecki, Nick Bonino, Greg Brown, Chris Clark, Kevin Colley, Chris Corrinet, Matt DelGuidice, Chris Drury, Justin Duberman, Ron Hainsey, Matt Hussey, Craig Janney, Keegan Lowe, Lane MacDermid, Matt Martin, Marquis Mathieu, Colin McDonald, Max Pacioretty, Michael Paliotta, Jonathan Quick, Moe Roberts, Ryan Shannon, Jaime Sifers, Brian Sullivan, Colin Wilson, Chris Winnes

Delaware.................. 1
Mark Eaton

Florida.................... 7
Dallas Eakins, Brian Ferlin, Blake Geoffrion, Shayne Gostisbehere, Dan Hinote, Val James, Jayson Megna

Georgia................... 3
Eric Chouinard, Mark Mowers, Jean-Marc Pelletier

Idaho..................... 2
Guyle Fielder, Pat Shea

Illinois.................... 52
Conor Allen, Craig Anderson, Bates Battaglia, Andy Berenzweig, Mike Brown, Connor Carrick, Chris Chelios, Gerald Coleman, Joe Corvo, Shawn Cronin, Joe Day, Robbie Earl, Brian Fahey, Tom Fergus, Lee Fogolin, Jr., Tony Granato, Bob Hall, Andrew Hutchinson, Ivan Irwin, Bob Janecyk, Matt Jones, Todd Krygier, Peter Lappin, Mark LaVarre, Brett Lebda, Matt Lindblad, Chris Lipuma, Stefan Matteau, Al Montoya, John Moore, Scott Morrow, Harry Mummery, Gregg Naumenko, Mike O'Connell, Ed Olczyk, Tom Preissing, Greg Rallo, Todd Reirden, Danny Richmond, Steve Richmond, Jeff Rohlicek, Mike Rucinski, Blake Sloan, Tim Stapleton, Bill Sweatt, Lee Sweatt, Ryan Thang, Nikos Tselios, Dennis Vaske, Tommy Wingels, Andy Wozniewski, Rick Zombo

Indiana................... 8
Donald Brashear, Jack Johnson, Ken Klee, Fred Knipscheer, John-Michael Liles, Dale Purinton, Cameron Schilling, Alfie Turcotte

Iowa...................... 1
Scott Clemmensen

Maine.................... 6
Danny Bolduc, Jon DiSalvatore, Brian Dumoulin, Doug Friedman, Jeff Libby, Greg Moore

Maryland.................. 5
Jeff Brubaker, Jeremy Duchesne, Jamie Fritsch, Jeff Halpern, Jarred Tinordi

Massachusetts............. 182
Fred Ahern, Don Aiken, Bobby Allen, Tony Amonte, Bill Arnold, Keith Aucoin, Steve Baker, Tom Barrasso, Ed Barry, Ray Barry, Shawn Bates, Blake Bellefeuille, Rick Bennett, Pete Bessone, Chris Bourque, Phil Bourque, Ryan Bourque, Brian Boyle, Andy Brickley, Bob Brooke, Doug Brown, Gary Burns, Bobby Butler, Joe Callahan, Jim Campbell, Dom Campedelli, Jim Carey, Paul Carey, John Carlson, Bobby Carpenter, John Carter, Art Chisholm, Michael Colman, Carl Corazzini, Bob Corkum, Rich Costello, Charlie Coyle, Jim Craig, Ted Crowley, Cleon Daskalakis, Niko Dimitrakos, Rick DiPietro, Ted Donato, Ted Drury, Dale Dunbar, Richie Dunn, Norm Dussault, Brian Eklund, Jim Fahey, Bobby Farnham, Paul Fenton, Benn Ferriero, Mike Fidler, Tom Fitzgerald, Brian Flynn, Gerry Foley, Jon Fontas, Robbie Ftorek, Mark Fusco, Gerry Geran, Brian Gibbons, Hal Gill, Matt Glennon, Scott Gordon, David Gove, Bill Guerin, Scott Harlow, Leland Harrington, Jimmy Hayes, Kevin Hayes, Eric Healey, Steve Heinze, Josh Hennessy, Vic Heyliger, Mark Holden, Jack Hughes, Joe Hulbig, Paul Hurley, Dave Hynes, Doug Janik, Bob Jay, Dean Jenkins, David A. Jensen, Ed Jeremiah, Duane Joyce, Chris Kelleher, Chris Kreider, Bob Kudelski, Mark Kumpel, Dan Lacouture, Albert Lacroix, Dick Lamby, Myles Lane, Peter Laviolette, Jeff Lazaro, Stephen Leach, Pat Leahy, Ray LeBlanc, Art Lesieur, John Lilley, Clarence MacKenzie, Greg Mauldin, John McCarthy, Bill McCreary Jr., Gerry McDonald, Shawn McEachern, Mike McHugh, Marty McInnis, Bob McManama, Mike Milbury, Bob Miller, Jay Miller, Paul Miller, Billy Moe, Jon Morris, Mike Morrison, Mike Mottau, Eric Nickulas, Chris Nilan, Brian Noonan, Brad Norton, Jeff Norton, Jack O'Callahan, Bill O'Dwyer, Paul O'Neil, Tom O'Regan, Chris O'Sullivan, Jay Pandolfo, Mike Pandolfo, Adam Pineault, Larry Pleau, Brian Pothier, Tom Poti, Bob Ring, Pat Rissmiller, Mickey Roach, Jeremy Roenick, Ed Ronan, Steve Rooney, Tom Rowe, Michael Ryan, David Sacco, Joe Sacco, Corey Schneider, Dwight Schofield, Bobby Sheehan, Dave Silk, Frank Simonetti, Raymie Skilton, Garth Snow, Tom Songin, Paul Stanton, Kevin Stevens, Jim Stewart, Paul Stewart, Brian Strait, Mike Sullivan, Bob Sweeney, Tim Sweeney, Dean Sylvester, Peter Taglianetti, Bob Taylor, Clifford Thompson, Billy Tibbetts, Keith Tkachuk, Louis Trudel, Darren Turcotte, Jim Vesey, Carl Voss, Chris Wagner, Kurt Walker, David Warsofsky, Noah Welch, Donald Wheldon, Bill Whelton, Brian White, Joe Whitney, Ryan Whitney, Kevin Wortman, Keith Yandle, C.J. Young, Scott Young

Michigan.................. 153
Justin Abdelkader, Gerry Abel, Taffy Abel, Keith Aldridge, Jason Bacashihua, Cliff Barton, Mark Beaufait, Chad Billins, John Blum, David Booth, Reid Boucher, Drayson Bowman, Pat Brown, Tony Bukovich, Charlie Burns, Adam Burt, Gord Buynak, Dan Bylsma, Jack Campbell, Ed Carpenter, Jimmy Carson, Shawn Chambers, Chris Cichoki, Danton Cole, Ian Cole, Sean Collins, Erik Condra, Chris Conner, Andrew Copp, Jim Cummins, Tony Curtale, Patrick Davis, Dave Debol, Danny DeKeyser, Larry Depalma, Vic Desjardins, Mike Donnelly, Matt Elich, Corey Elkins, Dave Feamster, Brian Felsner, Denny Felsner, Jeff Finger, Justin Florek, Alex Foster, Nathan Gerbe, Tim Gleason, Luke Glendening, Rob Globke, Alex Goligoski, Andy Greene, Matt Greene, Mike Grier, Adam Hall, Mark Hamway, Mike Hartman, Derian Hatcher, Kevin Hatcher, Dwight Helminen, T.J. Hensick, Andy Hilbert, Mark Howe, Marty Howe, Matt Hunwick, Shawn Hunwick, Al Iafrate, Bob Johnson, Brent Johnson, Brad Jones, Steve Kampfer, Dan Keczmer, Ryan Kesler, Ike Klingbeil, Torey Krug, Ben Lapraire, Drew Larman, Chad LaRose, David Legwand, Ken Leiter, Bryan Lerg, Chris Luongo, Peter Mannino, Alec Martinez, Pat Mayer, Mike McDougal, Don McSween, Andy Miele, Andrew Miller, Kelly Miller, Kevin Miller, Kip Miller, Ryan Miller, Jeff Mitchell, Mike Modano, Gary Morrison, Ken Morrow, Dave Moss, Pat Neaton, Jim Niekamp, Jordan Oesterle, Steven Oleksy, Rob Palmer, Aaron Palushaj, Scott Parse, Greg Pateryn, Craig Patrick, Pat Peake, Jeff Petry, Kevin Porter, Corey Potter, Wayne Presley, Brian Rafalski, Erik Reitz, Bobby Reynolds, Andy Roach, Doug Roberts, Gordie Roberts, Brian Rolston, Dale Rominski, Mike Rucinski, Bernie Ruelle, Pat Rupp, Bryan Rust, Ron Serafini, John Sherf, Jim Slater, Dennis Smith, Ted Speers, Jim Storm, Chris Summers, Damian Surma, Chris Tamer, Chris Tancill, Matt Taormina, Tim Thomas, Corey Tropp, Zach Trotman, Jacob Trouba, Dean Turner, Robert Valicevic, John Vanbiesbrouck, Mike Vellucci, Kris Vernarsky, Don Waddell, Austin Watson, Doug Weight, Carl Wetzel, James Wisniewski, Luke Witkowski, Craig Wolanin, Mike York, Jeff Zatkoff, Rudy Zunich

Minnesota................ 238
Will Acton, Rudy Ahlin, Andrew Alberts, Steve Alley, Earl Anderson, Russ Anderson, Mike Antonovich, Les Auge, David Backes, Bill Baker, Keith Ballard, Mike Baumgartner, Tim Bergland, Adam Berkhoel, Stu Bickel, Nick Bjugstad, Scott Bjugstad, Jason Blake, Brandon Bochenski, Brian Bonin, Casey Borer, Henry Boucha, Justin Braun, Joe Bretto, Frank Brimsek, Milt Brink, Aaron Broten, Neal Broten, Paul Broten, J.T. Brown, Bill Butters, Dustin Byfuglien, Jack Carlson, Steve Carlson, Ryan Carter, Jon Casey, Tom Chorske, Dave Christian, Steve Christoff, Ben Clymer, Bob Collyard, Tim Conboy, Mike Crowley, Mark Cullen, Matt Cullen, Jim Cunningham, John Curry, Chris Dahlquist, Cully Dahlstrom, Brad DeFauw, Bob Dill, Joe Dziedzic, Bryan Erickson, Chad Erickson, Cade Fairchild, Kelly Fairchild, Mike Farrell, Joe Finley, Rusty Fitzgerald, Zack Fitzgerald, Jeff Frazee, Trevor Frischmon, Gary Gambucci, Jake Gardiner, Ken Gernander, Tom Gilbert, Stan Gilbertson, Leroy Goldsworthy, Tom Gorence, Guy Gosselin, John Gruden, Al Hangsleben, Ben Hankinson, Casey Hankinson, Ben Hanowski, Keith Hanson, Tim Harrer, Brett Hauer, Adam Hauser, Peter Hayek, Eriah Hayes, Mark Heaslip, Bret Hedican, Seth Helgeson, Matt Henderson, Matt Hendricks, Darby Hendrickson, Sean Hill, Jack Hillen, Tom Hirsch, Phil Hoene, Paul Holmgren, Phil Housley, Don Jackson, Steve Janaszak, David H. Jensen, Joe Jensen, Steve Jensen, John Johannson, Craig Johnson, Erik Johnson, Jim Johnson, Mark Johnson, Virgil Johnson, Mike Karakas, Chris Kenady, Trent Klatt,

APPENDIX

Scot Kleinendorst, Matt Koalska, Jim Korn, Tom Kurvers, Bryce Lampman, Jamie Langenbrunner, Dave Langevin, Josh Langfeld, Reed Larson, Mike Lauen, Drew LeBlanc, Nick Leddy, Anders Lee, Brian Lee, Jordan Leopold, Pete LoPresti, Sam LoPresti, Mike Lundin, Chris Marinucci, John Mariucci, Paul Martin, Steve Martinson, Bob Mason, Chris McAlpine, Jamie McBain, Jack McCartan, Rob McClanahan, Ryan McDonagh, Jim McElmury, Bruce McIntosh, Mike McNeill, Philip McRae, Joe Micheletti, Pat Micheletti, Corey Millen, Warren Miller, Travis Morin, Joe Motzko, Rick Mrozik, Peter Mueller, Brock Nelson, Aaron Ness, Jeff Nielsen, Kirk Nielsen, Matt Niskanen, Craig Norwich, Jim O'Brien, Todd Okerlund, Kyle Okposo, Mark Osiecki, Joel Otto, Aldo Palazzari, Doug Palazzari, Jarod Palmer, Joe Papike, Bob Paradise, Zach Parise, Jeff Parker, Mark Parrish, Mark Pavelich, Tom Pederson, Derek Peltier, Mike Peluso, Toby Petersen, Lance Pitlick, Tyler Pitlick, Derek Plante, Shjon Podein, John Pohl, John Polich, Mike Polich, Nate Prosser, Chris Pryor, Nate Raduns, Mike Ramsey, Erik Rasmussen, Chad Rau, Damian Rhodes, Todd Richards, Travis Richards, Jon Rohloff, Todd Rohloff, Doc Romnes, Shaun Sabol, Scott Sandelin, Gary Sargent, Craig Sarner, Kurt Sauer, Michael Sauer, Butch Schaeffer, Clarence Schmidt, Nate Schmidt, Jordan Schroeder, Dan Sexton, Steve Short, Randy Skarda, Matt Smaby, Dale Smedsmo, Wyatt Smith, Carl Sneep, Dave Snuggerud, Alex Stalock, Robb Stauber, Derek Stepan, Ryan Stoa, Colin Stuart, Mark Stuart, Mike Stuart, Al Suomi, Jeff Taffe, John Taft, Dean Talafous, David Tanabe, Jeff Teal, Sean Toomey, Dan Trebil, Chris VandeVelde, Mark Van Guilder, Steve Wagner, Jim Warner, Jim Watt, Erik Westrum, Blake Wheeler, Tommy Williams, Warren Williams, Clay Wilson, Mike Wong, J.T. Wyman, Ken Yackel, Tom Younghans, Doug Zmolek

Missouri 15
Mark Alt, Brandon Bollig, Jim Boo, Chris Butler, Cal Heeter, Cam Janssen, Pat Lafontaine, Adam Lowry, Patrick Maroon, Scott Mayfield, Mike McKenna, Paul Ranheim, Travis Turnbull, Joe Vitale, Landon Wilson

Montana 1
Bill Lindsay

Nebraska. 2
Johnny Matz, Jed Ortmeyer

New Hampshire. 10
Kent Carlson, Mark Fayne, Brian Foster, Jeff Giuliano, Ben Lovejoy, Hubie McDonough, Freddy Meyer, Deron Quint, Tim Schaller, Jeff Serowik

New Jersey 14
Kenny Agostino, T.J. Brennan, Jim Dowd, John Gaudreau, Matt Herr, Brian Lawton, Paul Mara, Drew Miller, Bobby Ryan, Bobby Sanguinetti, James van Riemsdyk, Trevor van Riemsdyk, David Williams, Randy Wood

New York. 106
Matt Anderson, Tom Askey, Tony Bitetto, Zach Bogosian, Jason Bonsignore, Francis Bouillon, Jesse Boulerice, Rich Brennan, Greg Britz, Dustin Brown, Jack Brownschidle, Jeff Brownschidle, Billy Burch, Ryan Callahan, Pete Ciavaglia, Adam Clendening, Erik Cole, Tim Connolly, Craig Conroy, Bobby Crawford, Jerry D'Amigo, Craig Darby, Dan Dorion, Stan Drulia, Mike Dunham, Tim Erixon, Robert Esche, Jeff Farkas, Ted Fauss, Chris Ferraro, Peter Ferraro, Rory Fitzpatrick, Marcus Foligno, Nick Foligno, Nick Fotiu, Matt Gilroy, Brian Gionta, Stephen Gionta, Sean Haggerty, Richie Hansen, Guy Hebert, Chris Higgins, Jimmy Howard, Mike Hurlbut, Earl Ingarfield, Jr., Hugh Jessiman, Patrick Kaleta, Patrick Kane, Tim Kennedy, Keith Kinkaid, Connor Knapp, Mike Komisarek, Les Kuntar, Mike Lalor, Brian Lashoff, Matt Lashoff, Jay Leach, Edward Lee, Alex Levinsky, Todd Marchant, Jason McBain, Tom McCollum, Dan McFall, Max Middendorf, Aaron Miller, Jeremy Morin, Chris Mueller, Brian Mullen, Joe Mullen, Matt Murley, Eric Nystrom, Kyle Palmieri, Nick Palmieri, Glenn Patrick, Jim Pavese, Frank Peters, Nicholas Petrecki, Tracy Pratt, Shane Prince, Kevin Quick, Peter Ratchuk, Armand Raymond, Marty Reasoner, Dave Reece, Andre Roy, Philippe Sauve, Pete Scamurra, Joe Schaefer, Mathieu Schneider, Robbie Schremp, Rob Scuderi, Tim Sestito, Tom Sestito, Kevin Shattenkirk, Shane Sims, Paul Skidmore, Lee Stempniak, Brandon Sutter, Scott Thomas, Tony Tuzzolino, Ryan Vesce, Mike Walsh, Derek Whitmore, Michael Zalewski, Steve Zalewski, Jason Zent

North Carolina. 2
Jared Boll, Ben Smith

North Dakota. 13
Bob Bergloff, Scott Fankhouser, Paul Gaustad, Fern Headley, Danny Irmen, Tim Jackman, Ryan Kraft, Ron Moffat, Josh Olson, Mike Peluso, Ryan Potulny, Fido Purpur, Barry Tallackson

Ohio. 24
John Albert, Aris Brimanis, Carter Camper, Ab Demarco, Jr., Cecil Dillon, Dave Ellett, Curt Fraser, Dan Fritsche, Jeff Hamilton, Brett Harkins, Todd Harkins, Peter Harrold, Rick Hayward, Brian Holzinger, Ed Hospodar, Pat Jablonski, Moe Mantha, J.T. Miller, Ian Moran, Connor Murphy, Mike Rupp, Ben Simon, Bryan Smolinski, Doug Volmar

Oklahoma 5
Tyler Arnason, Matt Donovan, Jonathon Merrill, Burr Williams, Dan Woodley

Oregon. 5
Jere Gillis, Derek Gustafson, Ian Kidd, Grant Sasser, Jordan Smotherman

Pennsylvania. 32
Pete Babando, Matt Bartkowski, Bob Beers, Yank Boyd, Tom Brennan, Matt Campanale, Jay Caufield, Colby Cohen, John Gibson, Nate Guenin, Christian Hanson, Chad Kolarik, Grant Lewis, Ryan Malone, Justin Mercier, Ryan Mulhern, Gerry O'Flaherty, George Parros, Dylan Reese, Mike Richter, Brandon Saad, Henrik Samuelsson, David Sloane, Jesse Spring, Ray Staszak, Eric Tangradi, Bill Thomas, Vince Trocheck, R.J. Umberger, Mike Weber, Patrick Wey, John Zeiler

Rhode Island. 18
Bill Bennett, Harvey Bennett, Bryan Berard, Brian Boucher, Dave Capuano, Jack Capuano, Keith Carney, Tom Cavanagh, Clark Donatelli, David Emma, Rob Gaudreau, Paul Guay, Jeff Jillson, Steven King, David Littman, Tom Mellor, Scott Shaunessy, Chris Terreri

South Carolina 1
Ryan Hartman

Texas. 8
Chris Brown, Mike Christie, Seth Jones, Brian Leetch, Tyler Myers, Stefan Noesen, Zach Redmond, Jon Rheault

Utah. 4
Richard Bachman, Steve Konowalchuk, Trevor Lewis, Dylan Olsen

Vermont. 2
John LeClair, Graham Mink

Virginia 5
Chris Bala, Scott Darling, Scott Lachance, Jim Walsh, Eric Weinrich

Washington. 12
Bob Attwell, Tom Bissett, Patrick Dwyer, Curtis Hamilton, Wayne Hicks, Justin Johnson, Tyler Johnson, Ty Jones, Scott Levins, T.J. Oshie, David Wilkie, Duane Wylie

Washington D.C. 2
Kevyn Adams, Bill Nyrop

Wisconsin 30
Marc Behrend, Bob Blake, Alex Brooks, Adam Burish, John Byce, Kevin Dean, Jake Dowell, Davis Drewiske, Alex Galchenyuk, Troy Grosenick, Dave Hanson, Roger Jenkins, Phil Kessel, Craig Ludwig, David Maley, Jake McCabe, Joe Pavelski, Joe Piskula, Dan Plante, Joel Rechlicz, Barry Richter, Bobby Robins, Mike Sislo, Jack Skille, Craig Smith, Drew Stafford, David Steckel, Gary Suter, Ryan Suter, Brad Winchester

THE WORLD (listed alphabetically)

AUSTRIA 9
Christoph Brandner, Andre Burakovsky, Marko Dano, Reinhard Divis, Michael Grabner, Andreas Nodl, Thomas Pock, Michael Raffl, Thomas Vanek

BELARUS. 8
Alexander Andrijevski, Sergei Bautin, Raman Hrabarenka, Konstantin Koltsov, Andrei Kostitsyn, Sergei Kostitsyn, Oleg Mikulchik, Ruslan Salei

BELGIUM 1
Jan Benda

BORNEO. 1
Craig Adams

BRAZIL. 2
Mike Greenlay, Robyn Regehr

CROATIA 1
Borna Rendulic

CZECH REPUBLIC 213
Patrik Augusta, Jaroslav Balastik, Michal Barinka, Jaroslav Bednar, Ladislav Benysek, Josef Beranek, Karel Betik, Radim Bicanek, Zdenek Blatny, Radek Bonk, Pavel Brendl, Jiri Bubla, Jan Bulis, Petr Buzek, Peter Cajanek, Jan Caloun, Roman Cechmanek, Frantisek Cernik, Roman Cervenka, Milan Chalupa, Jiri Crha, Jakub Cutta, Tomas Divisek, Jiri Dopita, Miroslav Dvorak, Radek Dvorak, Patrik Elias, Martin Erat, Jiri Fischer, Tomas Fleischmann, Michael Frolik, Miroslav Frycer, Michal Grosek, Radko Gudas, Miloslav Guren, Jaroslav Halak, Radek Hamr, Roman Hamrlik, Martin Hanzal, Dominik Hasek, Martin Havlat, Jan Hejda, Milan Hejduk, Ales Hemsky, Tomas Hertl, Jan Hlavac, Ivan Hlinka, Jaroslav Hlinka, Milan Hnilicka, Milos Holan, Bobby Holik, Roman Horak, Miloslav Horava, Martin Hostak, Jan Hrdina, Jiri Hrdina, Petr Hubacek, Jiri Hudler, Ivan Huml, Jaromir Jagr, Tomas Jelinek, Jaroslav Jirik, Michal Jordan, Tomas Jurco, Frantisek Kaberle, Tomas Kaberle, Petr Kalus, Tomas Kana, Petr Kanko, Lukas Kaspar, Jakub Kindl, Jakub Klepis, Rostislav Klesla, Petr Klima, Tomas Kloucek, David Koci, Ladislav Kohn, Pavel Kolarik, Ales Kotalik, Milan Kraft, Lukas Krajicek, David Krejci, Kamil Kreps, Jaroslav Kristek, Robert Kron, Vlastimil Kroupa, Filip Kuba, Tomas Kubalik, Pavel Kubina, Frantisek Kucera, Kristian Kudroc, Tomas Kundratek, Tomas Kurka, Zdenek Kutlak, Robert Lang, Rick Lanz, Jiri Latal, Martin Lojek, Jan Ludvig, Marek Malik, Josef Marha, Martin Marincin, Radek Martinek, Marek Mazanec, Josef Melichar, Milan Michalek, Zbynek Michalek, Petr Mika, Stan Mikita, Jaroslav Modry, Tomas Mojzis, David Moravec, Petr Mrazek, Frantisek Musil, Stanislav Neckar, Vaclav Nedomansky, Vaclav Nedorost, Petr Nedved, Zdenek Nedved, Jan Nemecek, Andrej Nestrasil, Michal Neuvirth, Filip Novak, Jiri Novotny, Milan Novy, Rostislav Olesz, Jaroslav Otevrel, Ondrej Palat, Richard Panik, David Pastrnak, Pavel Patera, Ondrej Pavelec, Jakub Petruzalek, Karel Pilar, Kamil Piros, Ales Pisa, Libor Pivko, Michal Pivonka, Tomas Plekanec, Vaclav Pletka, Tomas Plihal, Roman Polak, Vojtech Polak, Tomas Popperle, Marek Posmyk, Jaroslav Pouzar, Petr Prajsler, Martin Prochazka, Vaclav Prospal, Petr Prucha, Martin Prusek, Karel Rachunek, Robert Reichel, Michal Repik, Pavel Rosa, Michal Rozsival, Martin Rucinsky, Vladimir Ruzicka, Alexander Salak, Robert Schnabel, Marek Schwarz, Jiri Sejba, Jiri Sekac, Andrej Sekera, Jaroslav Sevcik, Roman Simicek, Michal Sivek, Martin Skoula, Pavel Skrbek, Jiri Slegr, Richard Smehlik, Ladislav Smid, Radek Smolenak, Vladimir Sobotka, Jaroslav Spacek, Martin Spanhel, Tomas Srsen, Patrik Stefan, Martin Straka, Petr Straka, Andrej Sustr, Jaroslav Svejkovsky, Jaroslav Svoboda, Petr Svoboda (b. 1966), Petr Svoboda (b. 1980), Michal Sykora, Petr Sykora (b. 1976), Petr Sykora (b. 1978), Tomas Tatar, Peter Taticek, Petr Tenkrat, Milan Tichy, Jiri Tlusty, Pavel Trnka, Roman Turek, Dominik Uher, Vaclav Varada, Josef Vasicek, Tomas Vincour, Tomas Vlasak, Tomas Vokoun, David Volek, Jan Vopat, Roman Vopat, Jakub Voracek, Petr Vrana, Radim Vrbata, Vladimir Vujtek, David Vyborny, Libor Zabransky, Miroslav Zalesak, Marek Zidlicky, Tomas Zizka

DENMARK. 10
Frederik Andersen, Mikkel Boedker, Lars Eller, Jannik Hansen, Nicklas Jensen, Philip Larsen, Oliver Lauridsen, Frans Nielsen, Poul Popiel, Peter Regin

ENGLAND. 21
Red Beattie, Kevin Brown, Byron Dafoe, Joe Hall, Alan Hepple, Ken Hodge, Lou Holmes, Walter Jackson, Peter Lee, Norm Mann, Paul Messier, Brian Perry, Eric Pettinger, Gord Pettinger, Fred Robertson, Alex Smith, Daniel Taylor, Steve Thomas, Ken Thompson, Jack Tomson, Chris Worthy

FINLAND 185
Antti Aalto, Peter Ahola, Sami Aittokallio, Mika Alatalo, Joel Armia, Niklas Backstrom, Aleksander Barkov, Aki-Petteri Berg, Sean Bergenheim, Timo Blomqvist, Arto Blomsten, Toni Dahlman, Miika Elomo, Kari Eloranta, Mikko Eloranta, Valtteri Filppula, Markus Granlund, Mikael Granlund, Tuomas Gronman, Jari Gronstrand, Kari Haakana, Ari Haanpaa, Matti Hagman, Niklas Hagman, Riku Hahl, Teemu Hartikainen, Erik Haula, Ilkka Heikkinen, Riku Helenius, Sami Helenius, Raimo Helminen, Jukka Hentunen, Jani Hurme, Hannes Hyvonen, Jarkko Immonen, Risto Jalo, Kari Jalonen, Marko Jantunen, Hannu Jarvenpaa, Martti Jarventie, Iiro Jarvi, Arto Javanainen, Jesse Joensuu, Mikko Jokela, Jussi Jokinen, Olli Jokinen, Jyrki Jokipakka, Timo Jutila, Jari Kaarela, Tomi Kallio, Hannu Kamppuri, Niko Kapanen, Sami Kapanen, Jere Karalahti, Jarmo Kekalainen, Veli-Pekka Ketola, Marko Kiprusoff, Miikka Kiprusoff, Ville Koistinen, Tom Koivisto, Mikko Koivu, Saku Koivu, Petri Kontiola, Lauri Korpikoski, Mikko Koskinen, Lasse Kukkonen, Jarno Kultanen, Jari Kurri, Markku Kyllonen, Teemu Laakso, Antti Laaksonen, Janne Laukkanen, Jori Lehtera, Jere Lehtinen, Petteri Lehto, Antero Lehtonen, Kari Lehtonen, Mikko Lehtonen (b. 1978), Mikko Lehtonen (b. 1987), Ville Leino, Mikko Leinonen, Sami Lepisto, Tapio Levo, Juha Lind, Petteri Lindbohm, Perttu Lindgren, Jyrki Lumme, Pentti Lund, Mikko Luoma, Toni Lydman, Olli Maata, Mikko Makela, Tomi Maki, Kari Makkonen, Olli Malmivaara, Masi Marjamaki, Jussi Markkanen, Markus Mattsson, Anssi Melametsa, Antti Miettinen, Jarmo Myllys, Joonas Nattinen, Antti Niemi, Antti-Jussi Niemi, Ville Nieminen, Janne Niinimaa, Antero Niittymaki, Petteri Nokelainen, Mika Noronen, Fredrik Norrena, Petteri Nummelin, Teppo Numminen, Kai Nurminen, Pasi Nurminen, Janne Ojanen, Joni Ortio, Oskar Osala, Iiro Pakarinen, Timo Parssinen, Ville Peltonen, Harri Pesonen, Janne Pesonen, Lennart Petrell, Tomi Pettinen, Thomas Pihlman, Antti Pihlstrom, Ilkka Pikkarainen, Lasse Pirjeta, Esa Pirnes, Joni Pitkanen, Jukka Porvari, Al Pudas, Teemu Pulkkinen, Mika Pyorala, Antti Raanta, Karri Ramo, Joonas Rask, Tuukka Rask, Pekka Rautakallio, Pekka Rinne, Rasmus Rissanen, Rasmus Ristolainen, Jani Rita, Reijo Ruotsalainen, Christian Ruuttu, Jarkko Ruutu, Tuomo Ruutu, Jussi Rynnas, Simo Saarinen, Anssi Salmela, Tony Salmelainen, Sami Salo, Miikka Salomaki, Tomas Sandstrom, Tommi Santala, Teemu Selanne, Jyrki Seppa, Risto Siltanen, Ilkka Sinisalo, Ville Siren, Petri Skriko, Kai Suikkanen, Raimo Summanen, Kari Takko, Iiro Tarkki, Teuvo Teravainen, Esa Tikkanen, Jussi Timonen, Kimmo Timonen, Hannu Toivonen, Jari Torkki, Antti Tormanen, Vesa Toskala, Lauri Tukonen, Marko Tuomainen, Ossi Vaananen, Petri Varis, Jarkko Varvio, Sami Vatanen, Vesa Viitakoski, Hannu Virta, Tony Virta, Yuha Widing, Petteri Wirtanen, Yuha Ylonen

FRANCE. 9
Pierre-Edouard Bellemare, Philippe Bozon, Stephane Da Costa, Pat Daley, Cristobal Huet, Paul MacLean, Andre Peloffy, Antoine Roussel, Max Sauve

GERMANY 30
Sven Butenschon, Leon Draisaitl, Christian Ehrhoff, Jean-Marc Gaulin, Randy Gilhen, Brian Glynn, Marcel Goc, Sascha Goc, Erich Goldmann, Mikhail Grabovski, Thomas Greiss, Philipp Grubauer, Dany Heatley, Jochen Hecht, Uli Hiemer, Korbinian Holzer, Willie Huber, Udo Kiessling, Uwe Krupp, Michel Larocque, Marcel Mueller, Timo Pielmeier, Tobias Rieder, Christoph Schubert, Dennis Seidenberg, Marco Sturm, Alexander Sulzer, Walt Tkaczuk, Stefan Ustorf, David Wolf

APPENDIX

HAITI 1
Claude Vilgrain

HOLLAND................. 1
Ed Kea

INDONESIA 1
Richie Regehr

IRELAND 6
Sid Finney, Bobby Kirk, Jim McFadden, Sammy McManus, Owen Nolan, Jack Riley

ITALY 3
Nelson Debenedet, Victor Posa, Luca Sbisa

JAMAICA.................. 1
Graeme Townshend

JAPAN 2
Yutaka Fukufuji, Ryan O'Marra

KAZAKHSTAN 8
Nik Antropov, Vitaliy Kolesnik, Maxim Kuznetsov, Evgeny Nabokov, Alexander Perezhogin, Konstantin Pushkarev, Pavel Vorobiev, Vitali Yeremeyev

LATVIA................... 20
Kaspars Astashenko, Helmut Balderis, Oskars Bartulis, Kaspars Daugavins, Zemgus Girgensons, Kristers Gudlevskis, Viktor Ignatjev, Arturs Irbe, Raitis Ivanins, Martins Karsums, Ronalds Kenins, Arturs Kulda, Sandis Ozolinsh, Karlis Skrastins, Peter Skudra, Janis Sprukts, Viktor Tikhonov, Herbert Vasiljevs, Harijs Vitolinsh, Sergei Zholtok

LEBANON.................. 1
Ed Hatoum

LITHUANIA................ 2
Darius Kasparaitis, Dainius Zubrus

NIGERIA.................. 2
Akim Aliu, Rumun Ndur

NORWAY 8
Jonas Holos, Bill Johansen, Espen Knutsen, Anders Myrvold, Bjorn Skaare, Patrick Thoresen, Ole-Kristian Tollefsen, Mats Zuccarello

PARAGUAY................. 1
Willi Plett

POLAND................... 8
Mariusz Czerkawski, Nick Harbaruk, Joe Jerwa, Ed Leier, John Miszuk, Krzysztof Oliwa, Peter Sidorkiewicz, Wojtek Wolski

RUSSIA 206
Dmitry Afanasenkov, Maxim Afinogenov, Nikita Alexeev, Artem Anisimov, Denis Arkhipov, Evgeny Artyukhin, Yuri Babenko, Maxim Balmochnykh, Andrei Bashkirov, Ruslan Batyrshin, Anton Belov, Sergei Berezin, Maxim Bets, Sergei Bobrovsky, Alexandre Boikov, Nikolai Borschevsky, Sergei Brylin, Ilya Bryzgalov, Pavel Bure, Valeri Bure, Alexander Burmistrov, Vyacheslav Butsayev, Yuri Butsayev, Ilya Byakin, Dmitri Bykov, Vladimir Chebaturkin, Denis Chervyakov, Igor Chibirev, Stanislav Chistov, Artem Chubarov, Evgeni Dadonov, Pavel Datsyuk, Evgeni Davydov, Alexei Emelin, Fedor Fedorov, Sergei Fedorov, Anatoli Fedotov, Vyacheslav Fetisov, Nikita Filatov, Dmitri Filimonov, Alexander Frolov, Maxim Galanov, Stanislav Galiev, Jan Golubovsky, Sergei Gonchar, Viktor Gordiouk, Johnny Gottselig, Evgeni Grachev, Denis Grebeshkov, Mikhail Grigorenko, Alexei Gusarov, Sergei Gusev, Ravil Gusmanov, Val Hoffinger, Dmitrij Jaskin, Alexei Kaigorodov, Dmitri Kalinin, Valeri Kamensky, Jan Kaminsky, Vitali Karamnov, Valeri Karpov, Alexander Karpovtsev, Alexei Kasatonov, Alexander Kerch, Nikolai Khabibulin, Sergei Kharin, Alex Kharitonov, Alexander Khavanov, Alexander Khokhlachev, Yuri Khmylev, Anton Khudobin, Anton Klementyev, Sergei Klimovich, Leo Komarov, Maxim Kondratiev, Evgeni Konstantinov, Vladimir Konstantinov, Dmitri Korobov, Evgeni Korolev, Igor Korolev, Alexander Korolyuk, Ilya Kovalchuk, Andrei Kovalenko, Alexei Kovalev, Viktor Kozlov, Vyacheslav Kozlov, Igor Kravchuk, Mikhail Kravets, Sergei Krivokrasov, Vladimir Krutov, Nikita Kucherov, Alexei Kudashov, Nikolai Kulemin, Mikhail Kuleshov, Dmitri Kulikov, Evgeni Kuznetsov, Dmitri Kvartalnov, Olèg Kvasha, Igor Larionov, Enver Lisin, Andrei Loktionov, Andrei Lomakin, Roman Lyashenko, Andrei Makarov, Sergei Makarov, Vladimir Malakhov, Evgeni Malkin, Alexei Marchenko, Andrei Markov, Daniil Markov, Maksim Mayorov, Alexei Mikhnov, Boris Mironov, Dmitri Mironov, Alexander Mogilny, Alexei Morozov, Sergei Mylnikov, Dmitri Nabokov, Evgeni Namestnikov, Vladislav Namestnikov, Andrei Nazarov, Viktor Nechayev, Sergei Nemchinov, Nikita Nesterov, Valeri Nichushkin, Nikita Nikitin, Andrei Nikolishin, Alexander Nikulin, Igor Nikulin, Ivan Novoseltsev, Roman Oksiuta, Dmitri Orlov, Alexander Ovechkin, Grigori Panteleev, Dmitri Patzold, Alexander Pechurski, Oleg Petrov, Sergei Priakin, Vitali Prokhorov, Alexander Radulov, Igor Radulov, Kirill Safranov, Sergei Samsonov, Oleg Saprykin, Petr Schastlivy, Sweeney Schriner, Alexander Selivanov, Alexander Semak, Alexei Semenov, Anatoli Semenov, Alexander Semin, Konstantin Shafranov, Evgeni Shaldybin, Vadim Sharifijanov, Sergei Shirokov, Timofei Shishkanov, Mikhail Shtalenkov, Andrei Skopintsev, Alexei Smirnov, Sergei Starikov, Alexander Suglobov, Maxim Sushinsky, Alexander Svitov, Vladimir Tarasenko, Daniil Tarasov, Mikhail Tatarinov, Dmitri Tertyshny, Alexei Tezikov, German Titov, Denis Tolpeko, Pavel Torgayev, Andrei Trefilov, Nikolai Tsulygin, Denis Tsygurov, Vladimir Tsyplakov, Fedor Tyutin, Igor Ulanov, Semyon Varlamov, Andrei Vasilevsky, Andrei Vasiliev, Alexei Vasiliev, Alexander Vasyunov, Ivan Vishnevski, Anton Volchenkov, Alexandre Volchkov, Vladimir Vorobiev, Slava Voynov, Igor Vyazmikin, Sergei Vyshedkevich, Vitali Yachmenev, Bogdan Yakimov, Mikhail Yakubov, Nail Yakupov, Alexei Yashin, Alexei Yegorov, Dmitri Yushkevich, Nikita Zadorov, Valeri Zelepukin, Alexei Zhamnov, Vladimir Zharkov, Alexei Zhitnik, Sergei Zinovjev, Andrei Zubarev, Ilya Zubov, Sergei Zubov, Andrei Zyuzin

SCOTLAND................. 21
Andy Aitkenhead, Tom Anderson, Chuck Blair, Adam Brown, George Carey, Gordie Clark, Jim Conacher, Bobby Connors, Sandy Fitzpatrick, Irv Frew, Charlie Gardiner, Alex Gray, George Grigor, Sam McAdam, Dunc Munro, Jack Pratt, Jim Ross, Steve Smith, Bill Thomson, Bob Whitelaw, Alex Wood

SLOVAKIA 72
Jergus Baca, Josef Balej, Ivan Baranka, Lubos Bartecko, Peter Bartos, Milan Bartovic, Jiri Bicek, Mario Bliznak, Peter Budaj, Zdeno Chara, Martin Cibak, Ivan Ciernik, Jozef Cierny, Zdeno Ciger, Marian Cisar, Pavol Demitra, Robert Dome, Ivan Droppa, Vitezslav Duris, Marian Gaborik, Stanislav Gron, Michal Handzus, Radoslav Hecl, Marcel Hossa, Marian Hossa, Miroslav Ihnacak, Peter Ihnacak, Milan Jurcina, Ladislav Karabin, Juraj Kolnik, Tomas Kopecky, Milan Kytnar, Jan Lasak, Igor Liba, Richard Lintner, Ivan Majesky, Tomas Malec, Andrej Meszaros, Branislav Mezei, Vladimir Mihalik, Ladislav Nagy, Andrei Nedorost, Jaroslav Obsut, Peter Olvecky, Vladimir Orszagh, Zigmund Palffy, Dusan Pasek, Robert Petrovicky, Ronald Petrovicky, Andrei Podkonicky, Branko Radivojevic, Stefan Ruzicka, Miroslav Satan, Peter Sejna, Lubomir Sekeras, Peter Smrek, Radovan Somik, Rastislav Stana, Anton Stastny, Marian Stastny, Peter Stastny, Martin Strbak, Jozef Stumpel, Radoslav Suchy, Tomas Surovy, Marek Svatos, Robert Svehla, Roman Tvrdon, Lubomir Vaic, Boris Valabik, Lubomir Visnovsky, Richard Zednik

SLOVENIA 1
Anze Kopitar

SOUTH AFRICA 1
Olaf Kolzig

SOUTH KOREA.............. 2
Jim Paek, Richard Park

SWEDEN 279
Thommy Abrahamsson, Tommy Albelin, Daniel Alfredsson, Adam Almqvist, Erik Andersson, Joakim Andersson, Jonas Andersson, Kent-Erik Andersson, Mikael Andersson, Niklas Andersson, Peter Andersson (b. 1965), Peter Andersson (b. 1991), Magnus Arvedson, Viktor Arvidsson, Hardy Astrom, P-J Axelsson, Johan Backlund, Mikael Backlund, Christian Backman, Nicklas Backstrom, Daniel Bang, Niclas Bergfors, Stefan Bergkvist, Bo Berglund, Christian Berglund, Patrik Berglund, Thommie Bergman, Jonas Bergqvist, Josef Boumedienne, Per-Olov Brasar, Fredrik Bremberg (formerly Lindquist), Jonas Brodin, Fabian Brunnstrom, Robert Burakovsky, Anders Carlsson, Patrik Carnback, Andreas Dackell, Klas Dahlbeck, Ulf Dahlen, Kjell Dahlin, Johan Davidsson, Jacob de la Rose, Per Djoos, Rolf Edberg, Alexander Edler, Mattias Ekholm, Pelle Eklund, Nils Ekman, Oliver Ekman-Larsson, Anders Eldebrink, Andreas Engqvist, Jhonas Enroth, Tobias Enstrom, Jonathan Ericsson, Anders Eriksson, Joacim Eriksson, Loui Eriksson, Peter Eriksson, Roland Eriksson, Thomas Eriksson, Jan Erixon, Erik Ersberg, Dennis Everberg, Jesper Fast, Viktor Fasth, Christian Folin, Anton Forsberg, Filip Forsberg, Peter Forsberg, Gus Forslund, Tomas Forslund, Johan Franzen, Max Friberg, Jonas Frogren, Johan Garpenlov, Thomas Gradin, Petter Granberg, Nicklas Grossman, Carl Gunnarsson, Bengt-Ake Gustafsson, Erik Gustafsson, Per Gustafsson, Jonas Gustavsson, Peter Gustavsson, Carl Hagelin, Roger Hagglund, Anders Hakansson, Mats Hallin, Inge Hammarstrom, Johan Harju, Niclas Havelid, Anders Hedberg, Johan Hedberg, Pierre Hedin, Victor Hedman, Jonathan Hedstrom, Peter Helander, Magnus Hellberg, Niklas Hjalmarsson, Jonas Hoglund, Goran Hogosta, Johan Holmqvist, Michael Holmqvist, Tomas Holmstrom, Patric Hornqvist, Kristian Huselius, Ulf Isaksson, Calle Jarnkrok, Andreas Johansson, Bjorn Johansson, Calle Johansson, Jonas Johansson, Magnus Johansson, Marcus Johansson, Mathias Johansson, Roger Johansson, Kim Johnsson, Hans Jonsson, Jorgen Jonsson, Kenny Jonsson, Lars Jonsson, Tomas Jonsson, Jacob Josefson, Patrik Juhlin, Jonas Junland, Anders Kallur, Kyosti Karjalainen, Andreas Karlsson, Erik Karlsson, Henrik Karlsson, Melker Karlsson, William Karlsson, Christer Kellgren, Patric Kjellberg, Linus Klasen, Oscar Klefbom, Carl Klingberg, John Klingberg, Niklas Kronwall, Staffan Kronwall, Marcus Kruger, Dan Labraaten, Eddie Lack, Anton Lander, Gabriel Landeskog, Adam Larsson, Johan Larsson, Per Ledin, Tommy Lehmann, Robin Lehner, Nicklas Lidstrom, Andreas Lilja, Anders Lindback, Oscar Lindberg, Pelle Lindbergh, Johan Lindbom, Lars Lindgren, Mats Lindgren, Elias Lindholm, Hampus Lindholm, Mikael Lindholm, Joakim Lindstrom, Willy Lindstrom, Hakan Loob, Peter Loob, Bengt Lundholm, Henrik Lundqvist, Joel Lundqvist, Tord Lundstrom, Jacob Markstrom, Tony Martensson, Bjorn Melin, Roger Melin, Jan Mertzig, Fredrik Modin, Lars Molin, Oscar Moller, Johan Motin, Doug Murray, Markus Naslund, Mats Naslund, Patrik Nemeth, Marcus Nilson, Anders Nilsson, Kent Nilsson, Ulf Nilsson, Cristopher Nilstorp, Janne Niskala, Niklas Nordgren, Robert Nordmark, Jonas Nordqvist, Joakim Nordstrom, Peter Nordstrom, Mattias Norstrom, Michael Nylander, Gustav Nyquist, Bob Nystrom, Johnny Oduya, Mattias Ohlund, Fredrik Olausson, Christer Olsson, Jimmie Olvestad, Linus Omark, Magnus Paajarvi, Sami Pahlsson, John Persson, Ricard Persson, Stefan Persson, Andre Petersson, Jorgen Pettersson, Peter Popovic, David Printz, Rickard Rakell, Victor Rask, Marcus Ragnarsson, Mikael Renberg, Mattias Ritola, Bert Robertsson, Leif Rohlin, Jonas Ronnqvist, Magnus Roupe, David Rundblad, Thomas Rundqvist, Borje Salming, Tommy Salo, Andreas Salomonsson, Kjell Samuelsson, Martin Samuelsson, Mikael Samulesson, Philip Samuelsson, Ulf Samuelsson, Daniel Sedin, Henrik Sedin, Jakob Silfverberg, Lars-Erik Sjoberg, Tommy Sjodin, Fredrik Sjostrom, Carl Soderberg, Tommy Soderstrom, Viktor Stalberg, Anders Steen, Thomas Steen, Ulf Sterner, Roland Stoltz, Anton Stralman, Niklas Sundblad, Mats Sundin, Ronnie Sundin, Johan Sundstrom, Niklas Sundstrom, Patrik Sundstrom, Peter Sundstrom, Per Svartvadet, Niklas Svedberg, Leif Svensson, Magnus Svensson, Henrik Tallinder, Dick Tarnstrom, Mattias Tedenby, Mikael Tellqvist, Mats Thelin, Michael Thelvin, Andreas Thuresson, Mattias Timander, Daniel Tjarnqvist, Mathias Tjarnqvist, David Ullstrom, Alexander Urbom, Niclas Wallin, Peter Wallin, Rickard Wallin, Tom Wandell, Mattias Weinhandl, Alexander Wennberg, Tommy Westlund, Johan Witehall, Henrik Zetterberg, Lars Zetterstrom, Mika Zibanejad

SWITZERLAND.............. 26
David Aebischer, Sven Andrighetto, Sven Baertschi, Reto Berra, Damien Brunner, Raphael Diaz, Kevin Fiala, Patrick Fischer, Martin Gerber, Mark Hardy, Timo Helbling, Jonas Hiller, Pauli Jaks, Roman Josi, Simon Moser, Mirco Mueller, Nino Niederreiter, Tim Ramholt, Michel Riesen, Tobias Stephan, Mark Streit, Julien Vauclair, Reto Von Arx, Yannick Weber, Roman Wick, Thomas Ziegler

TAIWAN, CHINA 1
Rod Langway

TANZANIA 1
Chris Nielsen

UKRAINE 14
Anton Babchuk, Peter Bondra, Ruslan Fedotenko, Alexander Godynyuk, Dmitri Khristich, Sergei Petrenko, Alexei Ponikarovsky, Denis Shvidki, Oleg Tverdovsky, Sergei Varlamov, Alexander Vasilevski, Vitali Vishnevski, Dmitri Yakushin, Nikolai Zherdev

VENEZUELA................ 2
Rick Chartraw, Don Spring

WALES................... 3
Wilf Cude, Jack Evans, Cy Thomas

YUGOSLAVIA.............. 4
Goran Bezina, Ivan Boldirev, Jan Mursak, Stan Smrke